# Russia Twenty Years After

## REVOLUTIONARY STUDIES

Series Editor: PAUL LE BLANC

China, Marxism, and Democracy
*Edited by Thomas Barrett*

China's Urban Revolutionaries
*Gregor Benton*

A Dreamer's Paradise Lost
*Paul Buhle*

Trotskyism in the United States
*George Breitman, Paul Le Blanc, and Alan Wald*

Socialism from Below
*Hal Draper*

War and Revolution
*Hal Draper*

Max Schachtman and His Left
*Peter Drucker*

World Revolution 1917–1936
*C. L. R. James*

Marxism in Latin America from 1909 to the Present
*Edited by Michael Löwy*

On Changing the World
*Michael Löwy*

The Place of Marxism in History
*Ernest Mandel*

Revolutionary Marxism and Social Reality in the 20th Century
*Ernest Mandel*

Women and the Revolution
*Ethel Mannin*

The Heroic and Creative Meaning of Socialism: Selected Essays of José Carlos Mariátegui
*Edited and Translated by Michael Pearlman*

The New South Africa and the Socialist Vision
*Thomas K. Ranuga*

Russia at Twenty Years After
*Victor Serge*

The Left and the French Revolution
*Morris Slavin*

C. L. R. James and Revolutionary Marxism
*Edited by Scott McLemee and Paul Le Blanc*

The Marxist and the Jewish Question
*Morris Slavin*

The USSR 1987–1991: Marxist Perspectives
*Edited by Marilyn Vogt-Downey*

The Responsibility of Intellectuals
*Alan M. Wald*

Rudolf Hilferding
*F. Peter Wagner*

# Russia Twenty Years After

## Victor Serge

Translated by Max Shachtman

New Edition Prepared by
Susan Weissman

Includes
"THIRTY YEARS AFTER
THE RUSSIAN REVOLUTION"

HUMANITIES PRESS
NEW JERSEY

First published in 1937 by Hillman-Curl, Inc.

New edition published in paperback 1996 by
Humanities Press International, Inc., 165 First Avenue,
Atlantic Highlands, New Jersey 07716



**Library of Congress Cataloging-in-Publication Data**

Serge, Victor, 1890–1947.
Russia twenty years after / Victor Serge ; translated by Max Shachtman ; new edition prepared by Susan Weissman. — New ed.
p. cm. — (Revolutionary studies)
Originally pub.: New York : Hillman-Curl, 1937.
Includes index.
ISBN 0-391-03855-9 (pbk. : alk. paper)
1. Soviet Union—Politics and government—1917–1936. 2. Soviet Union—Foreign relations—1917–1945. I. Shachtman, Max, 1903–1972. II. Weissman, Susan. III. Title. IV. Series.
DK267.S4513 1996
947.084—dc20 95-49359
CIP



Printed in the United States of America

10 9 8 7 6 5 4 3 2 1

# Contents

# Victor Serge: The Forgotten Marxist

VICTOR SERGE—A NAME ALL BUT UNKNOWN IN THE FORMER Soviet Union—was one of the most lucid observers of the political developments of the young Soviet state, chronicling in his many works its brutal departure from the ideals of the October Revolution. Serge contended that Stalin's takeover and terroristic dictatorship amounted to a counter-revolution–and one of the bloodiest in history—due to the tenacious resistance of the revolutionary generation of Bolsheviks that Stalin was compelled to obliterate lest a critical voice survive.

Victor Serge was one who did survive, and he was determined to let his literary voice speak for those who were silenced. As far as Serge is known, he tends to be regarded as a revolutionary novelist. But Serge was more than that. He was a revolutionary historian, the historian of the Left Opposition. Serge spent the years from 1919 to 1936 in the heart of the revolution, and his own personal journey followed that of the revolution itself, from Petrograd to Orenburg, from the revolutionary struggle to the Stalinist gulag. He documented his experiences in both fiction and histories, sometimes blurring the line between the two. In his own autobiography, *Memoirs of a Revolutionary*, Serge confessed that he used the novel as his vehicle to get at the inner truth of the tumultous political struggles in which he and his comrades participated. His fiction was meant to communicate that truth in a way that his histories alone could not. Yet his histories also bear the stamp of his artistic prose, and it is the writing that makes Serge's work so powerful. This is also what makes Serge's work so Russian. Serge's chosen method of communication follows the tradition of Russian historians, even though he wrote in French for an international audience. In Russian the same word—*istoriia*—is used for "story" and for "history." Since the eighteenth century, Russian history has been written in fiction and nonfiction, as history was written by major writers and poets and not by professional historians.[1] What this means is that the line between historiography and literature has not been severed in Russia, and Serge's novels and histories are a reflection of this tradition, making the experience of reading his work all the more moving and memorable.

Reprinted here are two of Serge's most valuable and heretofore neglected works, whose significance has increased since the rapid disintegration of the Soviet Union. They are both retrospectives. The first, *Russia Twenty Years After*,[2] published in 1937 while Serge was translating Trotsky's *The Revolution Betrayed*, serves as a sort of companion volume to Trotsky's well-known study. Writing to Leon Sedov, Trotsky's son, Serge stated that he found Trotsky's book "*wonderful* and useful"[3] and added that he was "happy that in many places, my conclusions completely coincide with his, while overall both books shoot in exactly the same direction."[4]

Serge's work is both a social-scientific survey and analysis of the Soviet Union on its twentieth birthday. It is also a passionate polemic against Stalin's embezzlement of the revolution's promise—the creation of a concentration camp universe unashamedly called a workers' paradise. In *Russia Twenty Years After*, Serge's writing about the economy and society under Stalin transforms empirical data into a moving, compelling chronicle. His description of the crash industrialization of the first five-year plan is summed up in two phrases: "Build, build, build, export, shoot, build" and "industrialization is directed like a march through conquered territory."

The significance of Serge's *Russia Twenty Years After* is not limited to its analysis of the advent of the bureaucractic totalitarian state, called the bureaucratically administered command economy, or "barracks socialism," in current Soviet lexicon. It is an important document from the Stalin period. Serge was able, because he and his writings survived, to make a serious contribution to our understanding of the mechanism of repression and the fate of the repressed. Serge's concern with the nameless and faceless victims lost to Stalinism was singular. His writings, in a sense, served as their voices. He wrote pages and pages devoted to simply giving names and telling stories. His books are living testaments of the men and women who struggled and resisted—some more resolutely than others—the crushing of the revolution and its ideals by Stalin and his faction. *Russia Twenty Years After* devotes six chapters to outlining who filled what prisons; what individual and collective resistance took place there; the fate of workers, youths, peasants, scientists, writers, and teachers; and it tells us in great detail the fate of the anarchists, the socialists, the communists, the life and death of the Oppositionists, the Capitulators, and even of Stalin's coterie. In this manner *Russia Twenty Years After* was also part of the campaign arsenal of the surviving left, who remained to champion the truth against the lies of the Moscow Trials, not simply in the hope of saving individual lives of comrades languishing in the gulag but "to raise in a particular manner the issue of proletarian democracy—in the shape of freedom for Socialist opinion in the Soviet Union." This, Serge wrote Trotsky in May 1936, was part of engaging in "a practical rediscovery of what workers' democracy means . . . proving . . . that we are not in anyway the kind of people who build an enormous prison for anyone who disagrees with us." (Serge to Trotsky in *The Serge-Trotsky Papers*, ed. David Cotterill [Pluto Press, 1994], pp. 59–60)

Following the 1937 work is Serge's 1947 article titled "Russia Thirty Years After." It is one of the most penetrating, compact analyses of the significance of the defeat inflicted by Stalin. Yet it is suffused with hope for the future. It was impossible for Serge to surrender to the phase of reaction overtaking the Soviet Union. Instead he sought to understand these dark years and to leave behind some glimmer of what was attempted and how it went wrong. He concluded:

> The technical imperatives of production . . . combine with the desire for social justice and a new-found freedom to once again place the economy at the service of the community. . . . Since this realistic and deeply felt hope remains to us, all is not lost. (Undated article, Serge Archives, held by Serge's son Vlady Kibalchich in Mexico)

Typically "Russia Thirty Years After" found publication only in a far-left French journal with a tiny circulation.[5] This essay is a fine example of the mature Serge who was still preoccupied with the fate of the first socialist revolution. After Trotsky's assassination, Serge and Natalia Sedova were the only Left Oppositionists in the

West from the revolutionary generation; they were keenly aware that their ideas must survive Stalin's attempt to exterminate them.

In this essay and several other unpublished essays written during his Mexican exile, we see Serge's solitary struggle to go beyond orthodoxy in understanding the new world conjuncture after the war. No shibboleth was too sacred to leave unscrutinized, even the revolution itself. All his thinking about the character of the world was informed by his intimate understanding of the nature of Stalinism. His perception, which is perhaps even more true today after the demise of the USSR, was that the immense crisis of the modern world forcefully put socialism on the order of the day but coincided with an astonishing poverty of socialist thought. It was left to Serge to salvage revolutionary Marxism from the wreckage of Stalinism, to draw out its essential humanism and its fundamental optimism, despite the twin defeats of fascism and Stalinism. Serge spent his last months working on "Russia Thirty Years After," and it is the last piece he published. Its publication on the thirtieth anniversary of the October Revolution was followed only ten days later by Serge's lonely death. This is its first publication in English, some forty-six years after it was written.

Taken together *Russia Twenty Years After* and "Russia Thirty Years After" record the results of the revolution's early decades and draw the lessons for those who would prepare future revolutions; they also serve as correctives to the drivel written about the Soviet Union from both official Communists and their capitalist foes. In "Russia Thirty Years After," Serge set out to break the tendentious myths about everything from the revolution as a Bolshevik coup d'état (now writ large by Richard Pipes, Harvard historian and Reagan's National Security Officer and mimicked in Yeltsin's Russia by all manner of born-again marketeers) to the thesis that Stalin represented the logical continuation of Lenin's policies, a thesis now elevated to the status of a "truism" in today's former Soviet Union.

Serge's approach was dialectical. In this essay he explained what it was the early Bolsheviks aspired to and how political circumstances altered their goals. Stalinism represented a break with Leninism. Bolshevik thought did contain germs that spread under Stalin, but "to judge the living man by the death germs which the autopsy reveals in a corpse—and which he may have carried in him since his birth—is this very sensible?"[6]

Victor Serge was uniquely suited to sum up the experience of the revolution after twenty and thirty years. Yet after seventy-five years, we still are forced to introduce the readers to Victor Serge, just as Max Shachtman was compelled to do in the original introduction to the 1937 edition of *Russia Twenty Years After*.

### *Who was Victor Serge*

Dissident Communist, former anarchist, on the left of the Left Opposition, Serge is one of the many "blank pages" in Soviet political history. The ideas and theories so hotly contested in the 1920s were suppressed and kept from ordinary Soviet citizens, just as the proponents and supporters of these ideas were repressed in the brutal purges of the 1930s. Both decades of Soviet history were literally written off in the USSR. With the republication of Serge's *Russia Twenty Years After*, we fill in another of the Soviet Union's blank pages.

Serge wrote to correct the official record of falsifications that passed for Bolshevik history. He hoped future revolutionaries would be able to draw lessons from this experience. His unique life experience and his revolutionary writings are an eloquent challenge to orthodox notions of the Soviet Union. Twenty years before Khrushchev's Secret Speech about Stalin's crimes, and fifty years before Gorbachev's *glasnost*, Victor Serge was trying to alert the world to what was happening in Stalin's Russia. His words fell largely on deaf ears. Serge's antipathy to both the capitalist West and the Soviet state assured his marginality. His life and works not only oppose Stalinism but also present an alternative to the Bukharinism—or concessions to the market—that appeared in Serge's lifetime and reappeared in the guise of repeated reform efforts from Riutin to Khrushchev to Gorbachev's *perestroika*.[7]

Given the failure of the Soviet system, why is it still important to listen to Serge's voice? It is virtually impossible to understand today's problems in the former Soviet Union without examining its history, particularly the defeat of alternatives to Stalin's policies and how his policies shaped the production relations that developed in the Soviet Union. Serge's works are a valuable, neglected addition to the existing literature. They shed light on this formative chapter in Soviet political history.

What makes Serge's voice significant is his unique perspective as an insider/outsider/chronicler/participant. Serge wrote as a partisan with a particular point of view: Left Oppositionist. The question of "Stalinism versus Bolshevism" has been the most divisive within Soviet studies. It is the quintessential interpretive question having to do with the whole of Soviet historical and political development since the revolution. Whatever one's own view on this issue, Serge's insight proves valuable. Since the rapid disintegration of the Soviet Union at the close of 1991, the equation between Stalinism and Bolshevism, and even Marxism has been strengthened, making Serge's contribution even more critical.

Serge's political experience led him not to renounce socialism once Stalin had triumphed but to bring to it a declaration of the rights of man, enriching socialist goals. He opposed the one party system, declaring as early as 1918 and again in 1923 that a coalition government, although fraught with dangers, would have been less dangerous than what was to transpire under Stalin's dictatorship of the secretariat and the secret police. Serge criticized the New Economic Policy (NEP) for bringing back inequality and misery while not revitalizing democracy and a multiparty system. Serge's proposals for economic reform included "workers democracy" and a "communism of associations" instead of rigid, top-down, antidemocratic "plans".

Reading Serge's body of work on the Soviet Union, including his memoirs, histories, and novels, is indispensable for anyone who wants to get a feel for the atmosphere of the 1920s and 1930s inside the Soviet Union and the Communist movement; it is a testimony to his literary achievement, political acumen, and resolute honesty. The Serge "resurgence" is underway with many of his novels still in print, the republication of his history *Year One of the Russian Revolution* in 1992, and now the republication of *Russia Twenty Years After*.

*Serge's Political Journey to Russia.*

Victor Serge lived from 1890 to 1947. He was politically active in seven countries, participated in three revolutions, spent more than ten years in captivity, published more than forty books, and left behind thousands of pages of unpublished manuscripts, correspondence, and articles. He was born into one political exile and died in another. He was hounded and imprisoned. A sort of permanent political oppositionist, he opposed capitalism as a socialist; he opposed certain Bolshevik practices with his anarchist leanings; he opposed Stalin as a Left Oppositionist; and finally he opposed fascism and capitalism's Cold War as an unrepentant revolutionary Marxist.

Serge wrote from deep within the Soviet revolutionary experience as both a political actor and a victim of the degeneration of the revolution. As an insider he knew the men and women who made the revolution and those who destroyed it. He wrote of them in his political works and fleshed them out in his novels. Serge was not a dispassionate objective reporter but an ardent Left Oppositionist whose political outlook framed his exposition. He wrote with a novelist's eye for penetrating detail, posing essential questions, pointing out contradictions that he often left unresolved. Serge was not an original theorist; there is no such thing as a Sergist. His writing is passionate and honest and sometimes poetic, but it always remains critical and always retains his allegiance to the ideas of the revolutionary generation of Bolsheviks.

His written legacy includes seven novels, two volumes of poetry, three novellas, a collection of short stories; more than thirty books and pamphlets of history and politics including biographies of Lenin, Stalin, and Trotsky; an autobiography, his diary, or personal notebooks; and scores of journalistic articles and essays on a variety of themes. Although he was born in Belgium and wrote in French, Serge is arguably more "Russian" than anything else.

Born to an exiled Russian couple who belonged to "Narodnaya Volya" or "People's Will," Serge was raised in extreme poverty in Belgium. With no formal education (his father was contemptuous of the "stupid bourgeois education for the poor"[8]), Serge nevertheless inherited his parents" passion for knowledge, imbibed their conversations, and educated himself by ransacking encyclopedias and making the rounds of museums, libraries, and churches. For Serge learning was not separate from life but was life itself.

Serge was drawn into active politics as a youth, joining a socialist organization (the Jeunes-Gardes Socialistes) in Belgium at age fifteen. He moved to France and became an anarchist-individualist; experimented with alternative lifestyles, including vegetarianism; and became associated with the infamous Bonnot gang of anarchist outlaws. Serge was repulsed by the violence and madness of the Bonnot gang's exploits, though he sympathized with their motives. When the law caught up with the Bonnot gang, Serge refused to break solidarity with his comrades by condemning them. He ended up with a five-year prison sentence, an experience so unbearable that he could only free himself from what he called the "inward nightmare" by writing it in the novel *Men in Prison.*

Upon his release and expulsion from France, Serge went to Barcelona and plunged into the syndicalist insurrectionary street fighting of July 1917. Serge was politically disillusioned with anarchism, which he found manifestly unprepared for power. He was disgusted with European social democracy and had his sights on revolutionary Russia, the country of his "roots" and his language, which drew him like a magnet. He set off for Russia via France but wound up behind barbed wire in a French prison camp, accused of being a Bolshevik himself. There Serge languished, barely escaping the deadly "Spanish flu" epidemic of 1918, studying Marxism and revolution[9] with other Bolshevik prisoners for fifteen months. After the Armistice Serge was released in a prisoner exchange, and in February 1919 he found himself in revolutionary Petrograd.

*In Revolutionary Russia: Serge's Soviet Experience.*

After a few months of intense observation, participation, and discussion with the various revolutionary tendencies in Russia, Serge joined the Bolsheviks. As a revolutionary his allegiance to the Bolsheviks was based on what he saw as the correctness of their political positions, although he was always critical of their authoritarian excesses.

Serge threw himself into the struggle to defend the revolution and begin the construction of socialism. He was a machine gunner during the Civil War, became an intimate of the Bolshevik top leadership, and collaborated with Zinoviev in the first congresses of the Communist International.[10] He became a commissar in charge of the tsarist secret police archives, and after digging in the records of the Okhrana, he wrote an article in *Bulletin Communiste* in 1921 that was to become the book *What Everyone Should Know About State Repression.*[11] At the same time, Serge translated into French the works of Lenin, Trotsky, and Zinoviev, and he became friendly with poets, writers, anarchists, and Social Revolutionaries, mingling in richly varied political, social, and literary milieux. He belonged to "the last free thought society" and was probably their "only Communist member." This was the Free Philosophic Society led by the symbolist novelist Andrei Bely. As a confirmed, but critical Bolshevik, Serge was developing his Marxism.

Serge's brand of Marxism was fused with an anarchist's spirit and a primary commitment to socialism's international character. His Marxism was deeply humanistic, preoccupied with questions of personal development and individual freedom within the social whole. His central concern with the condition of life of the masses always meant that Serge saw democracy as an integral component of socialist development.

This critical spirit was not Serge's alone. The Bolsheviks' early history was characterized by lively debate, with members standing on different sides of every question. One only has to read the Bolshevik Central Committee minutes, and Daniel's book *The Conscience of the Revolution* to confirm this.[12]

One of what Serge called the tendentious myths of the Russian Revolution's historiography was that the Bolsheviks' immediate goal was to establish a monopoly on state power.[13] Serge wrote that the truth was just the opposite: the Bolsheviks were most afraid of being *isolated* in power. The left Social Revolutionaries participated in the government with the Bolsheviks from November until July 1918.

The Social Revolutionaries, among others, opposed the terms of the treaty of Brest Litovsk—the "peace of shame." So did Preobrazhensky and Bukharin, later to stand on opposite sides of the industrialization debates. They joined with others to put out the *Theses of Left Communists* in 1918.[14] They also warned against the growing bureaucratization of industry which would separate the proletariat from control over economic and political life, leading to increased dependence on bourgeois specialists and capitalist methods of labor organization, such as piecework and Taylorism.

Serge sided with Lenin on the question of Brest-Litovsk, although he sympathized with the antibureaucratic stance of the Left Communists. Writing that the Bolsheviks were forced into accepting the terms of the peace by the advancing German front, he nevertheless wrote forcefully of the consequences of this treaty: loss of huge tracts of Ukraine and the sacrifice of the Finnish revolution which was drowned in blood in 1918.[15]

Serge wrote in *Portrait de Staline* that the gravest error committed by the Bolsheviks was the establishment of the Cheka (Extraordinary Commission for the Repression of Counter-Revolution, Speculation, Espionage and Desertion), the security force formed to protect the revolution from counter-revolutionaries. He called it an inquisition.[16] In 1939 Serge wrote that the Bolshevik revolution died a self-inflicted death with the creation of the Cheka, instrument of Red Terror, forerunner of the GPU (State Political Administration), NKVD (People's Commissariat of Internal Affairs), and KGB (Committee for State Security), which exterminated the revolutionary generation of Bolsheviks. Thus Serge dated the beginning of the degeneration of the Russian revolution several years earlier than the more common figures of 1921 (Kronstadt) or 1924 (death of Lenin) or 1927 (defeat of the Opposition) or 1929 (forced collectivization, liquidation of kulaks, crash industrialization.)[17]

Yet in 1919–20 Serge was not publicly critical of the Cheka. In the conditions of Civil War, it appeared as a tragic necessity. Serge was working in the Comintern and used his offices to intercede on behalf of victims of the Cheka when he could. These were "early days" for the revolution, and Serge believed then that certain characteristics of Bolshevism, that is, its Marxist conviction, its view of the hegemony of the proletariat in the revolutionary process, its intransigent internationalism, and the unity between thought and action, gave it an innate superiority over the rival parties with which it shared a common outlook.[18]

Serge also concurred with Lenin on the question of industry. The Bolsheviks believed that socialism was impossible in such a backward setting but that a gradually socializing Russia would be an example for the European working class. Thus Lenin advocated not blanket nationalization of the means of production but workers' control over them instead. The Civil War changed everything, and made nationalization imperative for defense.

The intransigent internationalism of the Bolsheviks rested on their belief in the coming revolution in Europe. Lenin had said that in terms of world socialism, the German revolution, in an advanced capitalist country, was more important than the Russian revolution. If need be, the Russian Revolution would be sacrificed for the success of the first revolution in an advanced capitalist country.

Serge shared their analysis, but was less optimistic about successful revolution in the West. He wrote that the Bolsheviks were mistaken about the imminence of the European revolution, misjudging the parliamentary opportunism of the mediocre leaders of the European socialist movement. Nevertheless Serge understood that isolated Russia's only chance for survival was pinned on the West European extension of the revolution. He was convinced that revolutionary Russia, in the throes of hunger, isolation, and defeat, would collapse if left to itself. Ready to translate theory into practice, Serge threw himself wholeheartedly in support of the policy and volunteered to go to Germany to help prepare the insurrection by working in the Comintern (Communist International). He also confessed he was disgusted by the growing bureaucratization of the Bolshevik party and their counterterror,[19] and he was psychologically exhausted; a change of scenery and new activity would be welcome.

In Germany, Serge edited the French edition of the Comintern journal, International Press Correspondence, or *Inprecorr*. With the failure of the German revolution of 1923, Serge moved to Vienna, where he continued his work in the Comintern in the company of comrades such as Lukacs and Gramsci. Of his life at that point (1923), he wrote:

> All we lived for was activity integrated into history; we were interchangeable; we could immediately see the repercussions of affairs in Russia upon affairs in Germany and the Balkans; we felt linked with our comrades who, in pursuit of the same ends as we, perished or else scored some success at the other end of Europe. None of us had, in the bourgeois sense of the word, any personal existence: we changed our name, our posting and our work at the Party's need; we had just enough to live on without real material discomfort, and we were not interested in making money, or

> following a career, or producing a literary heritage, or leaving a name behind us; we were interested solely in the difficult business of reaching Socialism.[20]

The failure of the German revolution left the Bolsheviks isolated and in turmoil. The defeat paved the way not only for Hitler, but also Stalin—and an inward looking Bolshevik faction. During Serge's sojourn in Western Europe, he anxiously watched the growing inner party struggles at home and declared himself with the Left Opposition of the New Course in 1923. At the end of 1925, Serge demanded to return to the USSR to take up the fight within the Bolshevik party.

Critical of the use of terror, the bureaucratization of the party and the state, and the growing privileges that distanced the bureaucracy from the population and the aims of the revolution, the Left Opposition of Trotsky and others identified the bureaucracy as rooted in the new conditions of Soviet rule. Given that the original revolutionary working class had been largely decimated by Civil War and foreign intervention and the new working class was drawn mostly from a semiliterate peasantry, the Left Opposition argued that it was necessary for the Soviet state to promote an early and gradual industrialization as a precondition for the regeneration of class consciousness of the newly formed proletariat, with just one foot out of the countryside.

During the period 1923–26, Stalin packed the various bureaus of the Party with his people, making the outcome of party congresses and debates preordained. As a spokesman for the Left Opposition in the Leningrad party organization, Serge found it impossible to make a speech without being hooted down by Stalin's cohorts. This meant that if Trotsky and his supporters wanted an audience for their alternative political program, it would have to be taken outside the party, something neither Trotsky nor the others in the Left Opposition were prepared to do.

By 1927–28 the combination of lack of industrial policy and the growth of the private sector in agriculture led to a grain crisis. The low prices peasants were offered for their grain, coupled with the high prices charged for scarce industrial goods, were a powerful disincentive to produce more than the peasant needed for himself and his family. Then a series of poor harvests threatened both the state's export plans and food supplies. The peasants boycotted grain requisitions, and Stalin responded by ordering extraordinary measures to collect the grain. Red Army soldiers began to take the grain from the peasant at gunpoint.

The question of which way forward was now unavoidable. to proceed by increasing NEP and the private sector would lead back to capitalism and subjection to international capital and the world market; to institute genuine workers control of industry and democratic planning would make the bureaucratic structure superfluous. Both alternatives meant Stalin and the bureaucracy would lose power. As Serge (as well as Trotsky and other Left Oppositionists) so powerfully explained, neither option was realistic for a bureaucracy whose raison d'être was to maintain its privileged position in power.[21] They operated to maximize their own self-interest. Therefore Stalin took the only road open to him: eliminate the challenge from the peasantry, the party, and the working class without creating either capitalism or socialism—neither plan nor market. The ground was laid for ruling society through bureaucratic fiats, rapid industrialization with five-year "plans" administered from the top down, and forced collectivization.

At the same time, Comintern policy became a rubber stamp for Stalin's directives which flowed logically from the politics of "socialism in one country." Back in the Soviet Union and active in the Leningrad section of the Left Opposition, Serge wrote a series of articles that were published in the French journal *Clarté*, criticizing Stalin's policy which forced the Chinese Communist Party into the Kuomintang of Chiang-Kai-Shek, leading to the beheading of the Chinese revolution of 1927 and the subsequent massacre of Chinese communists.

These articles sealed Serge's fate. He was expelled from the party, joining a by now honorable list of expelled Oppositionists. He was later arrested and held for seven to eight weeks in 1928. Upon his release, Serge nearly died of an intestinal occlusion. Remarkably he refused to cooperate or confess anything while he was in jail; this saved his life in 1936 when his record was checked for admitted offenses before he could be released. Although Serge survived his illness, he suffered a political death. Open political activity was now closed to him, forcing Serge's decision to exchange political activism for the pen. He committed himself to writing and sketched out in his mind the series of documentary novels about these "unforgettable times."[22] He was determined to preserve the ideas, experience, and memory of the men and women with whom he had brushed shoulders and shared struggles.

In the period 1928–33, Serge survived in precarious liberty, living off his writings which he sent to France for publication. He also worked as a French translator of Lenin's works for the Lenin Institute. The translations were checked line by line "by experts charged with the task of uncovering possible sabotage in the disposition of semicolons."[23] Serge lived for a while in the countryside with Panait Istrati, the Rumanian writer, and traveled enough to have a chance to observe closely the effects of Stalin's policies.

Serge began to write about the effects of industrialization and collectivization, the creation and consolidation of the Stalinist system. In 1929 Panait Istrati published under his own name Serge's *Soviets 1929*.[24] In the next four years, Serge published in France and Spain his monumental history, *Year One of the Russian Revolution*, as well as three novels: *Men in Prison*, *Birth of Our Power*, and *Conquered City*. None of his books were published in the Soviet Union until 1989, when the provincial literary magazine *Ural* serialized his *The Case of Comrade Tulayev*.

Serge experienced Stalin's campaign of terror directly: he was arrested in 1933, held in solitary confinement for eighty days in the infamous Lubianka, and subjected to relentless nocturnal interrogations. He was then deported to Orenburg, where he and his son Vlady nearly starved to death.[25] During his deportation he wrote a further four books which were subsequently confiscated by the Soviet regime upon Serge's expulsion from the Soviet Union in 1936. Despite attempts to secure their "release" by his family, scholars, and politicians, these four books have never seen the light of day. The way these books were stolen by the GPU was quite dramatic and indicated that the papers were often more important than the man. Despite making eight copies of these books and depositing them in various places and despite a concerted campaign that this author undertook in 1985, which has been continued by the Victor Serge Association with the help of Soviet "friends of Serge," they remain locked from view. These books included two novels: one about the French anarchist movement titled *The Lost Men*, and the other a novel about war communism in 1920 titled *The Torment*. This second novel, which Serge described as conveying "the grandeur of the revolution," forms a sequel to his *Conquered City*. The third manuscript was a book of poems that he reconstructed in exile, and the fourth was his history *Year Two of the Russian Revolution*. Serge said he had never had the luxury of time to polish as he did with these books, which makes their loss all the more tragic. It also makes their recovery all the more urgent.

Serge was already known in France and Spain for his pamphlets and political articles; the publication of his history and three novels in the years 1930–32 established him as a serious revolutionary writer. His reputation in the West saved him from oblivion and death, a fate not shared by many Russian writers who had no such international following. A campaign was waged on Serge's behalf by Parisian intellectuals, embarrassing Communist "friends of the Soviet Union" Romain Rolland and André Malraux. Rolland interceded in Serge's favor with Stalin when he visited Moscow. In April 1936, just months before the first of the Moscow trials, Serge was removed from Orenburg, put on a train, but he was "relieved" of his suitcases, bulging with manuscripts and memorabilia, and expelled with his family from the Soviet Union. He was then stripped of his Soviet citizenship, making him a man without a country in Western Europe, where skies were already darkening with fascism and war.

The dramatic end to Serge's seventeen-year sojourn in the country of "victorious revolution" is a story worth telling: at the last station on the Soviet frontier, Negoreloye, Serge and his family were made to disembark for a final "search." Liuba and fourteen-month old Jeannine were led off in one direction, Serge and seventeen-year old Vlady in another. They were ordered to undress for a strip search. Vlady recalled that he was still in his underwear, with his trousers around his boots. The GPU agent prodded him to hurry and asked what was he hiding in his socks? Vlady retorted, "a submarine!" At that moment the whistle blew and the train started to pull away from the station. Serge and Vlady broke into a run, pulling their clothes up at the same time. They couldn't see Liuba and Jeannine. Horrified, Serge thought they would be left behind. He began screaming, "Mama, mama, I won't leave without you!" Vlady jumped on the train, saw his mother and baby sister, and shouted to his father, "They're here, see for yourself." Just before it was too late, Serge caught sight of Liuba and jumped on the moving train. He looked back to the GPU agents: they were pointing to Serge's suitcases, containing his manuscripts, photos, and personal belongings.[26] In 1992 Serge's KGB file was released from Orenburg. His manuscripts are still missing.

From 1936–40, Serge lived a precarious existence in Brussels and Paris, campaigning against the persecution of his comrades left behind in Stalin's gulag. Active politically with non-Stalinist groups and Trotsky's Fourth International, Serge watched the drama of the Spanish Civil War, the opportunism of the Popular Front, and the decline and ultimate defeat of the European left. A Communist Party campaign of slander effectively prevented Serge from publishing in all but the tiniest far left journals in France.[27] Despite severe economic hardship and constant danger from both the GPU and the Nazis, Serge continued to write in profusion. While he was in Europe, Serge produced *Midnight in the Century*, a novel about the resistance of the Opposition to Stalin from within the gulag. He also translated Trotsky's *Revolution Betrayed* and analyzed the political, economic, and social effects of Stalin's policies in *From Lenin to Stalin*, written in one 15-day stretch in 1936. He also wrote *Destiny of a Revolution* (1937; here republished with the American title of *Russia Twenty Years After* and *Portrait of Stalin* (1939) published several booklets on the Moscow Trials and campaigned publicly for recognition of the crimes against the revolutionary generation of Bolsheviks by Stalin, which was met with indifference in France where the reality of fascism and the impending war blinded many eyes to what was happening in the Soviet Union.[28] Serge continued his battle nevertheless, remaining in Paris until 1940, literally leaving the South of Paris as the Nazis invaded the North. He fled to Marseille, escaping certain death at the hands of the Gestapo, where he spent months fighting for a visa out of the nightmare. He lived for a while in a villa with surrealists and "degenerate artists" (so identified by Hitler). The United States refused to admit Serge. Only Mexico, the last refuge of Trotsky, offered a place to Serge and his family.

In Mexico, Serge found publishing left critiques of the USSR even more difficult than in Europe. In fact one house was ruined after publishing his *Hitler Contra Stalin*. Politically isolated and deprived of a livelihood, Serge wrote mostly for the desk drawer, producing some of his best work: *Memoirs of a Revolutionary*; what is arguably the finest novel about the purges, *The Case of Comrade Tulayev*; his novel about the experience of defeat and exile called *The Years Without Reprieve*; and a large collection of essays, correspondence, and articles on World War II, the future of socialism, fascism, the Jewish question, psychology, literature, and the evolution and nature of the Soviet system.

The end of the war found Serge in a weakened physical condition, his head brimming with writing projects. He tried to return to Europe but was stopped by a fatal heart attack in November 1947. He died after just hailing a cab, before he could tell the driver where to go. His clothes were threadbare, and he had holes in his shoes; the driver thought he had picked up a pauper.

Serge left behind him a lifetime of struggle, a commitment to the truth no matter how uncomfortable, "a victorious revolution and massacres in so great a number as to inspire a certain dizziness," (Serge, quoted in the introduction to his novel, *Midnight in a Century*, ed. Richard Greeman [New York: Writers and Readers, 1982], p. 17) and a certain confidence, born of his critical intelligence, in the possibilities of the future.

### *Serge's Critique of the Stalinist System.*

Serge's contribution to our understanding of the system Stalin created in the thirties is increasingly relevant today not only because it is critically examined from within the former Soviet Union, but because it was during the period Serge described that the class relations of the USSR were formed. If one wishes to understand the difficulties of the attempt at a transition to capitalism in the former Soviet Union today, one must make sense of the forces involved. To do that one must examine their formation. Stalin's system had a certain dynamic and logic that affected the lives of millions. Further the particular relations that were established between regime and worker under the dizzying conditions of crash industrialization and forced collectivization became permanent and reproducible features of the system. The chief characteristics of the relationship were that democratic planning was excluded as a possibility and instead the plans drawn up were "command documents" issued from the center without accurate information to assess the real possibility of carrying them out. In addition because the workers' needs were not taken into account, the workers or implementers adapted the instructions to fit their own needs, which meant that the plans broke down or were disrupted by the individualistic responses of the workers to the system being forced on them. In turn the next chain in the economy was affected as supplies were disrupted, causing the workers to change instructions similarly to fit their own needs. The result was that the more the center tried to centralize to maintain tight control over economic events, the less control it actually had as workers, in short supply, looked to their own interests, and managers lied to make themselves look good on paper. This form of "planning" became antiplanning: in place of a rational organization of production, an anarchic, irrational and costly system developed. Unreliable information and a form of atomized and involuntary sabotage were the results. The workers disrupted because their interests were *not* the same as those of the planners (under genuine socialist planning there would be no antagonism as the planners and implementers would be one and the same). The end result was that Stalinist planning (as Serge finally called it[29])—the allocation and mobilization of resources without democratic input—could not guarantee a recognizable correspondence of outcome of instructions to the instructions themselves.[30] As everyone falsified information in their own interests, a highly inefficient and wasteful system was created.[31] According to Serge: "there is disorder, panic, terror . . . passive resistance, atomic as it were. . . . all the statistics, all the balances, all the figures are false because nobody ever dares tell the truth."[32]

The methods employed caused the workers to become hostile to industrialization and to resist in an atomized, individualized rather than collective, manner by producing poorly, or not on time. What began as a response to forced tempos during a time of extreme labor shortage became a form of protest to the system.[33] In the heart of Stalin's terror machine, the elite gained political control over the population through force but not over economic events, though it tried hard.[34]

Serge illustrated the basic dilemmas of regime-worker relations described above graphically, without theorizing. He began with the forced collectivization of agriculture, designed to break the collective resistance of the peasantry, who had revolted against the bureaucratic measures imposed on them. To break their resistance, Stalin declared war on the resisters, who were "called kulaks, designated as enemies of the people . . . to be 'liquidated as a class.'"[35] Serge pointed out that full collectivization was never intended. The plan, which had been in development since 1925–26, only envisioned collectivizing as much land as could be supplied with agricultural machinery.[36] The whole point of collectivization was that agricultural production would be *industrialized* and provide an attractive alternative to the small farms of the peasantry. The *Kolkhoz* without tractors made no sense. Total collectivization was unforeseen and not planned for; as a result giant factories had to be created to produce agricultural machinery, using up resources intended for other sectors, to their detriment. As Serge noted collectivization produced a shortage of raw materials, hostility, and a ruined agriculture, and it destroyed the plan for industry. As hostile peasants hoarded grain and destroyed their livestock, agricultural output dwindled; Stalin demanded higher quotas and extracted every last grain in Ukraine for the cities and export, causing a state-organized famine that killed millions of peasants in 1932–33.[37] Serge noted wryly that collectivization produced anarchy rather than a plan. He said, "Instead of applying a political pattern, Stalin is reduced to improvisations."[38]

The bureaucratic and ill-thought out haste of Stalin's industrialization had far-reaching implications for future growth and quality of goods. Industrialization was financed through extreme pressure on the working class, producing intolerable conditions, which Serge cataloged in *Russia Twenty Years After*. He said "Industrialization is directed like a march through conquered territory." The intensification of labor meant that the worker, to meet quantity quotas, had to forget paying attention to quality. This is corroborated by Christian Rakovsky, Andrew Smith,[39] and other observers. Defective goods produced at one point entered into circulation as the means of production of future products that would also be defective,[40] building entire factories that were erected of defective construction materials and equipped with machines made from inferior metal. This was indeed an expensive and highly wasteful way to industrialize, both for the machines and the people.[41] Serge described the constant breakdown of machinery because of improper usage. There was never enough time as Stalin demanded the five-year plan be fulfilled in four or even three years! Precious resources, needed elsewhere, had to be used increasingly to repair exhausted machinery. Spare parts were in short supply and often got lost in delivery—holding up production. Serge noted that Stalin's answer to every problem was to squeeze the workers more; make them work harder, consume less; hold up their pay, cut their wages. This produced a very high rate of labor turnover, with a negative impact on production. Quoting official statistics Serge noted that in Ukraine whole factories were turned over in three months as the workers moved on looking for food, housing, and better working conditions. "You travel because wherever you are you feel bad."[42]

In *Soviets 1929* Serge pointed to the wasteful and high cost of production: lack of coordination meant that in some places whole factories were produced but lay idle because there were no power stations to feed them; in other places power stations were constructed but awaited the building of factories. On paper and in growth statistics it might look good, but in both instances the construction was useless and wasted.[43] In some areas factories were only 70 percent constructed (you can't use 70 percent of a factory); in other instances Serge described factories that produced 50, 60, even 100 percent defective goods, which often entered into circulation nonetheless.[44] Serge blamed the bureaucratic system for the costly, wasteful production and lamented that the self-interest of the bureaucracy was the only logic of the system, taking precedence over the needs of agriculture, industry, and the population.[45]

Although alluding to the problems and obviously aware of Rakovsky's analysis as expressed in his oppositional article "*Na s'ezde i v strane*," Serge did not present an overall theory. Instead he characteristically surveyed the effects of these vast forces on ordinary people, looking at life in town, country, and factory. He examined the horrifying conditions of workers who starved while working. The same conditions often forced women into prostitution after work to provide bread for their children. Grandparents were refused bread cards because they did not work (being too old), and roving bands of children existed because their parents had been whisked into labor camps. The lives of starving peasants in the state-organized famine of 1932–33, were contrasted to the lavish lifestyle of the "parvenus." Serge barely hid his cynicism for a system that called itself socialist and produced inequalities as grotesque as those of capitalism. Although Serge demonstrated that the economy grew despite Stalin's industrialization because the industrial work force expanded and machinery was introduced where it did not exist previously—not to mention the efforts of a truly massive slave labor sector in the camps[46]—he asked the essential question pertaining to this growth: Growth intended for whose benefit? What kind of growth?[47] And he described what went with this growth: pilfering, sabotage, misery, famine, passport laws, repression, and terror. Stalin's methods, according to Serge, were antisocialist but were officially justified by using an "amoral vulgar Marxism."

Serge discussed the draconian labor legislation and the various schemes employed to speed up production and squeeze more from the workers, such as shock work (*udarnichestvo*), "socialist competition," and Stakhanovism, pointing out these schemes were doomed because they were basically a fraud, rigged by opportunist managers and workers in collusion to win bonuses for themselves.

> Stakhanov did not work alone or just anywhere in general, but with a full-selected crew and in a favorable spot; that the Stakhanovist crews exerted such exhausting efforts that they included a supernumerary to replace the worker who might faint on the job; that the Stakhanovists prepared their work for one or two hours before and one or two hours after the "day" of production, which raised the real duration of their labor from two to three hours.[48]

When workers resisted outright, which they inevitably did, Serge conveyed the somewhat contradictory response of the regime to resistance while showing graphically what happened to those who dared to contest their situation collectively. The youths were often the most militant, and there is evidence of strikes. Serge described the strike at the textile plant in Ivanovo-Voznessensk in April 1931, where the workers had but one slogan to express their demands: "We are hungry!" The authorities yielded, blaming the local leadership. Food was sent in, work resumed, and then the purge quietly began. The Trotskyists among the strikers were shot, and not a word seeped out, except abroad.[49] In this one episode, Serge expressed the basic contradiction of the regime that manifestly feared the proletariat because it had usurped their political power. The same pattern of regime response to strikes remained for the duration of the Soviet period. Even in today's post–Soviet Union, the response is similar. Demands are quickly acceded, though infrequently fulfilled.

What the strikes showed was that the regime had to deal with organized resistance from youth and a section of older workers who had somehow survived the Civil War, NEP, and famines with some collective memory, bred on the ideas of Marxism, from the days of the Revolution. Serge noted that Stalin fought the workers and the peasants, and he beheaded the party. The regime also had to cope with the results of its policy—unfulfilled plans, high turnover, alcoholism amid extreme scarcity—all the while preparing for war. Serge made the point simply and forcefully: an underfed and malnourished workforce, living a joyless existence, could not be depended on to work well. What capitalist society had learned from the experience of slavery had been lost on the Stalinists.[50]

Serge answered his own questions about the nature of economic growth with examples of workers coerced into inhuman conditions who were not being paid enough to stave off hunger, slave labor engaged in construction in the camps, and peasants whose resistance was met with deportation and expropriation. The situation led to demoralization of the working class accompanied by a sense of futility. Pointing to the ubiquitous secret police who were stationed in all establishments, Serge evoked the life of ordinary citizens under these conditions:

> hemmed in by police, by poverty, by lies . . .[the] worker is preoccupied with obtaining, stamping, checking and re-registering a bread card which is refused half the workers on various pretexts; his wife runs from one empty store to another, registering in a queue at doors of fishstalls in the evening in order to wrangle the next morning over a ration of salt fish . . . exposed to

> spying in the shop . . . coming home to tell who was arrested last night.[51]

What Serge revealed is how the conditions of physical coercion and intimidation in the context of scarcity and speed-up left the population with nothing to think about but their own survival and self-interest. Serge's style was to accumulate concrete examples: the process of atomization of the population is empirically demonstrated but not theoretically argued.

*The Bloody Rupture.*

Stalin could only enforce his methods by wiping out all opposition. Serge noted the system was highly unstable, resting on brute force alone. The purges, though unplanned and proceeding from an internal dynamic set in motion by Stalin's methods of industrialization and rule, created new social relations. None of the basic problems of the society were resolved at the end of the blood purges, but millions paid with their lives. All forms of collective resistance were broken and any residual resistance was atomized as the weary population concerned itself with survival, not politics. Following the exultant first ten years of the revolution were what Serge called ten black years, from 1927–37. These later years constitute the struggle of the revolutionary generation against totalitarianism and the regime's war against its own people in the form of industrialization, famine, deportation, and execution. The founders of the revolution, who favored early industrialization, and gradual collectivization, democratic planning, militant internationalism, democratization of party and society, and a fight against bureaucratization, passed "from power into prison, deportation, and death." Serge called the "Stalin counter-revolution" the bloodiest takeover in history, in which the resistance of the revolutionary generation was so tenacious that it was necessary for the regime to eliminate it entirely to consolidate itself.[52] In his words,

> Bolsheviks perished by the tens of thousands, Civil War veterans by the hundreds of thousands, and Soviet citizens who were tainted by the condemned ideals by the millions. A few dozen companions of Lenin and Trotsky found themselves capable of dishonoring themselves by a supreme act of devotion to the party, before being shot. Thousands more were shot in basements. The largest concentration camps in history were set up to oversee the physical elimination of the vast masses of condemned.[53]

The new state, which Serge called a bureaucratic police state, was "reactionary in every important way with respect to ideals of the revolution. A Marxism of dead slogans born in offices takes the place of a critical Marxism of thinking men."[54] Further Stalin was able to "hold the souls of the opposition through their party patriotism, which he used to divide and devour them." The cult of the leader was born, the bureaucratic parvenus of the emerging totalitarian system parroted the words of the leader and hailed the theory of socialism in one country.

At the end of his life, Serge reaffirmed his commitment to the politics of the Left Opposition, but with certain qualifiers. Rather than label the Soviet Union with a descriptive slogan, Serge preferred to discuss its dilemmas and note its features. He was not precise in his characterization of the bureaucracy, alternately calling it a caste and a class; he did say exploitation occurs, but he did not call the regime capitalist.[55] He finally called the system "bureaucratic totalitarianism with collectivist leanings." He stated that the USSR would need a new revolution—and worried that without it the bureaucracy would do a deal with capitalism to exploit Soviet workers jointly.[56] Serge developed "revisionist" ideas about the role of the technocracy and had rather "heretical" notions about the party. Although he affirmed, "We badly need an organizational framework, " he cautioned us to a healthy suspicion of centralization, discipline, and guided ideology.[57]

Pessimistic that the USSR had created a "concentration camp universe," blocked socialism, and helped create Nazism, Serge nevertheless was more optimistic than ever at the end of his life that the only solution was socialism, which would put the economy at the service of its freely associated producers. Although the Mensheviks around the *New Leader*, many Trotskyists, and so-called centrists claimed Serge moved toward social democracy and away from Marxism, Serge himself posited the socialist transformation of capitalist society and the abolition of bourgeois rule. He wrote that the revolution must be more than just proletarian, that is, it must be socialist in the humanist sense, "more precisely, socializing though democratic libertarian means."[58] For Serge it was vital that the revolution pay attention to the question of liberty. Serge was an intransigent internationalist, a revolutionary committed to the utmost personal freedom within the revolutionary process. Unlike many other former revolutionaries whose "god had failed them," Serge did not see Stalinism as the natural outgrowth of Leninism but rather as the corruption of it. He argued that there were seeds contained in Bolshevik thought that grew to full blown weeds under Stalin, but there were also many other seeds that could have flowered into a new democracy had the circumstances existed for their germination.[59]

*Conclusion.*

This extended sketch of Serge—called "the forgotten Marxist" by Alex Buchman, one of Trotsky's bodyguards—establishes "that few writers about the Soviet Union have better credentials—or credentials half so good—to present to the reader. The material contained in this book will show, I think, that these credentials were well merited."[60]

To this present edition I'd like to add a note about Victor Serge's mature reflections. Toward the end of his life, Serge surveyed the world from the vantage point of a solitary surviving Left Oppositionist, who, while upholding the principles of revolutionary Bolshevism, tried to make sense of a new reality unperceived by his comrades. He decided that the essential tendencies of the modern world were "collectivist," controlled by an antidemocratic, technocratic elite. The nemesis to this totalitarian collectivism, he believed, was the historically conscious collectivism that would emerge from decomposing capitalism and enfeebled Stalinism. Forty-five years later, what has changed? Capitalism is still decomposing, and enfeebled Stalinism has finally succumbed. Post-Stalinism retains much of Stalinism's characteristics, which reveal themselves in the myriad reform "plans" to achieve the spontaneity of the market. The reformers are true products of the system they are trying to escape, still using top-down methods which amount to forcing the population into their schemes. The historically conscious collectivism Serge saw as the solution is yet to emerge.

Serge redefined the goals of socialism in 1943, which must include "the realization of a rational economy and the liberation of mankind, the realization of a human destiny that achieves a new dignity." If we examine this, we see that Stalinist society relieved humans from the undignified position of standing on street corners asking for work in exchange for food, but did not liberate humankind, or achieve any meaningful advance in human dignity. The ending of the Stalinist system creates the possibility for the beginning of a legitimate realization of socialist goals. To borrow a phrase from Serge, humanity is "on the eve."

## Notes

Susan Weissman has broadcast a weekly program on the Soviet Union in Los Angeles since 1981. She teaches in the Government Department at St. Mary's College of California and is on the editorial board of *Critique*, a journal of Soviet Studies and socialist theory and *Against the Current*. Victor Serge is the subject of her doctoral dissertation and scholarly attention. Her book, *Victor Serge: The Course is Set on Hope*, will be published by Verso in 1996/7. Parts of this introduction were first published in *Against the Current*, Nos 10–11, 13–14, and *Cahiers Leon Trotsky*, No. 37.

1. Andrew Wachtel, "Incarnations of Clio in the Age of Pushkin," in *An Obsession with History: Russian Writers Confront the Past*, *Slavic Review*, Fall 1992, p. 537.
2. First published as *Destin d'un Révolution* in France, and as *Destiny of a Revolution* in Britain.
3. *'ochen khoroshei i poleznoi' knigi.*
4. Postscript in letter from Serge to Sedov (in Russian), 18 August 1936. Boris Nikolaevsky Collection, Hoover Archive, Stanford University.
5. Published in November 1947, in *La Révolution proletarienne*

which was edited by the French syndicalist Alfred Rosmer.

6. Victor Serge, *The New International* (February 1939), p. 54.
7. In reality once the left was defeated by Stalin in 1927–37, the only alternative to emerge wag a "right" alternative, or a capitalist one. Gorbachev's replacement by Boris Yeltsin was an implicit recognition that the system, in fact, could not be reformed; it had to be scrapped.
8. Victor Serge *Memoirs of a Revolutionary* (New York: Writers and Readers, 1984), p. 7.
9. According to the *Memoirs of a Revolutionary*, (pp. 63-66) and *Birth of Our Power* (pp. 199–208), they studied Marx's *Civil War in France*, kept abreast of events in Russia, and discussed all the questions facing the Bolsheviks.
10. Serge organized the administration of the Executive Committee of the Comintern in Petrograd, creating the organization which was to be the seat of world revolution from scratch.
11. The book was reissued by the French police as an internal educational document during the 1968 events.
12. The debates were passionate and committed; in the minutes one finds that every member of the Central Committee threatened to resign at least once during the course of different debates, that is every member except Stalin, who never threatened resignation.
13. See "Trente Ans Après La Révolution Russe" in *La Révolution Proletarienne* (November 1947), no. 309, a retrospective Serge wrote on the Revolution's thirtieth birthday.
14. See "Theses of the Left Communists (1918)" published in the first number of the Moscow produced journal *Kommunist* on 20 April 1918, translated and published as a pamphlet by *Critique* (Glasgow, 1977).
15. See Victor Serge, *Year One of the Russian Revolution*, (New York: Holt & Rhinehart, 1973), pp. 182–91.
16. Victor Serge, *Portrait de Staline* (Paris: Editions Bernard Grasset, 1940), pp. 57–58.
17. But according to Serge, Thermidor was only realized in November 1927, ironically on the tenth anniversary of the October Revolution. This coincided with the defeat of the opposition within the party and the subsequent expulsion, arrest and deportation of its members, as well as the sacrificing of the

Chinese proletariat for the prestige and power of Stalin. See Serge, *Memoirs*, pp. 215–43.

18. Serge, "Trente Ans" p. 7.
19. For Serge the errors and mistakes of power were exposed with the handling of the Kronstadt rebellion in 1921. The sailors were protesting against the economic regime of War Communism and the dictatorship of the party, but according to Serge they only revolted because of the brutality with which Kalinin refused to listen to them. He agreed the Bolsheviks were right to fight to hold on to power, but their mistake was "to panic at the Kronstadt revolt, which they could have handled . . . with persuasion and understanding." Nevertheless, Serge declared himself on the side of the Party, against the "infantile illusions" of the backward workers of Kronstadt. See Victor Serge, *Memoirs*, pp. 124–32, "Trente Ans Après," and *New International*, (July 1938 and Feb. 1939).
20. Victor Serge, *Memoirs of a Revolutionary*, p. 177.
21. See, inter alia, Victor Serge, *Russia Twenty Years After* (New York: Pioneer Pub, 1937) and *From Lenin to Stalin* (New York: Pioneer Pub, 1937). Also, Leon Trotsky, *The Revolution Betrayed* (New York: Ment Publishers, 1965), among other works.
22. Victor Serge, *Memoirs of a Revolutionary*, p. 161.
23. Ibid., p. 273.
24. Istrati published the book as the second part of his trilogy, *Vers L'Autre Flamme* (Paris: Rieder, 1929). Republished in Paris 1980, by Fondation Panait Istrati, Union Générale D'Éditione. He used his name to give the book a wider audience and to protect Serge, who was still at large in the Soviet Union.
25. Serge's experiences in deportation are captured in his novel *Midnight in the Century*, superbly translated by Richard Greeman. Serge was joined in Orenburg by some thirty other members of the Left Opposition. Many of the discussions and meetings of the Opposition are recounted in the novel.
26. Interviews with Vlady Kibalchich, Mexico City and Moscow, March 1989. A fuller account of Serge's last days in the Soviet Union is found in Susan Weissman, *Victor Serge: Political, social and literary critic of the USSR, 1919–1947* (doctoral thesis), (University of Glasgow, 1991), pp. 288–296.
27. There was one notable exception: the Belgian *La Wallonie*

provided a platform for Serge from 1936–40.

28. Serge also became active with the International Left Opposition, took part in the congresses of Trotsky's Fourth International, and with the outbreak of Civil War in Spain, joined the POUM (Partido Obrero de Unificación Marxista), which was one of the causes of his rupture with Trotsky and the Fourth International.
29. Serge's insights into the problems that would arise under the Stalinist production system were particularly astute and remarkable for their farsightedness at the time. A more complete analysis of production relations in the 1930s has emerged today, and although Serge couldn't have known how things would turn out, he understood more clearly than most.
30. See the debate on "market socialism" in *Critique 14*.
31. For a full discussion of the relation that developed between the Soviet regime and its working class, the wasteful nature of the Soviet economy, see Hillel Ticktin, *Critique 1* (1973) and *Critique 6* (1976). For a discussion on the implications of Soviet social and economic organization on the formation of class relations in the period of the first three five-year plans, see Donald Filtzer, *Soviet Workers and Stalinist Industrialization* (New York: Sharpe, 1986).
32. Serge, *Russia Twenty Years After*, pp. 297-98.
33. The demand for labor was so high that during the first-five year plan, the workforce virtually doubled. The workers were well aware of the shortage and used it to their advantage. If a worker was fired for an infraction and was not arrested, he knew another job could be found somewhere else. Managers began to hoard workers as consumers hoard sugar during shortages. This led to a certain collusion between managers and workers regarding the tempo and rules of work. Thus the labor shortage gave the workers a certain protection that allowed them to determine partially the way they work, or, as Ticktin terms it, the worker gained a certain measure of control over his own work process. The trade-off for this relative independence of the worker is the undermining of efficiency, which led to contracting more labor and further compounding the problem of labor shortage, even where there was an apparent overstaffing. See also, Filtzer, *Soviet Workers*, chap. 6, pp. 152–78.

34. Serge's analysis of this period coincides with that of certain Left Oppositionists, mainly Rakovsky and Trotsky, whose work he complements and popularizes, and the Left Mensheviks around the journal *Sotsialisticheskii Vestnik*. Working independently of one another in conditions of repression and clandestinity in the late 1920s and early 1930s, a current of thought emerged that criticized the nature of economic growth and the chaotic state of planning or rather the lack of socialist planning. They called it planlessness (*besplannovost*). Serge's work on the question of planning showed some identification and sympathy with this current. The current mentioned above is discussed in the afterward to Rakovsky's article published in *Critique 13* (pp. 53–54) and in Filtzer's book, *Soviet Workers*, p. 39.
35. Serge, *Russia Twenty Years After*, p. 163.
36. Trotsky had noted that an entire class could not be eliminated by administrative methods but only by a change in technology and the mode of production. It was no more possible to create large-scale mechanized agriculture out of wooden ploughs and *kulak* horses than it was to create a ship by adding up fishing boats. "It is impossible to build kolkhozy today without tractors of the future." *Byulleten' Oppozitsii* IX (1930), 3, 7. quoted in Richard Day, "Leon Trotsky on the Problems of the Smychka and Forced Collectivization," *Critique 13*, 1981.
37. Serge, *Russia Twenty Years After*, p. 170. See also Bohdan Krawchenko, "The Famine in the Ukraine in 1933," *Critique 17*, 1986, pp. 137–47, and Robert Conquest, *Harvest of Sorrow*, (New York: Oxford University Press, 1986).
38. Serge, *Russia Twenty Years After*, p. 163.
39. See Khristian Rakovsky's significant article "The Five Year Plan in Crisis," originally published as "At the Congress and in the Country" (*Na s'ezde i v strane*), *Byulleten' oppozitsii* 25/26 (1931), pp. 9–32. Translated and published in *Critique 13*, 1981, pp. 13–54. Also Andrew Smith, *I Was a Soviet Worker*, 1937 (New York: E. P. Dutton, Inc), 1936.
40. Khristian Rakovsky, "The Five Year Plan," pp. 9–32.
41. Serge devotes an entire chapter to this in *Soviets 29* (Paris: Reider, 1929), entitled "Le Gaspillage Bureaucratique Dans L'Industrie", pp. 47–60.
42. Serge, *op.cit.*, p. 175.

43. The conception of waste as a characteristic of Soviet economic development is theoretically developed by H. H. Ticktin in "The Political Economy of the Soviet Union," *Critique 1*, 1973. He shows how waste partially nullifies the results of production, while showing an apparent growth on paper. This growth turns into nongrowth as it cannot be applied usefully to create either means of consumption or usable means of production. Thus it is production that does not provide a productive base for future expansion or produces a defective base for future defective expansion.
44. Serge, *Soviets 1929*, pp. 48–52.
45. Serge, *Soviets 1929*, pp. 56–57, *Russia Twenty Years After*, and *From Lenin to Stalin*.
46. Serge estimated there were up to 15 million in the forced labor sector. See *Russia Twenty Years After*, and *Carnets*, p. 189. He based his figures on David Dallin's book *Forced Labor in Soviet Russia* (New York: Yale Univ. Press, 1947), and discussions with Trotsky, and camp correspondence, etc.
47. Typescripts, unpublished, undated, Serge Archive, Mexico.
48. Serge, *Russia Twenty Years After*, p. 20.
49. Ibid., pp. 15–16. *Sotsialisticheskii Vestnik* also describes the same strike.
50. Serge, *Russia Twenty Years After*, pp. 163–78.
51. Ibid., p. 185.
52. Serge, "Trente Ans Après la Révolution Russe," p. 22 (p. 321 of this volume).
53. Ibid.
54. Ibid.
55. Like Trotsky, Serge noted that the bureaucracy was tied to the revolution and to the preservation of collective property and a managed, though not planned, economy. See his conclusions, *Russia Twenty Years After*.
56. Serge, unpublished manuscript, no date, archives, Mexico.
57. Serge, "Russia Thirty Years After," p. 23 (p. 326 of this volume).
58. Serge, unpublished manuscripts, no date, archives, Mexico.
59. Serge expressed this thought in various essays. See for example, his letter to Sidney Hook of 19 July 1943, called "Marxism et Démocratie."
60. Max Shachtman, in the original Introduction to *Russia Twenty Years After*, p. ix.

# Introduction

EVEN AFTER TWENTY YEARS OF EXISTENCE THE RUSSIAN Bolshevik Revolution has not ceased to be a source of lively and absorbing interest throughout the world, and a subject of fierce controversy. The Stalin régime, successor to the government of the original architects of the revolution, has, in recent times, been uncritically and lavishly praised by literary tourists as well as by writers who made their observations and drew their conclusions from afar. The fact that the Soviet régime has existed for such a long time, and has grown increasingly conservative and consequently respectable, is perhaps one of the basic reasons for the eulogistic literature that has flooded the market for the past few years. The apparent solidity and success of the new state has made criticism the heresy that acceptance was some fifteen years ago.

Nevertheless, there are still critics. Generally speaking, they fall into two broad categories. One is not only hostile to the present Stalin régime, but hostile also to the very ideal of the new social order towards which the Russian Revolution originally aimed. This critic concludes that the evils which the Soviet Union suffers from are the ineluctable results of any attempt radically to alter the capitalist—order—thus justifying the complainant's original faith in capitalism or his disillusioned abandonment of the socialist ideal which he held before he "saw it in real life." The other category contains a smaller number of critics. Without renouncing the fundamental ideas of the Russian Revolution, they argue that it is the present régime that has departed from these concepts, which can be restored and richly realized only by removing the Soviet bureaucracy and, while retaining the fundamental economic set-up of a nationalized means of production and exchange, by establishing a political system of workers' democracy.

Into the latter group falls the author of the present volume, Victor Serge. In many respects he is uniquely equipped to sum up the pluses and minuses of twenty years of the Russian Revolution. He is not a casual tourist-in-revolution, of either the dyspeptic or the dithyrambic variety, nor a dull grubber into statistics; not an enemy of the revolution nor a dilettante "friend." The past two decades of his life have been spent in the very heart of the Russian Revolution itself. He knows the revolutionary movement as only an active insider can know it. He knows the men who made the revolution possible, and the men who took their places later on. He has seen the revolution pursue its course on the highways, into the bypaths, and over disheartening detours.

But perhaps it is better to introduce the author to American readers—in France and Belgium this would be a work of supererogation—by means of a brief biography.

Victor Serge is a pseudonym for Victor Lvovich Kibalchich, born in Brussels on December 30, 1890, the son of Russian revolutionary émigrés. His father, a former army officer and then a physician, was a friend of the renowned Populist movement: *Narodnaya Volya*. One of his relatives, a chemist of the party, was hanged in 1881 after the assassination of Tsar Alexander II.

After a childhood in Belgium and England, Serge became a photographer's apprentice in Brussels at the age of fifteen. Later he became successively a photographer, a draughtsman, an office worker, a linotype operator after learning the trade in anarchist print-shops, then a journalist and translator. At fifteen, too, he joined the Socialist Young Guards in Ixelles; then the Brussels "Revolutionary Group." In 1910, after several years of activity in the movement, he became editor of *l'Anarchie*. In 1913 he was tried in the famous political assassination case of the anarchists Bonnot, Garnier, Callemin, and others. Although he was entirely innocent of any complicity in their acts, he courageously defended the ideas for which his movement stood and said nothing to inculpate the other defendants. His attitude saved a young girl comrade from a long term of imprisonment, but not himself, for he was sentenced to five years in the penitentiary.

Released in 1917, he went to Barcelona and became active among the syndicalists and anarchists in the National Confederation of Labour (C.N.T.), working as a linotype operator for his living and contributing to the anarchist journal *Tierra y Libertad*. He took part in the first revolutionary attempt made by the Catalonians in July 1917; when it was over he left for Russia. He was arrested in Paris, interned in a concentration camp by the Clemenceau government, and finally was exchanged in January 1919 as a Bolshevik hostage for an officer in the French Military Mission who was being held in Russia.

Upon his arrival in Petrograd he immediately became a member of the Communist party of Russia and a close colleague of Gregory Zinoviev in the Executive Committee of the Communist International, which had just been formed. He did not confine his activities for the Russian Revolution to airy sympathies. As member of a special communist battalion—"empty-bellied, revolver stuck in the belt, standing behind the armour plate of besieged Petrograd," as he has written—he defended the revolution not only with pen but also with rifle in hand.

He participated actively in the first congresses of the Communist International, was sent on hazardous confidential missions by the Soviet leaders, and for years was managing editor of the official world magazine, *Communist International.* He spent long periods of time in Germany, living secretly in the workers' quarters of Berlin, preparing for the 1923 revolution that never took place.

When the Trotskyist opposition was organized he became a supporter and an active spokesman. In 1928 he was expelled from the party, along with thousands of other Trotskyists, and imprisoned. In 1933 he was imprisoned again and deported to Orenburg. Only the most persistent agitation in France, Belgium, and elsewhere, conducted by his political friends as well as by the leading intellectual and literary personalities of those countries, forced his release in 1936. He was banished from the Soviet Union and deprived of his Soviet citizenship without any legal grounds.

In addition to being the translator into French of the works of Lenin, Trotsky, and Zinoviev, Serge (he continues to use the pseudonym he adopted in Barcelona in 1917 for reasons of legality) is an author in his own right. He has written a splendid history of the first year of the Russian Revolution, countless political and literary essays, and three novels of the revolutionary movement: *Les Hommes dans la Prison*, *Naissance de notre Force*, and *Ville Conquise.* Other works which he had already completed in manuscript form were retained by the Soviet censor when Serge was banished from Russia.

This brief sketch suffices to indicate that few writers about the Soviet Union have better credentials—or credentials half so good—to present to the reader. The material contained in this book will show, I think, that these credentials were well merited.

MAX SHACHTMAN
New York,
August 8, 1937

# Part One

# THE CONDITION OF MAN AND MIND

# I.

# *The Condition of the Workers—Wages*

AS IS KNOWN, THE DICTATORSHIP OF THE PROLETARIAT, EXERcised by the Communist party, makes the working class the ruling class and strives to build up a new classless society. Twenty years after the revolution, the condition of the workers varies according to the degree of professional instruction, the political quality (member of the party or the Communist Youth, right-thinker, suspect, relative or friend of a suspect or of a prominent communist), the enterprise, the region. The workers in the big plants are usually better paid for the same work than are those in the small ones. Those in the large centres are better paid than those in the remote provinces. The extreme inequality of wages bewilders the observer and makes possible various statistical camouflages, the least of which consists in recording an average wage that is really a good deal higher than the wage of the great majority.

According to a report of the late Kuibyshev to the Planning Commission, published on January 3, 1935, the average wage in Moscow was 149 rubles 30 kopecks per month.[1] At the same period, according to my personal information, the big majority of the workers of the Elec-

[1] At that time 1 ruble = approximately 20 cents; 1 kopeck = 2/10 of 1 cent.

trical Station of Moscow (*Elektrozavod*) received from 120 to 140 rubles per month. The state wage fund not having been appreciably increased since then (if the numerical increase of wage earners is taken into account), one may accept the following (monthly) salaries as the most current at the moment: labourers, 100 to 120 rubles; average worker, 150 to 200 rubles; skilled worker, 250 to 400 rubles; Stakhanovist, 500 rubles and over, running as high as 1,500 to 2,000 rubles in exceptional cases.

Women's wages are always somewhat lower, which is especially noticeable at the bottom rungs, that is, for the vast majority of women workers. Hundreds of thousands of Soviet women workers get between 70 and 90 rubles a month, a poverty wage entirely inadequate to feed the one who gets it. We are forced to conclude that the employer-state regards the woman's wage in reality as a bonus wage in the family budget. The theory does, indeed, say: Equal wages for equal work. But you will be told that the work is rarely equal. . . .

Wages in Leningrad and Moscow at the beginning of 1936: a scientific collaborator of a large establishment of higher study, 300 to 400 rubles; a stenographer knowing foreign languages, about 200 rubles; a newspaper editor, 230 rubles; miscellaneous employees, 90 to 120 rubles. Many women workers in Moscow textiles (*Krasnaya-Presnya*) were getting between 100 and 120 rubles, only quite recently. In the provinces, where I lived, the prevalent basis of women's wages ranged between 70 and 90 rubles. An economist got 350 rubles (unlimited working day); a bookkeeper (unlimited working day and penal responsibility for the running of the enterprise), 250 to 350 rubles; a responsible functionary of the party, 250 rubles and over; a director of an enterprise or the head of an office (communist), 400 to 800 rubles; high functionaries (communists) and big specialists, from 1,000 to 5,000 rubles. In the capitals, renowned specialists get as high as between 5,000 and 10,000 rubles per month. Writers have the same kind of income. The great official dramatists, the official painters who do the portraits of the important leaders over and over again, the poets and novelists approved by the Central Committee, may get a million a year and more.

These data require some supplementary explanations: the collaborator of a scientific institute gets only 300 to 400 rubles, but he works in two or three institutes, which comes to 1,200 rubles at the end of the month. The newspaper editor, at 250 rubles per month, collaborates on other publications, which trebles his income. The factory director, at 500 or 1,500 rubles, gets himself granted premiums for the execution of plans on the occasion of festivals and anniversaries. The party functionaries and the communist leaders receive gifts of garments made of fine cloth, are lodged by the party in comfortable quarters built for that purpose, have the benefits of watering places in the Caucasus or the Crimea, free of charge or at reduced rates. But the vast majority of the workers, those who live on low wages, is left entirely to itself, that is, to its poverty.

Let us make an accounting of the levies placed upon wages: the tax, the compulsory loans (15 days of wages per year, for the lower paid; 1 month and more for the others), dues in the party, the trade-union, the Aviation-Chemistry, the Red Aid,[1] etc.; the voluntary—in reality, the imposed—subscriptions for international solidarity, for the construction of dirigibles and aeroplanes, etc. The total real reduction of wages amounts to 15 to 20 per cent. In one hospital

[1] In 1935 the government prohibited the levying of payments for more than two so-called free societies. A platonic decision, but symptomatic.

(1935), I knew probationers who received 26 rubles per fortnight at a time when brown bread cost a ruble a kilogram; in addition, life insurance was imposed upon them, provided they were in good health. In the factories and shops the system of fines is rigorously practised: fines for poor work, tardiness, suspension of work, deficient discipline. This provokes scenes. You believe you are entitled to 100 rubles at the end of the month, and the management presents you with a list of fines of 30 rubles! It is saddening to recall in this connection that Lenin, in Siberia, began his work as a publicist with a pamphlet which was an indictment: *On Fines*.

The official propaganda makes a big to-do of *indirect wages*, represented by social insurance, free treatment in case of illness, country vacations, old-age pensions. What is substantially left of all this is the somewhat reduced wage paid in case of illness and also the allocations for pregnancy and nursing. Doctors still often receive only a limited number of sickness tickets for distribution. Free medicaments have recently been abolished. Sojourns in the better rest homes are free only to the very well-known "activists" who get offers from the trade-unions. In practice, a trip to the Crimea or the Caucasus is an entirely unrealizable dream for the worker receiving from 80 to 150 rubles per month, for it involves an outlay of about 700 rubles, in addition to which he must get a permit, which is no easy matter. The published figures fully confirm this personal observation, for only 181,000 workers visited the watering places in 1934 (out of 24,000,000 wage workers).

What is the purchasing power of these wages? The purchasing power of the ruble is about equal to that of the French or Belgian franc, except for the price of brown bread, which is lower in the U.S.S.R. (It costs 1 ruble or

90 kopecks a kilogram; in turn, however, real white bread is beyond reach: 4 rubles 50 and 7 rubles 50 a kilogram.) Here are some prices at the beginning of 1936: beef, 6 to 8 rubles a kilogram; pork, 9 to 12 rubles; butter, 14 to 18 rubles; sausage, 7 to 9 rubles; salami, 25 rubles; ham, 18 to 20 rubles; Gruyère cheese, 24 rubles; herring, 6 to 10 rubles; caviar, 32 to 40 rubles; coffee, 40 to 50 rubles; candy, 9 to 40 rubles; tea, 60 to 100 rubles; chocolate, 50 rubles; alcohol, vodka, 12 rubles a litre. Manufactured articles: overcoat, 100 to 500 rubles; leather-soled shoes, 80 to 150 rubles; a cotton suit, 200 rubles; a woollen suit, 600 to 1,000 rubles; dress, 70 to 100 rubles; woollen shirt, 200 rubles. Fuel: a cubic metre of firewood, cut and transported to the home, between 40 and 50 rubles (at least 6 cubic metres are needed to heat a modest lodging through the winter). Rental of a private unfurnished room in the provinces, 40 to 58 rubles a month; a furnished corner as a roomer, 30 rubles and over, dearer than in the large cities. To the high prices should be added the difficulty of getting food, cloth, woollens, footwear, wood. You are often compelled to go to a neighbouring town to get a pair of shoes or a plaid from which to make an overcoat. The shortage of merchandise is cause for a rise in prices on the illicit market; and the arrest and deportation of speculators, which took place throughout the summer of 1936 at the rate of a hundred a day in Moscow alone, according to the newspapers, remedy nothing.

The worker at 100 rubles a month, therefore, receives in 24 days of work a little more than 5 kilograms of butter or a hundred kilograms of brown bread. Since you can live on bread alone, at least for a fairly long time, he is no longer famished and rather contented with this improvement.

A French worker who lived in the U.S.S.R. for more than ten years had the ingenious idea of drawing up, for

1936, a comparative table of wages and prices in Moscow and in Paris, enabling one to calculate what working time is necessary, by category of workers (labourer, average, skilled), for the purchase of current articles and objects of consumption. He reached the conclusion that the Soviet labourer works 172 minutes for a kilogram of white bread, which represents 36 minutes of the time of a Parisian unemployed worker; that the Soviet worker works 1,584 minutes (the labourer) or 930 (the average worker) or 632 (the skilled worker) for the kilogram of butter that the French labourer gets in 180 minutes and the skilled worker in 114 minutes. These calculations are unassailable.[1]

Did they live better before the revolution? People of forty are unanimous in affirming it, in all three respects of food, clothing, and lodgings. Statistics confirm it. A worker of the textile industry who, in 1912–1914, received 300 kilograms of bread per month, a miner who received 600, today get an average of 150 (the equivalent of 150 rubles). More than once I heard mothers deploring the fact that their children have never known the good times when, during religious festivals, such nice things as pastries, preserves, and creams were made; and old women complaining of no longer even having tea to drink. . . . Most of the pensions of Civil War widows are 30 rubles a month. In 1926 the pre-war level seemed to be nearly reached; they are far from it today. In order to restore to the vast majority of Russian workers their material level of 1926 it would be necessary to double all the low wages. According to the head of the government, Molotov, in the three or four years

[1] Ch. Yvon, *Ce qu' est devenue la Révolution russe,* published in Paris by La Révolution Prolétarienne. This little book is probably the best study yet published on the condition of the Russian workers.

to come one cannot count on an increase of more than "a few dozen per cent" (let us say, 30).

A dozen years ago the labour aristocracy, getting more than 150 rubles per month, represented 5 per cent of the proletariat. Let us say, to give a generous figure, that it now reaches 10 per cent, even though the new highly mechanized enterprises need semi-skilled workers above all. *Nine-tenths of the Soviet workers thus live on low wages.*

How do they manage to live? Rent, being paid pro rata, absorbs only about a tenth of the budget. It is true that the quarters are usually a hole. The norm of "habitable area" allocated to the inhabitants is 8 square metres per capita in the large cities and less in the regional centres where the local authorities sometimes reduce it to 5 square metres. This means that workers are quartered at the rate of one family to a room; that they sleep in the corridors, in garrets, in lofts, in cellars; and since the houses are not fitted for such overcrowding, entire families occupy poorly ventilated rooms which other families must cross in order to come and go. Imagine the consequences, under such crowded conditions, of the lack of linen, of furniture, of clothing; the ignorance, the alcoholism, and the informing; and the bitter struggles that can occur, for example, over a room whose occupant, an old woman, seems to be on the point of dying. Many workers in the large plants live still more poorly, in barracks. In the provinces and in the large suburbs, people try to raise rabbits, pigs, a cow. These animals must then be lodged in the corridors, under the windows if not in the room itself, for thievery is a social scourge. And yet the most ingenious things are thought up in this primitive destitution to create a home. I have seen touching interiors, very clean and almost prepossessing, in which poverty is clothed in a sort of whiteness. Nothing there but well-washed and mended scraps out of old chests; the lamp glass patched up with transparent paper; the bed sheets are taken off at night, for they are irreplaceable. . . . Most tragic is the suffering felt by poorly nourished children from the great cold spells in wintertime.

Tragic also is alcoholism. Men, women, old folk, and many adolescents—everybody drinks. On the snow or in the August dust, in the fields or in the great arteries of the capitals, it is not unusual to see men fall down dead-drunk. On paydays and holidays, *a third* of the passers-by stagger along, humming and bawling, down the street. The day of Kirov's obsequies the sale of vodka was prohibited. "You understand," a communist, manager of a co-operative, said to me, "if the people got drunk today, we might hear them say too much. . . ."

The alcoholism of the Russian people derives from its indigent condition. No home, no well-being, few distractions—life is joyless. There remains alcohol, which drowns the blues and unleashes the brute liberated from conventions. Alcoholism in its turn is a cause of undernourishment and of countless scenes. In the hospitals where I stayed the personnel would settle down on the eve of the rest days, preparing themselves to treat broken jaws, fractures and injuries of all kinds. . . . Having lived with the poor of the country, I would not dream of reproaching them for getting drunk. I know too well the immense sadness of a life without escape and without joy. Alcoholism will diminish when well-being increases.

The low wage of the great number often makes the work unusable. The shoemaker, whom an artisans' co-operative would pay 150 rubles per month, has every interest in making at home, with leather he has pilfered, some clandestine repairs which bring him an additional income and which satisfy the client more, for they are fairly properly made. He takes care not to have himself turned into one of the unemployed; on the contrary, he does everything to remain registered as a worker. Speculation—that is, the resale of articles bought from the state, be it due to favours awarded or simply to spending a night at the door of the store—feeds millions of men. The resale of a pair of shoes brings in, in one morning, as much as eight days of work in the factory. In order to be registered as a worker, people go to the factory, but it is speculation that actually feeds them. And also theft: whatever isn't nailed down is lifted. The party periodically launches big campaigns against theft in the industrial enterprises and in the stores. Trials are staged to set an example, and the severest sentences are pronounced. But nothing can prevent the breadseller at 110 rubles a month from wolfing a small loaf and taking away another for her child, even at the risk of two years at hard labour; nor the worker at 150 rubles a month from taking thread from the plant, which he will easily resell at 3 rubles a bobbin. . . . Speculation explains the dissimulated unemployment of millions of persons; it torments and relieves the masses; the consumer suffers from it, so long as in many cases he can count upon it alone but, since he himself speculates, the advantages gain in the end over the disadvantages.

Pilfering a bit, reselling something, a worker's household with the nominal wage of 200 rubles (the husband 130, the wife 70), and two children, can almost double its income if it knows how to go about it. The worker feeds on vegetables, fresh in the summer and salted in the winter, on a little meat one or two days out of five, on dairy products when they are not too dear. If he has a cow or a goat, he is almost in clover, in spite of the odour of manure that fills the house. The big problems are those of clothing and fuel. In the provinces wood is pilfered from the parks, picket fences are stolen. One winter after another, I have seen the picket fence of a military hippodrome disappear.

It is a certainty that the sorry condition of the railroad men is one of the causes of the dilapidation of the rolling stock. The lines connected with countries abroad are the only ones that are well kept up. Then come a few of the trunk lines. As soon as you leave Moscow, the trains, always crowded, become dirty; the train conductors are poor devils whose very appearance reveals a desperate indigence. Railroad men, however, supplement their income by rendering illicit services to travellers and by transporting merchandise for petty speculation.

It is often asserted that in the U.S.S.R. there is neither unemployment nor a feeling of insecurity among the workers. It is true that there is rather a shortage of labour, because it is so poorly remunerated. Anyone who has looked for work in a city of the U.S.S.R. knows that, while he always ends by finding it, by the time he is hired he is so discouraged that he is ready to accept even the worst conditions. Anyone who has travelled knows that migratory throngs fill the railroad stations, manifestly people who are going neither to the factory, to the office, nor into the fields the following morning. Mass unemployment, such as ravages the capitalist countries, does not exist at the present moment; but other forms of unemployment, which governmental statistics deliberately ignore, affect millions of workers. Insecurity, under these conditions, also assumes a different form than in the West. You have neither reserves nor savings, you live in great want, so that a dismissal followed by a short period of unemployment (without allocations) may become a terrible experience. Then again, the work does not feed you entirely, so that a prisonlike insecurity has become the most ordinary thing for everybody.[1]

Among the people, the couple that is burdened with a family has a hard life. The man must "work" in order to have a legal status, after which the problem is to make arrangements in order to live. . . . The crèches for children, the laundries, and other public utility establishments serve only a privileged minority. The conditions of the masses are dismally, onerously primitive.

To sum up:

Excessive inequality of wages, running as high as 1 to 15 in the ranks of the working class. Wages of the great majority, very low, appreciably lower than the average wage of the statistician and plainly insufficient for the upkeep of the worker. Average wage (higher, we repeat, than that of the great majority), assuring a standard of living lower than the pre-war and much lower than that of the vast majority of the workers of the West. Anticipated growth of wages much too slow. A government, however little concerned with the genuine interests of the working class, would preoccupy itself with bringing back within the shortest possible interval the basic wages of the 1914 level, nearly attained in 1926. The bureaucratic régime prefers

---

[1] Up to 1934 the economic life of the U.S.S.R. rested upon inflation, and it still rests on low wages. The raising of wages is a vital necessity; so is the stabilization of the ruble, that is, financial reform. Unemployment has been eliminated only by means of a sort of inflation of the personnel consequent upon the monetary inflation. It is quite probable that the return to a stable budget calculated in real values, by obliging the enterprises to reduce their general expenses, will make them liquidate the superfluous personnel and will thus bring back unemployment, which it seems impossible to liquidate in reality save in a much more harmonious social organism of greater equalitarian tendencies.

to accentuate the social differentiation by creating diverse privileged categories to the detriment of the disinherited masses.

In comparison with the workers, the technicians enjoy a clearly privileged position. Their salaries are rarely below 300 rubles and most often they range between 500 and 1,000 rubles, a sum which they sometimes far exceed. The best qualified engineers get several thousand rubles per month. They profit by bonuses. Comfortable dwellings are built for their use. They have clubs. Scientific establishments, founded in great number, aim to provide them with the means of perfecting technique. But they are not authorized to form any associations. All their researches are under surveillance.

Their condition would appear excellent were it not for the often crushing burden of penal responsibilities that weighs them down. The management of the enterprises is in the hands of communists who merely carry out the instructions of the central organisms. Do these instructions prove to be inexecutable? Do they have unforeseen and vexatious consequences? Do low wages adversely affect the productivity of labour? Has the plan been discredited? Finally, has the engineer permitted himself to formulate objections? Did he keep still, out of prudent complacency, on the eve of an experiment that turned out badly? In all these cases and in many others, the technical personnel, accused of incompetence, of negligence, of bad faith, even of counter-revolutionary spirit or of conspiracy, is the object of mass punishments which always mean arrests and all too often end in executions. . . .

# 2.

# *The Condition of the Workers—The Work*

LOW WAGES CANNOT CONTINUE INDEFINITELY—THEY ARE TOO costly to the community. They increase the general costs of production instead of diminishing them. I know a clothing factory where the bad work reached such proportions that it had to refuse all deliveries. The workers there received from 80 to 150 rubles. No amount of agitation could stimulate them; the penalties and the fines only served to aggravate the evil. Every worker who was any good at her job hastened to quit the factory in order to sew cotton shirts at home which, when sold on the market, brought her in a larger sum. The plan was never carried out except on paper. In the club of the enterprise, men and women workers accused of sabotage were tried for cheating. Others, caught red-handed at stealing, went to prison. Both were subject to years of suffering and the factory lost several skilled workers thereby. Women workers, leaving their work at ten o'clock in the evening, were reduced to seeking out some drunken non-commissioned officer in the streets who would get them a dinner.

From the Donietz mines to the big factories the same evils have ravaged industry. In April 1931 the big textile plants of Ivanovo-Voznessensk suddenly went on strike. All their demands were contained in this cry: "We are hungry!" Hundreds of rank-and-file communists had kept secret the preparations of the movement. The central authorities yielded on every point and threw the responsibility for the inadequate nourishment upon the shoulders of the local authorities. The factories received foodstuffs, work was resumed without repressions, and the purge began quietly. I was assured that oppositionists (Trotskyists) were later shot, on the pretext of sabotage and treason. No word of it seeped into the press, except abroad.

Until the stabilization of the ruble,[1] the industrial directors tried to compensate for low quality and the low intensity of labour by eliminating leisure time. That is what the activity of the shock brigades and the brigades of enthusiasts boiled down to. Young workers, swept along by propagandists and stimulated by bonuses and the granting of various privileges (a little more substantial meal, slight improvement of the food, moving pictures without waiting a turn), formed themselves into brigades determined to work to the very limit of their strength. These brigades competed with each other, and that was the socialist emulation. Then the custom of Communist Saturdayings of the civil war days was remembered—the day of voluntary labour devoted to the common cause. But in 1919–1920 only the Saturday wage was contributed, after all, and you rested on Sunday. In 1931–1935 the men and women workers were called upon, under various pretexts, to do unpaid work for three rest days out of four. "Voluntary" days were arranged—by a decision of the trade-union, adopted in open meeting by raised hands—in order to fill up "the breaches in the plan," "to catch up with and outstrip" an-

[1] See later, p. 191, "A Turn: The Stabilization of the Ruble." Bread cards were abolished on January 1, 1935, and from that day on the ruble had the real value of one kilogram of rye bread.

other enterprise, to repair mistakes, to support the army, aviation, schools. . . . In the last 75 days of the construction of the Moscow subway 500,000 workers contributed voluntary and free days of labour (according to the Soviet press). It is to be noted also that in the same period, still according to the official papers, criminality was proportionately increased among the subway constructors.

The stabilization of the ruble made possible the return to the methods of labour exploitation established in the capitalist countries. Piecework wages, minute rationalization, job-timing, work by shifts. Enterprises equipped according to the last word in technique had a labour yield lower than that of the old "joints" in the vicinity of Paris or London, in which, to be sure, the lathe-hand does not go hungry. Upon a signal from the Central Committee the Stakhanov movement sprang up, all decked out with stunning records. The production norm of a Donietz mine being 7 tons of coal per day per digger (average in the Ruhr: 10 tons; maximum: 16 to 17 tons), Alexis Stakhanov cut 100 tons in one day, August 31, 1935. The next day he was a celebrity, the whole publicity machine having started on signal. His picture was to be seen everywhere. The radio stations broadcast his remarks. He left the mine for conferences. Bobkov, meanwhile, had cut 159 tons in a day. Then Issachenko, 201 tons (September 10th); later Artiukhov, 536 tons (November 4th); Borissov, finally, 800 tons (800!). In France and elsewhere miners, more competent than I, have judged these records, which are better evaluated in the light of the general results of Stakhanovism in the same mines. In Gorlovka the average production reached in 220 days of sustained effort was 34 tons. Far from 800 tons or even from the modest 100 tons of Stakhanov! But in October 1935 the mine where Stakhanov had worked yielded a production increase of only 7 per cent. In the Donietz region, it was from 15 to 20 per cent.

The Central Committee of the party feigned surprise in welcoming the initiative of the workers. It explained their passion for work by the improvement of the conditions of existence and *decreed the revision of all the norms of work.* The technicians who voiced objections were treated as saboteurs. The placards showed a gigantic Stakhanov overturning the old, pretendedly scientific norms. The renewing of the collective labour contracts was delayed for several months. The workers understood immediately what was involved:

1. The increasing of the norms of production without a corresponding increase in wages.

2. The creation of a numerically small, well-paid labour aristocracy, which would set working conditions in general on the wrong track and would help the directors keep the masses moving.

Almost everywhere they reacted sharply. Stakhanovists had their heads smashed. Some were killed. The young communist who, in order to get a bonus or to quit the plant later on, tried to beat the record was considered a traitor by his shopmates. This resistance was broken by means of repression, and Stakhanovism was attenuated by generalizing it. The name was speedily worn down, in a few months, amidst abuse and even ridicule. The party committees were forced to react against the exaggerations of Stakhanovism. I knew a hospital director who thought up a favoured treatment for his Stakhanovist patients. . . . What remains of this campaign pursued with a totalitarian ardour? An elevation of the norms which, all told, would hardly exceed 10 per cent, and a more appreciable growth of inequality among the workers, a small number of whom have gained the possibility of joining the privileged strata of society. A greater productivity of labour can be obtained, in general, only by more genuinely improving the material conditions of the workers.

I have read nothing more erroneous about Stakhanovism than these few lines culled from a French review[1]: "*In these creative surroundings* par excellence, *a collective and anonymous idea* had to germinate which found *by chance* in the person of Stakhanov its first *bold realizer. . . .*" I have underlined the falsest words of this sentence in which is revealed a bumptiousness greater even than the incompetence of the author. And I am at a loss to discover what it is that obliges intellectuals, perhaps of good faith, to deal with such subjects out of the fullness of their ignorance. "Creative surroundings"—poverty, the flagging labour of undernourished workers, the bargaining at the factory, the police notations in the passports of the discharged workers, the Draconian legislation? A "collective and anonymous idea"? Stakhanov himself has told how he prepared his record together with the communist directors of the mine (who were themselves only executing the instructions of their superiors); the publicity of the totalitarian state did the rest. The element of "chance" amounts to nothing in all this and Stakhanov, a zealous executor rather than a bold realizer, simply succeeded in making a career.

Many things, moreover, have been left unsaid about these exploits, such as that Stakhanov did not work alone or just anywhere in general, but with a full-selected crew and in a favourable spot; that the Stakhanovist crews exerted such exhausting efforts that they included a supernumerary to replace the worker who might faint on the

---

[1] M. R. Chanel, in *Europe*, April 15, 1936.

job; that the Stakhanovists prepared their work for one or two hours before and one or two hours after the "day" of production, which raised the real duration of their labour from two to three hours. That once their exploit was accomplished, these production aces left the mine or the factory in order to carry on studies. . . . It is patent that they could not stay on without discrediting themselves and discrediting the propaganda built around them, for they would not succeed in maintaining the level of their own records.

Since Stakhanovism, the wage relations between the ordinary worker and the privileged worker vary from 1 to 10 and even to 20.

The participation of the workers in the management of the enterprises practically ceased a long time ago. Of the shop democracy of the early days there subsisted a few vestiges up to 1935. The factory directors affected the air of former workers, made themselves accessible, and allowed themselves to be addressed familiarly. Since the ruble was resurrected, a contrary tendency has asserted itself. The well-dressed director must keep his distance.

# 3.

# *The Condition of Woman*

THE EQUALITY OF RIGHTS PREVENTS NEITHER PHYSIOLOGICAL inequality nor the consequences, particularly irksome for the woman, of the general indigence. The compulsory promiscuity of the overcrowded lodgings is especially painful to the young girl and the young woman. How many couples are unable to separate because it is impossible to find different lodgings! In such cases the man liberates himself more easily, and forced cohabitation is less oppressive to him. The venereal dispensaries are crowded with infected youth who declare that they cannot be cured at home because of the impossibility of isolating themselves. The very low wage of the vast majority of young women forces them to seek a husband who is making good money, a military man or a party member. The surreptitious prostitution of all those who owe a tolerably good job to the amiability of store managers and office heads escapes, fortunately for the moralists, all statistical calculation.

Prostitution, properly speaking, subsists in most cities. Less widespread than in the big cities of the West, it is also more wretched. No legal regulation deals with it; in practice, commissions provided with discretionary powers keep it under surveillance and sometimes prosecute it; from time to time, on the eve of holidays or international congresses, sudden raids clean up Moscow, Leningrad, Kiev, Odessa. Hundreds of women are arrested in one night and sometimes they are deported by administrative measure to the North or to Siberia. There they fall into the clutches of administrators and the police. The housing crisis and the repression of pandering make prostitution in the big Russian cities something at once infamous and sordid. The girls bring their clients to the rear of unlighted courts, to churches that are being demolished, to corridors, to abandoned gardens, to hovels. Night watchmen have been condemned for having rented to them the vestibules in front of the big stores. Bathhouses are sometimes their refuge. You can see the chauffeurs of trusts spending the night with their cars, picking up chance couples.

In 1928–1929 the Soviet press was ordered to suppress the section devoted to miscellaneous news. It has recently been re-established in the sense that the newspapers mention a burglary once a week in order to emphasize the promptness with which the guilty were captured. But in the days when the *Krasnaya Vechernaya Gazeta (Red Evening Gazette)* of Leningrad published, among other things, suicide lists, there were from twelve to fifteen a day; young women were the majority in these horrible statistics and they made free use of veronal which could still be obtained. We have no reason to say that suicides are less numerous today. The poverty which drives young women to kill themselves forces just as many onto the pavements. Extremely wretched, hounded by the militia and by the committees of the Housing Co-operatives, prostitution ends necessarily by joining the very numerous underworld, made up of burglars, swindlers, bandits, pimps, and guerrillas of all kinds. And the result is that if the same laws are not applied to it, at least the same rigours are. Deportees have told me of the executions, by administrative decision, of "incorrigible" prostitutes, put on the same basis as habitual criminals, their companions of the depths.

There exist in Moscow (and perhaps elsewhere) one or more model establishments for rehabilitation. I once read a description of them by Mme. Margareta Nelken, deputy to the Spanish Cortes. This lady saw girls living freely in the nice House, studying there, and making as much as 300 rubles a month. In that period I met pallid women workers who worked like beavers for half that sum and dreamed of getting, by protection, a pair of rubber shoes from the store reserved for the G.P.U. . . . They did not understand that it was necessary to begin by prostituting themselves in order to gain access to a House where they might finally earn a living! Yet I admit that there is some laudable truth in the model establishments which tourists are taken to visit. But what a small place they occupy in life!

So long as the big majority of the young working women do not get enough from their work to feed, clothe, and house themselves—for it is not only a question of work, but of being able to live on the pay—the evil will remain without cure. If, in spite of everything, prostitution in the U.S.S.R. has been much less important in the last few years than in most of the other civilized countries, it is due to the fact that it is more profitable and even easier to engage in petty speculation on the market or to steal from the shop than to patrol the streets. Moreover, the demand has diminished as a result of the general indigence and probably, in the years of famine, of a physiological depression. As is obvious, these temporary causes are not the result of an improvement in the condition of women. Nothing is easier for a man supplied with means than to buy a woman, even outside the sphere of prostitution as such.[1]

The freedom of abortion, a capital conquest of the revolution, ceased to exist in the summer of 1935. Previously, circular letters had quietly strangled it. Henceforward, abortion is permitted only for medical reasons; and it is punished by obloquy and fines for the patient, by prison for the operator. At the same time the law grants premiums to large families.[2] One sees very well, alas! the reasons for this policy of natality, based upon the calculations of military experts who will tell you without blinking an eyelid how many millions of lives will have to be sacrificed in two years of war. . . . The return to obligatory maternity in a period of indigence is nothing less, for the woman, than an enormous aggravation of her condition. Then there is the matter of her rights and her dignity: socialism seems to us called upon to bring about the triumph of conscious and not of imposed maternity. Since the doctors received the order to advise against and to refuse abortions, the clandestine clientele of the abortionists has grown, the price of a medical abortion has doubled, with the result of an immediate aggravation of dangers, of suffering, of costs, and of servitude for the poorest among the women.

The new legislation has been justified by arguments which sound like bitter pleasantries. Do we not enjoy a free and happy life? No more unemployment, all careers open to women. Why should they spurn the joys of ma-

---

[1] This also exists in special forms, superintended and even organized, in the large hotels reserved for foreigners.

[2] The encouragement given to large families is manifested in the allocations of 2,000 rubles a year for five years for every child beginning with the seventh and 5,000 rubles for one year for every child beginning with the eleventh and 3,000 annually for four years. These measures of serious support went immediately into effect. (Law of June 27, 1936.)

ternity? Things like this could be read throughout the Soviet press—which no longer publishes suicides. . . . Doctors have proved the injuriousness of abortions. On being interviewed, old serfs have related their happiness in having had sixteen children, exceeded today by their happiness in living under the tutelage of the well-beloved Leader. Nobody has raised the question of the wage of the woman worker or of the condition of the child.

Other legal measures taken at the same time put a tax on divorce "in order to strengthen the family": 50 rubles for the first time, 150 for the second, 300 rubles for any thereafter. The absolute ease of obtaining a divorce often worked against the woman, without a doubt; but do the officials imagine that they have done well in keeping ill-matched couples together by means of a fine? It may be expected that the legislator will soon go back upon another great reform achieved in the early years of the revolution: the legal recognition of the free union as having the same standing as marriage.

The establishment of paternity, the compulsory pension payable by the father for each child, with the amount fixed by the courts, paid vacations during pregnancy and nursing periods (recently raised from 42 to 56 days before and after birth), contraceptive freedom, the recognition of the free union, the freedom of divorce, the freedom of abortion, the equality of rights—these were what women gained from the proletarian revolution. One can see on what points these gains have been compromised, all the more so because the economic condition of woman and the place assigned to her in life by custom and physiology are still far from assuring her genuine equality.

The social differentiation obliges us to distinguish the various conditions of Soviet women. The upper strata of society, especially numerous in the centres, have produced the type of elegant and indolent lady, who follows the fashions, the theatre, the concerts, who is desolated when she is unable to get the latest dance records from abroad, who tans herself every year on the beaches of the Crimea or the Caucasus. I have heard the elegant in the literary salons praising the enthusiasm of the Donietz miners and the political wisdom of the Leader. I have seen others, fat and dressed in transparent silks, leaning on the arms of aviation officers, walking past children with bellies swollen from famine who moaned softly as they lay stretched out in the dust. Flies resting on their eyelids and lips tormented them. The ladies turned their heads away. After all, they were only little Kazaks or Kirghiz. . . .

Below this feminine aristocracy is the average housewife of modest means, as needy as she is everywhere else. Still lower—and she constitutes the majority—is the woman of the people, a worker or peasant, who does the washing, goes for water to the fountain or to the river (in winter, it is to a hole punctured in the ice), takes care of the animals, raises the children, receives the drunken man at the end of the week, stands in line in front of the stores, buys a few metres of satinette in order to resell them and, thanks to this brilliant stroke of business, is able to provide shoes for the youngest. The foreign littérateurs do not come to question her while travelling. Disfigured and aged at thirty-five, she sometimes takes to drink. Then you hear her—on the revolutionary holidays—singing in a discordant voice the old popular plaints. After her fiftieth year she draws a checkered cotton handkerchief or a black one (according to the religious tradition) around her head and from time to time walks for kilometres in her old shoes over dusty roads, through mud or snow, in order to kneel in the only church that has not been shut down and which is always far away—terribly far away. . . .

The gains of the revolution would be immense in the realm of morals if poverty and the lack of freedom did not compromise them. For the woman, as for her husband, the whole problem comes down to two propositions: a rise in wages and a restitution of rights.

# 4.

## *The Youth*

---

IN LITTLE LESS THAN TWENTY YEARS SEVERAL GENERATIONS of abandoned children have changed places in the depths of society. At first there was that of the civil war, numerically the least important. Then that of the great famine of the Volga (1922–1923), estimated at several millions. Later that of the collectivization. Millions of tillers were dispossessed and deported: this doomed millions of children to perish or to roam. I saw them in Leningrad and in Moscow, living in sewers, in billboard kiosks, in the vaults of cemeteries where they were the undisturbed masters; hold conferences at night in urinals; travel on the roofs of trains or on the rods below. They would emerge, pestiferous, black with sweat, to ask a few kopecks from travellers and to lie in wait for the chance to steal a valise. On foot, all along the roads, crouched at the back of cattle cars under warm and stinking litters, hidden between cases that they pilfered, they descended in the spring from the large cities towards the warm countries. They were driven back, but they began all over again. Neither Dickens nor Jack London ever wrote anything comparable to the backwater of their existence. Natural selection, assisted by repressions, eliminated many of them. The lucky ones established themselves as bootblacks at the beaches. Could they doubt, while enduring the feeble jokes of the high functionaries and their ladies, that they were witnessing the foundation of a classless society?

The autumn come, they went back to the capitals to sell matches, cigarettes, and cocoa, to install themselves in the vestibules of stores where it was warm and they could pretend to render a service to the client by opening the door when they had the chance. They gathered together to sleep in the still warm vat of tar used to repair streets. Tousled little heads, lousy as could be but full of shrewd wisdom, stuck out of it in a circle and the passer-by could overhear enigmatic remarks made in slang and adorned with filthy oaths. More than one dry stroke—without the shedding of blood—or a "wet" one, you understand?—was meditated there. I saw others starving to death in the ruins of demolished churches, in public gardens. Nothing could be done about it. The Children's Home refused to take in everybody and you were barely fed there. These children preferred to starve in liberty. The authorities ordered raids. But where are they to be hidden? "What's this," they said to the police, "you can't steal, you can't sell cigarettes, you can't sleep on a bench? So we can't even live, citizen? Aren't we human beings any longer?" I have heard such remarks, but I never heard an answer to them.

Most of them, of course, become criminals. Thereupon they are treated as such and no longer as young vagabonds. Concentration camps, the forests of the North, canal digging, prison, escape, summary execution of second offenders, the unrecorded finish of famished youth who perish in the course of an interminable transfer in an icy coach. . . . I have known several who, having fallen into some decent spot, under a humane and not stupid camp chief (there are more of them than is realized), became men, toughened at the job and handier than the average mortal. I have run into teachers, a poet, skilled workers who were former pickpockets. They had found the *Road to Life*, as in the film of that name—a fairly good film, truthful in its way. Others, just as numerous, whom the law had made liable to the death penalty, took other roads, unknown to the film-makers. . . . We were talking on the street, at the edge of the pavement. A drunkard lay a few steps away on the snow. Two urchins of about twelve came over to him, with the nimbleness of monkeys, drew off his boots, and plunged into the throng. Sly ones.

Those who were four or five years old at the beginning of the collectivization, and who survived it, are reaching their twelfth year: there must be quite a number of them. . . . In addition, poverty flings its annual contingent upon the streets and the highways. It is not yet finished.

Above the abandoned youth, in the social hierarchy, stands the working youth of town and country. In spite of everything, it is vigorous, alert, full of a consuming desire to live, untutored, rude, bellicose, inclined to drink, practical, not idealistic, hardened against pain and hunger, skilled in all the sports, narrow-minded, and sure of itself. It joins the Communist Youth because you have got to do that in order to get a better job or to carry on your studies more easily. It flings itself in throngs towards all the branches of technique and of knowledge. The relations between the sexes there are simple and rather healthy, in spite of the often affected brutality of the young male, the false disdain of petty bourgeois prejudices, the genuine sexual freedom. By and large, co-education all along the line yields good results. Young people seek each other's society, they fall in love, and the proportion of happy unions is certainly not less than it is anywhere else. Virginity has lost a part of its price without jealousy having appreciably declined. Poor, this youth is completely absorbed in the struggle for life. As soon as it has escaped hunger—more or less—it thinks of clothing itself; coquetting resumes its rights and, as the privileged set the example, it seeks ingenuously to imitate the clothing and the manners of the West. A French or German fashion magazine makes the round of the city, passing from hand to hand, violently disputed. (These magazines were prohibited for many years; I do not know if they have been authorized since dancing, formerly also forbidden, was recommended and since clothing-display salons were opened in Moscow.)

The major part of the city youth carries on its studies by taking advantage of the support of the state, of scholarships, subsidies, common lodgings. The students live merrily in a poverty that is sometimes heart-rending, in dirty dormitories, with dirty cots, furnished with benches of damp wood. However, I do have the impression that even in the towns remote from the centre, their condition is improving, and almost prepossessing and well-kept common lodgings are encountered with increasing frequency. There are two kinds of institutions of higher learning: those of the party and the others. The first, the more privileged, train the communist functionaries. The periodic or permanent purgings strike dark blows there. Access to the others is comparatively easy but higher studies, necessitating expenses and protection—for you must first of all be sent into a university city by the communist authorities—are in reality accessible only to the sons and daughters of the privileged, plus a contingent of students taken from among the workers by the services of the party. The very large majority of the young people must content itself with professional studies of an inferior or average degree. The custom of managed studies has been established, which provokes lively discontent. This city, this school, furnishes mechanics, agronomists, or veterinarians almost exclusively: and you will not change anything, you have no choice in the matter. After the managed studies—the administrative placing: you have pursued, under pressure, the course of an agronomical *tekhnicum* for three years. Your agronomist's certificate obtained, you are sent for several years, without anybody bothering to consult you, into some remote *colkhoz* [collective farm] a hundred kilometres from the railroad. You finally come out of it, with tenacity and address, but only after a long period of time. The young communist will succeed sooner than anyone else in establishing himself in an average city provided with baths and moving picture theatres. Above all, if he knows how to flatter and serve the authorities.

In the intellectual milieu, properly so-called, of the capitals is enacted the drama of the nonconformist youth. Should the student be ever so little suspect, he will not be allowed to finish his studies. I have known doctors, physicists, and engineers who for years multiplied their applications and their labours without being allowed to take the final examination which would give them the right to a diploma. One of them was told: "Renew an engagement for a year in a *colkhoz*, give proof of the right spirit, and we shall see." Another was given no answer at all.

This youth, it goes without saying, has no means whatsoever of expression, no moral activity. In 1936 the Communist Youth (the Comsomol) lost their feeble semblance of political activity, which they had carried on for the sake of form. Only the archives of the G.P.U. will someday throw light on their state of mind. They are divided into several profoundly different milieux under fairly uniform appearances. An important and influential minority of young communists, strongly worked upon by the bureaucratic apparatus, invested with a certain authority, better dressed, lodged, and fed than the other youth, faithfully professes the official ideology. Imbued with the new patriotism, it is preparing for the war. It carries out zealously all orders, and lives on oversimplified ideas and approved texts. "With us, socialism reigns—with them, in the capitalist universe, it is terror, the crisis, exploitation. Our army is the strongest in the world," etc. . . . It practises with ardour the cult of the Leader. It forms the subordinate cadres of the power and of the army.

More numerous, the youth of the middle stratum adapts itself passively to these young communists, imitates their manner of speaking, but with a profoundly different nature. On the whole, it is interested only in technique and in careers. Asphyxiating, mediocre single-track politics bores it without deceiving it or making it rebel (in view of the total futility of rebellion). It soon learns to show itself prudent in its reflections, assiduous in its studies, as zealous as it must be in the carrying out of orders, and it learns also to keep its dignity well concealed. Young communists and non-party youth unite with an emphatic absence of personality—how many superficial observers have taken it for a collective spirit!—an implacable individualism. The Comsomol student who astonishes you by his feigned or genuine inability to think differently from the editorials of *Pravda* will jostle a pregnant woman at the streetcar stop in order to get on ahead of her. He will carry on a shady struggle by means of intrigues, bribery, and denunciation in order to obtain a room, will march over the body of a comrade in order to have himself sent to Moscow. . . .

More primitive, still maintaining old traditions, both good and bad, like those of songs, of dances, of courting young girls, of family and local solidarity, of collective drinking bouts, of scraps of street against street and quarter against quarter, the poorest youth—and the most numerous—seems to me to be more appealing and less deformed by the bureaucratic régime. What handsome lads, what dazzling young girls, with somewhat heavy features, their nature so singularly unpolished in the intellectual sense of the word and yet so fine and rich, enduring and prodigious! Co-education and the moral equality of the sexes, as well as the effort to draw young girls into sports with a view to military preparation, make comradeships virile and sometimes mark out young couples who will end by being able to live. . . . At the other pole of this youth of the people is located, in the capitals, a gamy Bohemia and an intelligentsia among whom every kind of dissoluteness discreetly flourishes.

The entire youth is evolving towards a succinct realism. Smitten with technique, thirsting for well-being. Supple in adaptation, hardened against pain and hunger. The word "Americanism" still best expresses its spirit. Few general ideas, no formulated ethics, no conscious idealism, an aversion to politics. Even among Comsomols, conversational subjects touching upon politics are carefully avoided, less out of fear than out of boredom. It is so vain and so empty! They live on elementary notions, and pretty poor ones at times. The young man to whom you explain that twenty daily newspapers of different opinions appear at the same time in Paris will not understand you well, even if he consents to believe you. "But how is that possible?" he will ask, quite dumbfounded.

Nevertheless, all the needs of man ferment in this magnificent human dough. The Secret Service purges it unceasingly. Those under thirty years of age are in the majority in all the places of detention. Here are a few episodic facts that came by chance to my attention. In 1926–1928–1929 a strange movement of youth was born in the university centres. Communists and non-party men came together to form apolitical socialist study groups in order to pose all the problems among themselves. They hardly concealed themselves, not thinking that they were committing a crime. In Moscow and Kharkov they even published a review in manuscript: *The Struggle (Borba)*. The G.P.U. espied it without delay. They were all arrested and interned, the "ringleaders" were sent to those corners from which there is virtually no return. At the same time a Scout movement was also destroyed. The Jewish Zionist Youth has for many years been subjected to repressions, renewed from season to season. A Socialist Youth was formed at the beginning of the collectivization in Moscow and Leningrad, and the whole membership was flung into prison. The young Trotskyists today set the tone of the communist opposition, in the "solitaries" and in the concentration camps.

# 5.

## *Peasants, Artisans, Administrators, Believers*

*The Peasants.*—THERE ARE RICH *colkhozes*[1] AND THERE ARE poor ones. Within the *colkhozes* themselves, the distribution of work and of profits is unequal in the extreme. The administrators and their entourage of "activists" are first served. Then there are the poor agriculturists, the rich, and the average. That depends upon the individual parcel of land, upon the relations you have with the managers, upon the number of workers and of mouths there are in the family. The welfare of the *colkhoz* depends upon the land, the means of communication, and above all, upon the authorities who tax it. In the regions remote from railways, a good deal is consumed on the spot and life is better, but there are no newspapers, no manufactured articles. In certain frontier regions the population, after being carefully purged, enjoys a favourable treatment. In the regions provided with railways, state commerce offers the peasants phonographs, bicycles, rice powder, dentifrices, silk hosiery. They buy them; they have even been seen buying pianos, and the press has made a big to-do about these signs of enrichment. As usual, the truth is somewhat different.

[1] Collective agricultural farms; most of the agriculturists are organized in agricultural co-operatives of a sort, which are closely supervised by the party and the state.

The agriculturists buy everything they can in order not to hoard up a currency which they have good reason to distrust. To phonographs, they prefer low-cut shoes; to luxury articles, ordinary cottons; but they do not find any on the market, articles of prime necessity being produced in insufficient quantities. In order to restrict the purchasing power of the peasant while compelling him to sell his personal reserves of grain to the state (to the state which pays him for wheat a fifth or a seventh of what it receives for it as bread), there was conceived the system of receipts for the delivery of grain. The buyer is served in a store only if, when paying, he can prove that he has delivered so much grain to the state for so much money. He is allowed to make purchases in conformity with this sum. These receipts, naturally, become the object of speculation.

The vast majority of the peasants live more poorly than before the collectivization, that is, on the whole, at a level lower than the pre-war. In 1925–1926 what they gained from the nationalization of the soil they lost in part because of the dearness of manufactured articles. But after having known the terror and the famine, and having passed through the crises of revolt and despair, they have returned little by little to more pacific states of mind, especially since they were left with something to eat. In 1933–1934 they generally wished for war, in order to obtain arms and wait to see what would happen. . . . They made no secret of it. In 1935 I saw this desire give way to the fear of war.

Even less than the workers do the peasants have the right to move about. The system of interior passports does not permit them to establish themselves in the city. Before being sold a railroad ticket in a station, they are asked to present a paper from the *colkhoz* authorizing the trip; and this regardless of the passport, which is demanded in any case. It is true that trips are made afoot or by chance means and that a mass of petty complicities makes existence in the country easier than in the city.

On the whole, the peasants whom I knew did not appear to me to be reactionary in the old sense of the word. Nobody regrets the old régime, nor would he desire its return; but there is a thoroughgoing hostility to the local and central bureaucracy. The local functionaries perish fairly often in automobile accidents about which few entertain any illusions. Others, of less importance, have their faces banged up in dark corners. I even doubt if the spirit of individual property is deeply anchored in the Russian peasant, at least so far as the land is concerned; the advantages of large-scale collective cultivation are easily understood. The peasants would like a "real régime of the soviets," which would restore their rights to them and would let them organize as they please.

In 1936 a singular reform was achieved in the Northern Caucasus, in Central Asia, and in various points of the U.S.S.R. The *sovkhozes* [Soviet farms], agricultural exploitations of the state, in which the cultivators were only wage-workers, those huge grain factories about which such a noisy propaganda was once made, were liquidated in large number and their lands distributed to the *colkhozes*, that is, to the peasant collectives.

*The Artisans.*—Long encouraged for formality's sake, because their industries furnished a mass of consumption articles that the state produces insufficiently or not at all, the artisans were constrained by fiscal pressure to enter into *artels* or co-operative associations, controlled by the party. The thing was done very simply. The meagre possessions of the small watchmaker were confiscated without any form of due process, and he was told: "Go to work in the *artel!*" (This was in 1931–1932.) The amount of taxes required from a small shoemaker was trebled without reason. He shut up shop and went to ask for a job in the *artel.*

The *artel* makes the artisan work eight hours a day for a wage always below his income as an independent. It makes him pay a co-operator's share, which is usually large (several hundred rubles), and it imposes state loans upon him. The artisan finds himself deprived of his freedom, exploited, defrauded; he works badly. Everyone knows that if the *artels* work at low prices, their production is worse than mediocre. The only exceptions to this rule are those which, established on a commercial basis, have become fairly good businesses and illicit enterprises for their members. Returning home in the evening, the artisan works clandestinely for his private clientele and works honestly. The *artel* becomes the place of variegated combinations: it solicits and obtains credits or subsidies, it enters into semi-illicit or entirely illicit traffic. Its bookkeeping is always false. From time to time it goes bankrupt or amalgamates with other *artels,* a trick used to avoid paying off debts or to reimburse secured credits. A reorganization follows, which is primarily a change of signs. Sometimes the administrators go to prison like anybody else; but more often they get out of it, being in the party and provided with useful connections. There is no life without risks, is there? In the meantime, the combinations are everywhere.

*Business.*—We now come to the unique domain of *blatt,* a Russian slang term which signifies "combination." From the bottom of economic life to its summit the combination reigns. Heads of trusts, directors of banks or of plants, administrators of state commerce, administrators of *colkhozes* or of *artels,* store managers, employees—all resort to it every day. All the wheels of the colossal machine are oiled and fouled by it. Its rôle is as great as that of planning, because without it the plan would never be realized. The combination of a multitude of departments makes up for the insufficiency of wages, for the defects in statistics, for administrative negligence, for bureaucratic unintelligence; it piles miracle upon miracle. A shoe factory director receives, in accordance with the plan, a permit for a ton of leather to be taken from the neighbouring tannery in February. The tannery, even though it conforms with the directives, answers that it finds it impossible to deliver these raw materials before March. The production plan of the shoe factory is going up in smoke; but our director is not upset by it. He expected that. "Look here, old man," he will say to his colleague from the tannery, "you wouldn't pull a trick like that on me, would you!" Certainly not, we only need to get together on it. Service for service, eh? The tanners are lacking shoes, dear comrade, couldn't you have five hundred pairs for me within the fortnight? In the end, the tanners will be shod—not so well, to be sure, as their factory director and his family, whose boots the whole town will admire; and the shoe plant will execute its plan, which will bring its director premiums, a banquet, etc. It will be clearly perceived, when the problem of transporting the raw materials from one plant to the other arises, that there are neither cars nor trucks available, for entirely peremptory reasons; but here again the beneficent combination will intervene. Railroad men and truck drivers will find that it pays.

*The Believers.*—The campaign of dechristianization, officially closed in 1935, led to the destruction of most of the churches and among them a number of historic monuments.

A commission presided over by the academician Luppol had previously taken care to alter the classification of the major part of the monuments that it was supposed to conserve, in order to offer them to the crowbars of the wreckers. Right in Moscow, churches that were old works of art have disappeared. At the height of the persecutions and the demolitions, the authorities demanded of the Moscow clergy a public declaration affirming that it enjoyed the fullest freedom and that if the places of worship were closing up it was because the believers were losing interest in them. . . . The priests naturally signed everything that was wanted, and their statement was published. In the Kremlin, the Voznessensky and Chudov monasteries, dating from the fourteenth century, and the Voznessenskaya Cathedral, with five gilded cupolas, built in 1519 and reconstructed in 1721, have given way to one of the most comfortable barracks, whose façade rises above the Red Square. In Orenburg, where I was in exile until 1936, there were about fifteen churches: three dated back to the founding of the city, at the beginning of the eighteenth century, and memories of the rebellion of Pugachev were associated with them. All of them, except one that is without historical or artistic interest, have been demolished. But let us return to Moscow. Wreckers, who think themselves urbanists because they prefer a square of glistening asphalt to a masterpiece of centuries gone by, razed the admirable Sukhareva tower, a tall, red belfry built in the days of Peter I, one of the architectural beauties of the old city. The responsibility for this vandalism devolves exclusively upon the bureaucratic régime, because it goes without saying that if the population had had the slightest possibility of making itself heard, it would not have permitted either the persecution of believers, which was at once a revolting abuse and a political blunder, or the destruction of so large a part of its historic patrimony.

The anti-religious persecution coincided with the collectivization and was only a derivative of the general discontent of that epoch. Religious holidays were interdicted when the scarcity forbade any increased consumption on the occasion of the festivals; as soon as the scarcity diminished, the prohibition fell into desuetude and the authorities themselves began recommending the putting up of Christmas trees. Religious life seems to me to be downtrodden rather than actually wiped out. You arrive in towns where only heaps of brick are left of the churches. It is explained to you that the Soviet decided on these demolitions upon the unanimous request of the workers. Everybody knows how they vote for resolutions of this kind in the shops, how they vote for no-matter-what resolution, out of an inability to do otherwise and in their hurry to get home. It will be added that the believers offered no objections. You doubt that. They have even refused to renew the rental lease of the houses of worship. For that, it was enough to quintuple the rent. The Free Association of the Godless numbers 15,000 dues-paying members. . . . The well-intentioned tourist takes note of these results and meditates upon the end of the old beliefs.

He does not hear the women who walk through the icy streets, murmuring as they see a funeral that "we know what a man is worth today: less than a dog you throw into a hole." Be patient and observe. You will learn that the members of the atheistic society are recruited on paper in the enterprises and confine themselves to paying their dues without being invited to do anything else whatever; and that many of them are probably believers who find it wise not to make the fact public. Enter into the confidence of these people: you will see them celebrate all the religious holidays. You will learn that, in spite of everything, there is in the country a small church that remained open, discreet and perhaps forgotten, to which people come from fifty kilometres around. That they hold a collective mass there for all the dead of a year's quarter, piously enumerated. That it is crowded at Easter, because the whole countryside passes through it. That such and such a young communist was married in church. That the sects live on, burrowed in the families, accustomed to persecution for many centuries.

Nevertheless, the youth of the cities appears to be free-thinking. But such is its need of an intellectual and spiritual life that it is visibly ready to welcome any teaching with an immense receptivity; so much so that the return to a certain religious tolerance, especially given the prohibition of any living socialist propaganda, will certainly have the effect of bringing a part of this youth to the churches and the sects.

Mystics are treated as counter-revolutionists, arrested, interned or deported. I was able to follow, in the intellectual milieux of Leningrad, several cases of this sort.

*The Social Differentiation.*—Official statistics, far from furnishing us with figures on this cardinal subject, seem drawn up for the purpose of screening them from us. They classify the People's Commissar and the factory director under the head of employees on the same basis as the office boy. They do not distinguish between the president of the *colkhoz* and the most disinherited member of the peasant community; the Stakhanovist and the labourer are just workers; the servant is a worker or else she disappears under the head of miscellaneous. We shall pose the question in these terms: What part of the population enjoys an ease modestly defined by the satisfying of these needs—good food, good clothing, good lodgings? For it is plain that this part of the population is the only one interested in the maintenance of the régime.

It comprises: the cadres of the state, of the trade-unions, of the party (they are all one, for the party trains all the cadres); the cadres and the personnel of the Secret Service, its special troops included; the cadres of industry and trade, formed by communist administrators and non-party specialists or technicians; the cadres of education, with the exception of teachers whose condition is still precarious; the doctors, jurists, artists, writers; the cadres of the army and the fleet; the cadres of the *colkhozes*, administrators and communist organizers—say, a million persons out of the 250,000 *colkhozes*. The labour aristocracy.

My computations have led me to estimate these favoured elements at a minimum of 10,000,000 persons, a figure to be doubled to include the families. Trotsky estimates them at from 10 to 12 millions, say, about 25,000,000 souls with the families,[1] and concludes: "Twelve to fifteen per cent of the population, that is the authentic basis of the absolutist ruling circles." The rest of the population, 85 to 88 per cent, lives in primitive conditions, in discomfort, in want, in misery, or else it benefits from a well-being that is illicit and concealed, and therefore mingled with insecurity.

---

[1] Leon Trotsky, *The Revolution Betrayed.*

# 6.

# *Managed Science, Literature, and Pedagogy*

---

SOCIAL WARS CANNOT BE FAVOURABLE TO SCIENTIFIC RE-search and to literary creation. They imply, in this sense as in many others, a sacrifice to the future. The material and moral enrichment of the masses is acquired only after the victory and the healing of the wounds. The intellectual production of Russia, therefore, was feeble during the years of combat. With the coming of peace, since 1922, life was resumed in the new order with an astonishing joy, ardour and variety.

Soviet literature was born in the two to three years from 1921 to 1923, with names known before and now renewed and enhanced (Serafimovich, Alexis Tolstoy, Mikhail Prishvin, Lidin, Ehrenburg, Marietta Shaginian, Zamiatin), and a throng of new names of young writers already full of experience and pith: Boris Pilnyak, Constantin Fedin, Leonid Leonov, Vsevolod Ivanov, Fedor Gladkov, Yury Tinianov, Mikhail Zostchenko, Mikhail Sholokhov, Nicolas Nikitin. A little later, or in the second rank, appeared Tarassov-Rodionov, Lydia Seifulina, Libedinsky, Pavlenko, Tikhonov. Within a few years poets produced a magnificent work: Yessenin, Mayakovsky, Pasternak, Selvinsky, Tikhonov, Mandelstam. One is stupefied when one considers this glittering début of Soviet literature, or records the audacity and the candour of the writer under a régime barely emerged from the terror.

Many of the works of that period would no longer be publishable today; they are, moreover, either withdrawn from the libraries or scarcely tolerated. Intellectual freedom is being extinguished in every domain with the victory of the bureaucracy. A period is opening up of increasing sterility, of spiritless official propaganda, of stereotypes approved by the bureaux as in other times and places by the Congregation: "literature in uniform," in the just words of Max Eastman.

It would be tedious to retrace the vicissitudes of this progressive suffocation. In 1929 two masterful writers of the young generation were suddenly denounced by the entire press, upon a slogan emanating from the Central Committee, as public enemies—one for having written about life in the provinces a novel of a realism designated as "pessimistic and counter-revolutionary" (Pilnyak, *Mahogany*); the other for having published abroad in translation a work condemned by the censorship because it was a strong satire directed at bureaucratic state-ism (Zamiatin, *We*). Pilnyak consented to all the desirable concessions and even rewrote his book in the optimistic genre. Zamiatin, firmer, was forced to expatriate himself. The young generation swallowed it all without flinching, even though Gorky, questioned by a Leningrad writer who wanted to know "if the moment has come to have ourselves deported," is supposed to have replied: "It seems to me, yes." Nobody had read the incriminated works, but everybody condemned them. There is always an hour when the redeeming choice between cowardice and courage is possible. It was in 1929 that the Soviet writers abdicated their dignity. Their decay had already begun, it is true, and it required years, years marked by famous suicides: Sergei Yessenin, a lyrical poet, opened the funereal series; Andrei Sobol, prosaist and tormented revolutionist, followed him; Mayakovsky, social poet, renowned, rich, and loaded with honours, blew out his brains a few days after having adhered to the party's general line in literature. Young ones like Victor Dmitriev, passed away without noise. . . . Meanwhile, let us note, the writers have grown rich.

To work your hardest to create requires a tenacious courage that contrasts with the absence of any civic courage; and extraordinary faculties of adaptation and mimicry. Some writers take refuge in the centuries gone by. There at least they are fairly tranquil. To this evasion of the present we owe some good historical novels (Chapigin, *Stenka Razin*, Tinianov, *The Death of Vazir-Mukhtar*, Alexis Tolstoy, *Peter I*).

In April, 1932, the bureaucrats of the rod of the Associations of Proletarian Writers, who lorded it brutally over letters, learned one morning from the papers that they were suppressed: decision of the Leader. All the old literary groups were to be dissolved and refounded—after a purging—into a new association of Soviet writers, directed by its communist fraction. The men of letters proved themselves docile. They had been enrolled, enthusiastically, into shock brigades, obliged to produce on an industrial scale works on the Plan. Regardless of circumstances, they had voted all the death penalties that had been demanded from them, they had sung the praises of the hangmen in verse and prose, they had paraphrased the most unbelievable indictments, they had demonstrated in the streets against the Pope and the Second International, they had promised in solemn resolutions to give the régime "Dnieprostroys of literature" —to "catch up with and surpass" Tolstoy and Dostoyevsky.

. . . Without uttering a word of protest, they had allowed the arrest of all those among them that were scheduled for arrest. They had submitted to all the censures with a sort of euphoric resignation. And what censorships! Mutilated translations, bowdlerized biographies (the conversion of Rimbaud is suppressed from the Russian translation of J.-M. Carré's book, so that the Rimbaud case, in Russia, finds itself grossly simplified), entire works condemned. The Writers' Publishers of Leningrad was forced into bankruptcy under my very eyes, by the prohibition of several works that were on the point of appearing, previously authorized by the censor: a novel on the N.E.P. by Wolf Ehrlich, if my memory serves me well. . . . You would not believe it, the N.E.P. having been obsolete (it was in 1930–1931). A novel by Roman Goul on the revolutionary terrorism of times past: it might have given troublesome ideas to youth. A novel by Helen Tagger: this excellent writer was not right on the line; in addition, she was the wife of a deportee. Poems by Kliuev: too much Old-Russian sentiment in it. The monograph of a danseuse. . . . Was that a time for dancing? The novel of Kuklin on the Red Army: deplorably realistic because there were drunken officers in it. . . .

The director of literary publications in Moscow told me in 1928, after having called upon me to abjure: "Even if you produce a masterpiece every year, not a line of yours will appear!" Thereupon the translation of my novel, *Les Hommes dans la Prison*, already set up in pages with the censor's authorization to print 10,000 copies, was destroyed. None of my books appears in the U.S.S.R. When I was finally able to leave Russia in April, 1936, the censors withheld, along with my papers and personal souvenirs, all my handwritten works, the fruit of years of intense labour: an eyewitness account of the events that took place in France in 1910–1913, a novel, some poems. All of them were taken, in spite of the flagrant illegality of the procedure.[1]

Censorship in various degrees. The Writers' Union has its docket where every man of letters has a political label which is taken into consideration when deciding on publication, size of the edition, republication of his books. The editors pick a book to pieces before accepting it. The bureaux of the party, consulted in doubtful cases, sometimes designate functionaries to go over the work with the author. The manuscript then passes to the Board of Letters, attached to the Commissariat of Public Education, but in reality subordinated to the Secret Service. There it receives the necessary stamp of approval. Set up, the proof sheets are submitted to the censorship proper, likewise subordinated to the Secret Service, which casts a final glance at it, not without asking for all sorts of alterations if it so pleases. The work having appeared, it is not yet finished. It is up to the competent departments to recommend it to the libraries, which instantly assures it an unlimited sale, or to have it declared pernicious in the newspaper notes, which may mean its withdrawal from circulation. . . . The same works, the same authors, may be declared, in turn, excellent or detestable, for political reasons. Riazanov, the biographer of Marx, had just been consecrated as a great man in all the official publications (and his merits as a savant and a revolutionist are truly great), when he became irksome and was put behind bars. . . . The head of the cultural de-

[1] The Italian communist emigration knows Gatto Mammone well, as an old militant who lived in the U.S.S.R. for many years. For more than twenty years Mammone had been at work on a history of the labour movement of Europe. Taking refuge in Russia, he made the mistake of taking along his manuscripts and documents. *The Soviet censor robbed him of everything.*

partment of the Central Committee, Stetsky, immediately denounced him in *Pravda* as an overrated mediocrity. "We took him for a beacon," this blackguard writes textually, "he was only a candle." But with what can one compare people who are capable of mistaking a candle for a beacon? . . . Galina Serebriakova was still a reputed communist woman of letters on August 1, 1936, the author of highly esteemed works: *The Youth of Marx, The Women of the French Revolution.* At the end of the same month, flung into prison on suspicion of concealed inclination to opposition, she is treated by the semi-official *Literary Gazette* of Moscow as a counter-revolutionist devoid of any talent.

On the other hand, almost world-wide reputations are built up in a few days by publicity methods borrowed from the American trusts. The order need only be given to all the sections of the Communist International to have their publishing houses translate a seventh-rate work; the entire communist and communist-inspired press will proclaim its merits, and that may last for a certain time until it is perceived that it is nothing but a shabby fabrication. In the country itself, reputations are made as follows: Upon a sign from the bureaux, the communist cells in the factory start the discussion of a book, the "masses of readers" invite the author to lecture, the libraries boost him and so do the ships of the line, there is created a whole "spontaneous movement" which draws the admiration of old men of letters from abroad who are expressly invited. . . . Pilnyak never having succeeded in getting back completely into good graces, probably because he cannot help feeling and thinking like a man formed by the revolution, the favour of the Leader has granted first place in Soviet letters to Count Alexis Tolstoy, semi-official writer under the old régime, White émigré from 1918 to 1923, since rallied to the Soviet régime, rich and right-thinking. "My *Peter I*," said Alexis Tolstoy to a Western journalist, "was printed in 1,500,000 copies and you won't find one in the bookshops. . . ." The author being paid at the rate of 350 to 750 rubles—according to his personal quota—per form of 16 pages and printing of 5,000 copies, it is not difficult to calculate that this novel alone, where it was believed that flattering allusions to the Leader could be seen, brought him millions of rubles. Besides—let us permit him to speak—"the state gives the writer all the material facilities. It procures him ease, rest, tranquillity, homes in town and country. . . ." The profession of encomiast of the régime is thus one of the most remunerative; here we are carried off in a sublime flight a thousand leagues from the poverty wages in textile.

Only, there are risks. At the exact moment that this interview appeared the Union of Soviet Writers purged itself, and sanctioned with copious applause the expulsion, arrest, deportation, and execution of a number of its members.[1]

In ten years literature and science managed by these police methods have shown their sterility. Not because there is a lack of printing paper; but not a single powerfully-inspired work has appeared. Not a single Marxian work worth

---

[1] The terrible suspicion of Trotskyism thus befell Galina Serebriakova, Tarassov-Rodionov, Grudskaya, Trostchenko, Vegman, Selivanovsky, Ivan Katayev, Ivan Zarudny. Kamenev belonged to the Writers' Union, like another of those shot in the Zinoviev trial, Pikel. Long before that, there had been imprisoned or deported: the poet Vladimir Piast (said to have committed suicide in his deportation); Ossip Mandelstam, one of the masters of Russian verse today; the poet Nicolas Kliuev; the poet Pavel Vassiliev (who was tried as a common criminal); the children's writer Biankis; the philosopher Ivanov-Razumnik, author of a *History of Contemporary Russian Thought* and of a *Shtchedrin;* and many others. At the beginning of his deportation, Christian Rakovsky wrote a voluminous *History of the Revolution in the Ukraine*, a work all the more important because its author took an active part in the events. This work has not been published.

recalling, in the country of triumphant Marxism. The last philosophical school, that of Deborin, a dry and limited logician who ruled over philosophy for years, was destroyed, some time ago, by an administrative campaign. Deborin himself, before becoming an academician in order the better to hold his tongue, tried to commit suicide. Political economy? Rubin and Finn-Yenotayevsky are in prison. Forbidden to raise the questions of the exploitation of labour, of inflation, of the circulation of commodities, of the standard of living of the workers, of the per capita consumption of the population, of the distribution of the national income, of what part of it the bureaucracy consumes, of socialism in a single country. History? Political fortunes have been made by rewriting it to suit the taste of the day, like this Tal, author of the first history of the Red Army in which the name of Trotsky is not mentioned; like Lavrenti Beria who began his career by recasting the history of the Bolshevik organizations of the Caucasus in such a manner as makes a star out of Stalin. Anyshev—author of a good *Essay in the History of the Civil War*, the only one worth mentioning—and Nevsky—author of a history of the party, fairly good and withdrawn from circulation for just that reason—are both in prison. In prison also are the historians Seidel and Friedland, whose gentleness nevertheless remains inexhaustible. Maxim Gorky, after having altered, in a sense unfavourable to Trotsky, the remarks of Lenin which he had set down in his memoirs, was put at the head of the editorial board of a *History of the Civil War* in ten volumes, in which Trotsky is presented as the saboteur of the revolution and Stalin as its saviour. The *Memoirs* of Krupskaya have been done over again and edited by a special commission which did not permit the widow of Lenin to write a line freely. . . .

The Soviet encyclopædias are periodically revised in order to bring them up to date in the political sense of the term. In the second edition of the *Small Encyclopædia* you do not find the forecasts formulated in the first on the consumption of the masses at the end of the first Five-Year Plan. . . . The biographies of the former leaders of the party vary from edition to edition. An encyclopædia of three large volumes, which cost the state years of the labour of hundreds of specialists and millions of rubles, was torn up entirely in Leningrad in 1932. The libraries are continually purged, and if the works of Riazanov and Trotsky are not burned it is only because it is found more practical to tear them up quietly.

The natural sciences? Geologists have been imprisoned for having interpreted subsoil qualities differently from what was wanted in high places: ignorance of the natural wealth of the country, hence sabotage, hence treason. . . . Others have been shot. Bacteriologists have been thrown into prison for obscure reasons. The most celebrated one died in a Leningrad prison hospital. But the further removed laboratory research is from social life and technique the more chances it has of being pursued without impediment and even with encouragement (grants, honours). All this still does not prevent the activity of the Secret Service. The subsidies generously allotted to the physiologist Pavlov for his researches into conditional reflexes did not prevent the arrest of his collaborators and friends. The encouragement given to the academician Yoffe for his researches into the structure of the atom did not prevent the deportation of his collaborators. The physicist Lazarev, after having been put in the very front rank of Soviet science, was imprisoned, deported, and then amnestied.[1]

[1] The historian Tarlé suffered the same tribulations.

Managed literature and science permit the organization of festivities at which solemnity is mingled with the mirth of banquets, with ordered ovations, and with ridiculous things that are at once amusing and saddening. The surgeons assembled in congress swear eternal devotion to the Leader. The gynæcologists declare that they want to draw their inspiration forever from his teachings, The writers, whom he has called the "engineers of the soul," declaim litanies to him and adopt the canons of "socialistic realism," which is actually neither realist nor socialist, since it rests on the suppression of all freedom of opinion and expression.

What is to be said of intellectual intercourse with foreign lands? The postal censorship turns back pitilessly all the publications, all the books that do not emanate either from official communism or a sufficiently tame and moderate bourgeois spirit. *Le Temps* is the only French journal admitted into the U.S.S.R., together with *l'Humanité*. Too advanced reviews, like *Europe*, arrived up to recently only on occasion. In certain libraries the foreign reviews are put at the disposal of the public after all the undesirable pages have been torn out. Works of authors who are friendly to the U.S.S.R., like André Malraux and Jean-Richard Bloch, are prohibited. Moreover, a foreign author is judged exclusively by his attitude towards the Stalinist régime. André Gide, practically unknown to the Russian public and stupidly treated as a corrupted and corrupting bourgeois, becomes overnight a great revolutionary writer, only because he made certain declarations. For having scrupulously clarified his thoughts since then, he is insulted by the entire Soviet press. Foreign books enter with difficulty, not a bookshop offers them for sale; the rare books trade is subject to censorship.

When I was about to leave an old doctor to whom I was

saying my farewell begged me to send him the reviews of his speciality. "So many years gone by," he said, "and I haven't been able to keep abreast of anything." Suddenly he changed his mind: "No, don't send anything; they would think that I have connections abroad, and you know how dangerous that is. . . ."

At every turn in domestic politics, all programs and methods of education experience sudden transformations, not without resistance (usually simply inspired by good sense), which is broken down by administrative or police sanctions. Since 1935 there seems to be a desire to return to the old traditions. The students' committees have been suppressed, the directors restored, the discipline stiffened. The pupils will wear uniforms, as under the old régime. The organization of the Pioneers takes them in hand at an early stage in order to teach them the cult of the Leader, the goose-step with drums beating, the holding of meetings of approval or of protest, according to the rules. A recent decision has instituted stable study manuals (up to now they changed virtually every two years), and Stalin has intervened personally to condemn the overly stupid popularizations of history and the overly maladroit falsifications. In this way, there are no history manuals as yet. So far as I can judge, however, the school programs appear to me to be much better than those of the primary schools of France and Belgium. Soviet primary school education corresponds more to a middle school education in the West oriented towards technical studies. The programs are more scientific. The conditions of the teachers, miserable until recently, were improved in 1936; a sustained effort is being made to clean and decorate the schools. It is not without results; but school materials are lacking, copybooks are rare, the pupils often work with one book for three or four; there is a still greater lack of educated instructors, and the perverse selection made in the pedagogical circles as a result of the repression only aggravates the evil. The school directors have to be appointed from among the party members. For want of communist pedagogues, the director is sometimes the most ignorant man in the school.

But the greatest evil is not the poverty of means and of men. It is the bureaucratic spirit that prevails in the schools and is translated into suspicion, informing, the repetition of formulæ devoid of all content, the lessons of pure Stalinism crammed into children eight years old, the stifling of any critical spirit, the repression of all thought, and the hypocritical dissimulation to which the child accustoms himself out of necessity.

# Part Two

# THE SYSTEM

# I.

## *The Secret Service, Crimes of Opinion, Internal Passports*

---

THE TRAVELLER VISITING A COMMUNE IN THE MIDDLE AGES would have stopped to contemplate the belfry tower or the town hall, rising above the poor dwellings of the artisan and the bourgeois. The traveller visiting the cities of the U.S.S.R. today stops involuntarily, in Moscow, at the top of the Kuznetsky Most, the liveliest artery of the capital, to take in at a glance the latest architectural ensemble, the most imposing of the edifices of the G.P.U. . . . A building of fifteen stories, huge co-operative stores, dwellings, and offices; in the basement and at the rear of vast courts are perfectly silenced prisons; and somewhere behind those façades of fine, polished stone, those shop fronts, those screened windows where the lamplight flares up in the evening, somewhere at the rear of a cellar lighted by neon lights, are the cleverly conceived execution rooms.

In Leningrad the new building of the G.P.U., built on the spot of a modest Palace of Justice that was burned in the March, 1917, days, dominates the Neva by its tiered terraces and the Volodarsky Prospect by its granite columns. None of the old palaces of St. Petersburg can bear comparison with it. The same is true in all the centres of the U.S.S.R. The most imposing building is that of the G.P.U. And by a curiously preserved, old Asiatic custom, the cellars of the building usually serve as prisons. I was in those jails in Moscow and in Samara (Kuybishev). In most of the towns there is a great animation in the neighbourhood of the G.P.U. Automobiles, motorcycles, carriages, mounted couriers, the coming and going of policemen escorting wretched convoys. Sentinels, their weapons held ready for action, survey the streets, preventing passers-by from stopping. At night projectors light up the façade, sentinels are on guard in the blinding light. Symbols. Here they work twenty-four hours a day, more feverishly by night than by day. The secret operations, the raids, the arrests, the questionings, the executions–all begin towards ten in the evening and do not end until dawn.

Since 1934 the G.P.U.–State Political Administration–calls itself more frankly, in the Western manner, the Secret Service and is no longer anything but a department of the Commissariat of the Interior, or its abbreviation in Russian–N.K.V.D. Far from reducing the influence of the political police, this reform has increased it by subordinating the most important ministry to it. The head of the G.P.U., named Commissar-General, is the equal of a marshal, the Assistant Commissars have the rank of generals commanding an army and, in point of fact, do command special troops. Decorated with all the Soviet orders, Yagoda shows himself by Stalin's side on all solemn occasions. He is at once a head of the army, a great builder, a great policeman, a great, heavy-laden conscience, praised by Gorky and Romain Rolland.[1] Dependent upon the Commissariat are: the Secret Service and its intelligence services abroad, the militia (or the police proper), the criminal investigation department, the internal passport department, public works

[1] He was replaced at the end of the Zinoviev trial by an obscure functionary named Yezhov.–*Trans.*

employing penal labor, the road and highway maintenance service, the black cabinet, the concentration camps, the prisons, the "solitaries," deportation, the secret tribunal which is called the Special Conference. It is an omnipotent ministry of the police exercising a minute control of the entire population at every moment.

Up to 1934 the G.P.U. applied the death penalty widely, pronounced by secret commissions upon the report of examining magistrates, without hearing the accused. Since the Special Conference (*Osoboye Sovestchaniye* N.K.V.D.), it can no longer inflict penalties of more than five years of incarceration. It has at its disposal, therefore, deportation, the concentration camps, prisons, and the "solitaries." It sits in secret, its composition is secret, it decides the fate of the accused without having him appear before it, it admits no defence attorneys, it furnishes no explanation to the accused or to his relations, its decisions are practically irrevocable. During the entire duration of the penalty it exercises an absolute power over the condemned. In cases where the Secret Service deems the penalty of five years to be inadequate, the accused, since 1934, are turned over to the Special Colleges of the People's Tribunals and the Revolutionary Tribunals (*Osobaya Kolleghia Narssuda*, etc.).

The Special Colleges of the tribunals are composed of three judges appointed by the party committees. Sitting in judgment behind closed doors, they decide whether defence counsel is admitted or not. Up to now, so far as I know, they have never admitted it in political cases; the accused is heard, the witnesses are cited, a formal procedure is strictly observed. The general opinion is that the verdicts pronounced by these tribunals are much more severe than the purely administrative verdicts of the Secret Service. Most frequently, they vary from five to ten years of internment in a concentration camp. Here are a few typical cases. A worker in charge of maintaining the reading room of his factory goes to a store to get some placards. He laughingly refuses the portraits of Stalin and Kalinin that are to be seen everywhere. "I've enough of those heads, give me something else." He is arrested shortly thereafter, accused of throwing discredit upon the leaders of the party (counter-revolutionary agitation), turned over to the special tribunal, six years of internment. . . .

Two couples are driving in an auto, a tire bursts. They have drunk a little, they are laughing. One of the men cries: "A bomb under Stalin's behind wouldn't have made a bigger explosion!" A falling out between the women a few months later, and one of the group reports this remark. The two women and the guilty man are arrested, turned over to the tribunal under indictment of terroristic agitation and sentenced to terms ranging between five and ten years of internment—the two women for having failed to report the remark. The Soviet law makes informing a duty, and failure in such a case is a crime punishable by the strongest penalties.

In a factory dining room where sausage has been served for several successive days a worker asks banteringly if he is going to be made to "eat up the whole Budyenny cavalry. . . ." Indicted for anti-Soviet agitation and sent to a concentration camp.

At Orenburg, on November 7, 1935, communist deportees, Stalinists for the most part, that is, those having abjured dissident opinions that they had once held or that were once imputed to them, come together to celebrate the October Revolution. The metal worker Alexis Santalov, of Leningrad, an oppositionist who did not abjure—a very aggravating circumstance—flies into a passion and speaks of the "bureaucratic scoundrels." Denounced by a stool pigeon present, he is condemned to five years of internment and is sent to the Karaganda concentration camp. The typographical worker Ivanov, of Leningrad, and his wife, having abjured, are each given only three years of the same penalty for having heard the remarks without reporting them the very next day.

The arrests usually take place at night, occasionally in the daytime, but by surprise, so as to pass off unperceived and to remain secret. Families have great difficulty in finding the vanished person in prison; they do not always succeed.

As a rule, no visit of relations is authorized during the investigation, which always takes place in absolute secrecy. The prisoners may be kept in a cell for months on end, without reading matter of any kind, without the slightest contact with the outside, without walking around, without extra food. I underwent this regimen in Moscow for three months. The examination, using psychological terror, seeks thus to break them in order to extort confessions, the quality of which is of little importance but will serve to prop up a condemnation sought for in advance, to show the skill of the examining magistrate and to cover his responsibility in case of a check-up by the higher bodies of the party. The questionings take place at night, in order the better to play on the nerves of the accused. They sometimes begin with long conversations of which no minutes are kept. The minutes signed by the accused are generally written by the hand of the examining magistrate.

Only prisoners of note are given the benefit of an individual cell. In the large Butirky prison, in Moscow, rooms intended for a dozen persons hold as many as a hundred. The situation is worse in the provinces. A point is sometimes reached where small quarters are so filled up that the prisoners cannot sleep in them except in turn; they pass the day standing up or on their haunches, one against the other, and institute among themselves a rotation according to which they succeed each other at the stinking tub or at the dormer window through which a breath of air may come. In every season the humidity of the sweat and the breath covers the walls. If you can conjure up the filth, the illness, the exhaustion from hunger, the despair prevailing in such a cell, you will have an idea of the routine of the prisoners. Numerous comrades, men and women whose names I could cite, spent months in these hells. It is needless to detail the mortality rate among the prisoners under such conditions. In a little prison of the Orenburg region in 1933–1934 several hundred men died of undernourishment, of cold and misery; the "plan of work" of the prison not having been executed, their food had been cut off. Most of the prisoners were peasants jailed for infractions of the rules of *colkhozes* or bad application of the directives of the party.

A well-known saying in Russian revolutionary circles is: "So long as the man is in your hands, there is always a way of framing him," or else: "So long as you have the neck, the rope will be found somewhere." To frame a person means to find formal pretexts, evidence (which may be false, it matters little), an interpretation of texts in such a way as permits an explanation of the sentence without putting into it in so many words: "Because of his convictions . . ." For the past two or three years no effort has been spared in framing persons. In a large number of cases men are in reality—and quite obviously—seized only for having been fighters for the revolution under the old régime or for having been socialists, anarchists, or oppositional communists many years ago. I shall cite names in sufficient number. The power, having no illusions as to their feelings towards it, considers that having once been revolutionists they might, in case of a social crisis, become revolutionists again; and they try to suppress them.

Once in the toils of the Secret Service a person is well aware that he will never get out of them, or not for a dozen years anyway. The revolutionists and the genuine nonconformists will never get out. The system comprises a series of successive measures, the duration of which is rarely less than ten years and the effect of which may be prolonged, theoretically, for a lifetime.

A socialist or a left-wing communist has the courage to acknowledge that he has great reservations as to the general line of the party. Not even that much is needed in the vast majority of cases. It is enough to have at one time professed opinions other than the official doctrine of the day, of being or of having been in relation with socialists or other oppositionists, of having received a letter, told a story. . . . Condemned to three years of "solitary," that is, to incarceration. At the expiration of his three years, if he has any amount of personal importance at all, if he belongs to the cadres, he is brought up to the bureau of the prison and learns that the G.P.U. has *added* two years to his term. . . . At the end of the five years he is not liberated, but sent into deportation for three years in some remote territory. At the expiration of the first three years of deportation, he goes through the routine called the "minus" or "except for"; he is offered the possibility of choosing his new place of deportation out of a restricted list; in theory, he can live anywhere in the U.S.S.R. *except for* the large cities, the frontier regions, the industrial regions, and others. At the expiration of these additional three years of deportation, if the Secret Service doesn't think it has to make another decision on his case, he may finally receive a passport as a free Soviet citizen. But this passport will bear a special notation of the Secret Service and from then on he will be forbidden to register his domicile in any of the large cities or in the industrial, maritime, or frontier regions. His position will be that of a man perpetually forbidden a sojourn.

For the real militants, that is, for the men who have the courage to maintain their convictions—all political activity being impossible for them—things happen more simply: on various pretexts, and even without pretext, they are merely moved about from prison to deportation and from deportation to prison.

The custom of internal passports does not exist, I believe, in any large civilized state. Not even the fascist states have thought that they could rob their nationals of their freedom to move about in the country and to change residence. The *Small Soviet Encyclopædia*, published by the State Publishers, says in its edition of 1930 that "the custom of internal passports, instituted by the autocracy as an instrument of police oppression of the toiling masses, was suppressed by the October Revolution." It was re-established and terribly aggravated in 1932. The passports are delivered by special commissions in which the Secret Service has a preponderant voice. These commissions apply secret instructions so that no law, no known regulation guides their operations. Nobody knows if he will receive his passport. The refusal of a passport means that you must leave your place of residence within ten days and proceed to a locality 65 or 101 kilometres from a large city, as the case may be. There, moreover, you may also be refused a passport. Deportations resulting from the refusal of a passport have taken place and continue to occur en masse, tearing apart families, mercilessly breaking up lives—without explanation or appeal. Children have been seen separated from their parents, women snatched from their husbands, fathers torn from their families. At the beginning, the administrative excesses were such in Moscow that an epidemic of suicides resulted and—according to the public rumour, for nothing exact is ever known—Stalin had to intervene to put on the brakes. In so far as these things are talked about aloud, the passport is supposed to be refused in the large centres to former nobles, former capitalists, former military men, *former political prisoners*, those suspected of opposition, and to certain categories of condemned common criminals; it may be refused for loose morals, for homosexuality; and so indeed it is, without explanation, in the most revolting cases.

I knew the following cases: a student was expelled from Moscow because her father—himself authorized to reside in Moscow in his capacity as specialist—had once been a capitalist. In reality this young woman inclined to the anarchists, was known for "having ideas." . . . In Leningrad I saw the wife of a communist expelled from the city because in 1918 she had been married to an officer; this occurred in 1933 and the woman had a child by her second husband. . . . My parents-in-law were refused passports in Leningrad in 1933 because they were the parents-in-law of an oppositional communist, himself imprisoned for this reason alone. . . . The person involved was the old worker Russakov who had at that time more than forty years of labour behind him.

Passports are always refused to the families of those shot or of condemned men who have been given long terms.

These families are deported, as a rule. (Several wives of the young communists of Leningrad who were shot in 1934 have been sent to concentration camps.)

The possession of a normal passport, without a special notation by the Secret Service, only gives the Soviet citizen the right to reside in one locality. Everywhere else he may be refused registration; and he is refused. In other words, he has lost the right to move. A worker living in a small town cannot get registered in a large centre save upon the request of his employers and only for the duration of his work. A worker of Cheliabinsk who wants to live a while in Moscow, if only to shake off a little of the oppressive provincial unculturedness, has no possibility open to her except marriage with a Muscovite.

The passport is visaed at the place of work. With each change of employ, the reason for the change is entered into the passport. I have known of workers discharged for not having come on the day of rest to contribute a "voluntary" (and, naturally, gratuitous) day of work, in whose passports is written: "discharged for sabotage of the production plan."

# 2.

# *Penitentiaries, "Solitaries," Deportation, Right of Asylum*

*The Penitentiaries.*—THE CONCENTRATION CAMPS OCCUPY entire regions. The *Slon* (*Solovietsky Lager Osobovo Naznachenya,* Special Camp of Solovietsky) includes the whole littoral of the White Sea, the Solovietsky Islands, the Kola peninsula, the town of Kem. It is an entire, vast northern country with model establishments of which a propaganda film has been made and with filthy corners from which there is rarely a return. The penal labourers of the concentration camps exploit the apatite beds of Khibinogorsk (now Kirovsk) in the extreme North, the mines, the plantations, the new enterprises of Karaganda in Central Asia, the lumber industries in the north of Russia and of Siberia. They are employed throughout the U.S.S.R. in the construction of certain edifices (buildings of the Secret Service, prisons, etc.), in the digging of the Moscow-Volga canal, in the construction of the Leningrad-Moscow highway, in military-strategic works. It is absolutely impossible to know all their assignments. There are secret camps. A few years ago there was one greatly dreaded, on an island of the Caspian. A large camp exists at the mouth of the Pechora, within the Arctic Circle. Solovky, Karaganda, Oost-Pechora, and Mariisk are the best known. To my knowledge—casual and very fragmentary—many students have been sent to the Karaganda mines. But without doubt there are many of them in all the penitentiaries. Many Leningrad specialists were sent to Oost-Pechora after the Kirov affair (1934). As to the treatment inflicted upon the youth of the schools, the following fact was brought to my attention: A student of Ivanovo-Voznessensk, called upon to lecture on the end of the French Revolution, was accused of having made political allusions in the course of it when he spoke of the Thermidor. He spent several months in prison, in an overcrowded room, amidst squalor, hunger, illness, fear, oblivion; in the end his good faith was recognized and he was liberated. A few days later there was a meeting of the schools. He took the floor, following some fine speeches, and from the tribune told the story of what had happened to him. He was arrested the very same evening, indicted on the basis of Article 58 for counter-revolutionary agitation, and sent to Karaganda for ten years.

The routine in these penitentiaries has infinite variations. Its gradations run from the model establishment and semi-freedom to the most miserable conditions, to physical decay, to terror, to sadistically inflicted torture. It is no secret to anybody that a certain number of camp chiefs are shot every year for having conducted themselves criminally towards the interned. What cannot happen in a detachment of condemned men lost in the Siberian brush, including bandits, desperate or exasperated peasants, stool pigeons ready for anything, intellectuals and technicians, harshly treated politicals, all of them bound to a hard task, badly fed, and submitted to the absolute power of a policeman who is himself a condemned man!

The condemned are tied down to their work. The emulation—which we dare not call socialist out of respect for socialism—of the shock brigades, Stakhanovism, makes it possible to squeeze out of these labourers a maximum return guaranteed by the existence of Reinforced Companies of the Régime (R.U.R., *Rota Oosilennovo Regima*), where those who try to resist go to perish. Political prisoners, socialists, anarchists, and communists, the latter mainly Trotskyists or suspected of Trotskyism, sent to the concentration camps by the thousands, especially since 1934, carry on endless struggles there, in order to defend their dignity and a derisive minimum of political rights, by refusing to work, by hunger strikes, by suicide. (A few years ago five members of the Central Committee of the Turkish Nationalist party of the Caucasus, the "Moosavat," who demanded in the Solovietsky Islands that they be recognized as political prisoners and be transferred to the "solitaries," let themselves die of hunger.)

*The Prisons.*—Most of the prisons of the old régime are still used, and overcrowding is the rule within them. New model prisons are built in various places. The routine of the political prisons that are called "solitaries" varies according to the locality. In general it is endurable, with the reservations that I shall indicate. There are "solitaries" in Suzdal (the former monastery, a prison of the old régime), in Yaroslav, in Cheliabinsk, in Tobolsk, in Verkhne-Uralsk. The one in Yaroslav used to be—and may well yet be—reserved in part for foreigners and for politicals subjected to isolation. It is surely not the only one. The condemned live there in common, grouped in rooms. Walks twice a day, in groups. Food of inferior quality, based on oatmeal pastes, millet, etc., but fairly adequate. The smallest rights of the prisoners are the object of constant struggles with the administration, struggles which lead periodically to acts of savagery, hunger strikes, scenes of all sorts. The singing of the "International" on May 1st provoked terrible conflicts on several occasions, the prisoners having replied to the cruelties by big hunger strikes and by revolts. There have been hunger strikes against the automatic doubling of sentences. Sentinels have fired into cell windows. The administration has drenched the prisoners with icy water in their cells; and has forcibly fed hunger strikers whose death was feared. All these things have been witnessed. . . . A hunger strike of 450 Trotskyists in Verkhne-Uralsk lasted eighteen days in 1931. The one in December, 1934, was shorter, but was marked by the secret kidnapping of the strike committee (Dingelstedt, Byk, Krassinsky, Slitinsky), who were sent to the Solovietsky Islands. Our Trotskyist comrade, A. Tarov, who escaped at the end of 1935 from a place of deportation and crossed the frontier, writes:

"On January 22, 1931, the anniversary of Lenin's death, all the deported Bolshevik-Leninists of Akmolinsk [Kazakstan] were arrested and incarcerated in cells infected with typhoid. There were twelve of us, including two women; nine contracted typhoid. In the Petropavlovsk prison we found four oppositional communist workers. . . .

"In the Verkhne-Uralsk prison the Bolshevik-Leninists, to the number of 450, began a hunger strike to protest against the despotism of the local administration. The year before, in the course of a hunger strike, the director Biziukov gave the order to douse our comrades with cold water—this in winter and in Siberia! The order was executed. When our comrades began to barricade the cells, the jailers directed the water hose into their eyes. Our comrade Pogossian lost his sight. In 1931, a turnkey fired a shot through a grille into the chest of comrade Essayan. On the days of revolutionary festivals, we had serious conflicts with the administration. We were either incarcerated or beaten up because we sang the 'International.'

"In the Petropavlovsk prison I saw 35 women, eight of them with nursing babies, shut up in a cell of 25 square metres. The only access to air was through the peephole. I shall never forget those piteous and puny children! Taking turns, the mothers held them up to the peephole so that they might breathe a wretched ration of fresh air. . . .

"We began our hunger strike [in Verkhne-Uralsk, against the automatic doubling of sentences] on December 11, 1933. On the 20th, the hunger strikers were dragged from cell to cell because of a raid. They began to feed us forcibly. Unspeakable violence was the result, the voluntarily famished men battling with the jailers. Our comrades, of course, were trounced. At the end of our strength, they crammed rubber hose down our mouths and throats. The famished men were dragged to the 'feeding cell' like so many dogs. Nobody gave in. On the fifteenth day we decided to suspend the strike because the attempts at suicide were becoming too numerous. . . .

"The G.P.U. promised not to double the sentences any more. More than 130 comrades had participated in the strike. The strike committee was sent off to the Solovietsky Islands, but without an increase in sentence."

An arresting sequel to this story: the prisons of the monasteries of Solovietsky and of Suzdal were reserved for many centuries for heretics and for grand dignitaries who had fallen into disgrace.

The prisoners are entirely cut off from the world. From time to time they may, upon individual authorization, receive visits from their relatives, but the great distances make this a rather theoretical right. They may exchange six letters a month with their relatives (receive two and write four, or any other arrangement of this sort), the letters, of course, being censored, and many of them being lost either at the point of arrival or of departure. *All their intellectual works are confiscated when they leave.* In this connection it may be recalled that under the old régime Chernychevsky was able to write his great novel, *What to Do?* in the Petropavlovsk Fortress, where Kropotkin was also authorized to continue his works on geography. . . . The Chernychevskys and the Kropotkins of today are beaten down to their very minds. Nothing they think about reaches the world of life outside. Their works are classified by the Secret Service in its archives. When they come out of there, the world will see with stupefaction the portion of the intellectual production of an epoch that was thus choked off. . . .

The Butirky prison, famous in the last years of the autocracy, is a city within a city in Moscow. It includes secret quarters: for any number of years now it has not been known who is there. Recently, according to a good deal of tallying evidence that I was able to assemble, there was within it a fairly large number of foreigners: Germans, Poles, Italians, a Spanish anarchist, a Viennese Schutzbund man and numerous Russian railroad men who returned from Manchuria after the sale to Japan of the Chinese Eastern Railway. Because the political prisoners often resort to the hunger strike, a special quarter has been reserved for these strikers. As soon as he has signified his decision, the striker is transferred to a special cell where his clothing is taken from him to be replaced by a prisoner's uniform; he gets a pretty scanty pallet, precious little food, and he is deprived of reading matter. . . . He is abandoned to himself and the authorities wait until exhaustion has begun its work to convince him of the futility of resistance. Nothing of these struggles is known on the outside and most of the prison itself is unaware of them.

For more than ten years the political prisons have been under the personal control of two high functionaries of the G.P.U. who are known for their harshness, the citizeness Andreyeva and her deputy, Dukis.

*Deportation.*—One may be deported to a fairly large town like Tashkent, Kazan, Saratov, and find moderately good employment there, but this treatment is reserved, in general, for Stalinist deportees of note (very numerous at the moment), and to socialists who are well known abroad. Most of the deportees are subject to compulsory residence in localities without industry, sometimes in unhealthful villages or hamlets, or those known for their rigorous climate. Northern Russia and Northern Siberia, Central Asia, the desert regions of Kazakstan are the best known places of deportation. The number of political deportees must reach several tens of thousands.

The deportee cannot get any work without the specific consent of the Secret Service. If he is a worker, he will not be tolerated in a factory or a shop. If he is an intellectual, he will not be allowed to teach or to continue his studies. The so-called responsible employments, the only ones that are fairly adequately paid, are forbidden him. He is deprived of civil rights. His correspondence, closely supervised by the black cabinet, is often confiscated. He cannot have any kind of systematic relations with party members and, generally speaking, he is not welcomed into the local population which rightly fears to compromise itself. He is often raided, often arrested without explanation. In a word, he lives under the permanent threat of the Secret Service against which he has no defence whatever. At Arkhangelsk,

Yenisseisk, Minussinsk, in the Narim region, in Astrakhan, in Orenburg, in Semipalatinsk, etc., half the deportees are doomed to unemployment. The Secret Service, recognizing that it is materially impossible for them to find work under the conditions in which it puts them, grants them a dole that ranges from 30 to 75 rubles per month (1 kilogram of brown bread, remember, costs 1 ruble; a corner in somebody's home comes to 30 rubles).

The deportees are doomed, for the most part, to destitution and, by virtue of a surveillance that goes on every minute, in which stool pigeons and provocation play the biggest part, to a truly tragic moral condition. Their private life is shattered. Three or four times a year they will be shifted administratively from one region to another, for no known reason, apparently in order to wear down their nerves. The transfers take place in convoys, in prisoners' coaches, together with common criminals. They travel for months from prison to prison. They are often arrested and sent to concentration camps without being able to find out why. The testimony of Dr. Anton Ciliga, a Yugoslavian communist who recently left the U.S.S.R. after long struggles in the prisons, says: "During the summer of 1935 almost all the Bolshevik-Leninists deported to Central Asia, to Samarkand, Chimkent, Alma-Ata, Akmolinsk, Aktiubinsk, Pavlodar, were sent to concentration camps for five years." The year before, all the deportees of Semipalatinsk, about thirty, were imprisoned. In January 1936 all the Trotskyists deported to Tara (Siberia) were arrested. In 1935 almost all the socialist deportees of Ulianovsk and Kazan were arrested and subjected to new sentences because some of them had approved, in private letters, the formation of the united front in France.

Deportees live alone or in small groups in the villages of

the North, far from any civilization, far from the railways, devoured in the summer by mosquitoes, under orders not to move about for more than 500 metres from their home.

With the exception of some *kulaks* [wealthy peasants], representatives of the possessing classes are no longer to be found in the concentration camps and other places of captivity. The repression strikes with all its weight upon Soviet workers of various origins, nine times out of ten quite arbitrarily taxed with counter-revolution.

In the prisons, the concentration camps, etc., one finds the believers of various sects; priests, technicians, and intellectuals accused of sabotage; suspects—in large numbers—suspects solely because of their socialist origins or of their remote past; noblemen and sons of noblemen, former tradesmen, former military men or their descendants, persons having relatives abroad even if not in emigration, persons of German or Polish origin. . . . One finds mystics, occultists, Masons. From the political standpoint, all the parties are represented—these are the only places where they are even represented—Jewish (Zionist), Armenian, Georgian, Turkish, and Mongol nationalists, Social Revolutionaries, social democrats, non-party socialists, anarchists, syndicalists, oppositional communists of whom the Trotskyists are the majority, suspect Stalinist communists, the latter being exceedingly numerous. The present party purging, carried on by a checking up of every membership card and of the personal dossier of each member, means the expulsion, according to the figures published by the official press, of 10 to 14 per cent of the party membership. The expelled are immediately arrested and accused under Article 168 of the penal code (fraud and swindling) of having abused the confidence of the party by concealing from it something about their past or their social origins. From

150,000 to 200,000 communists, foreign to any opposition in reality, are thus being confined to the prisons or the penitentiaries at the present moment.

What can be the magnitude of the repression? I shall not speak here of the deportation *en masse* of several millions of well-to-do or reputedly well-to-do peasants for the requirements of the cause; nor of the technicians, workers, and functionaries condemned in connection with the poor execution of the Five-Year Plans and the collectivization plans, who number several tens of thousands (the functionaries sentenced during the collectivization have recently been amnestied, together with certain categories of peasants); nor of the Leningrad deportees who likewise number several tens of thousands. I have mentioned the 150,000 to 200,000 communists of the purge now taking place (Article 168). Thousands of communists of Leningrad, of the Zinoviev tendency, were sentenced in 1935. I think that the national parties must have several thousand representatives in the penitentiaries; the socialists and the anarchists, several hundred men each, a few thousands altogether. The oppositional communists, Trotskyists mainly, counted from 3,000 to 4,000 outlaws towards the end of 1929; there now remain a few hundred—hardly more than 500, it seems to me. The suspected Stalinist communists, among whom are many accused of "Trotskyism," must run into the thousands, even tens of thousands.

Upon my arrival in Orenburg in 1933, the little town numbered some 15 political deportees, anarchists, socialists and communists. Upon my departure, in April 1936, the town had from 150 to 200, of whom a maximum of 30 really had anarchist, socialist, or Trotskyist convictions. There were a dozen Trotskyists and perhaps a half hundred suspects of Trotskyism. There were, in addition, about a thousand deportees from Leningrad. One can see from this monographic view the crescendo of the repression in 1935–1936.

It is proper to throw some light here on the application of the right of asylum in the U.S.S.R. The foreign political refugees who arrive in the U.S.S.R. without passing through the channels of the International Red Aid [International Labour Defence] are generally imprisoned upon their arrival as espionage suspects.

A large number of foreign communists are imprisoned under diverse pretexts, administratively tried, and sentenced in secrecy. The Hungarians, the Rumanians, the Poles, the Germans, are particularly numerous in the Solovietsky Islands. Dr. Anton Ciliga recently made known the deportation of a score of Yugoslavian oppositional communists. Many Italian anarchists and communists are at present deported (Gaggi, Merino, Calligaris). Bulgarian communist militants are likewise to be found in the prisons and places of deportation. The illegal parties, whose members could in no case resort to consular protection, are the principal sufferers from these police persecutions. A group of Polish communist refugees, including a former deputy of the Warsaw Diet, were recently shot in the U.S.S.R. upon the charge of espionage, after an absolutely secret trial. This fact was made public by the *Bulletin* of the Russian Communist Opposition (published in Paris) in its April 4, 1936, number.

For several years now, Italian refugees living in the U.S.S.R. have been granted authorization to leave the country only if they agreed to be repatriated through Odessa, that is, turned over to the Fascists. The anarchist Petrini went through there in 1935, after many years of internment and deportation.

It is quite possible that the new Soviet constitution will mitigate a state of affairs that has become a danger to the régime and one that can *neither be acknowledged nor justified* in the eyes of international opinion. The abundance of labour in the penitentiaries certainly does not compensate for the injury done to production by the brutal elimination of a high percentage of skilled workers. The digging of canals of strategical importance does not compensate for the effects of the mass discontentment with the state power. The abuse of the terror exercised against the toiling classes is a boomerang against the régime and threatens to be rather costly to it one of these days. The government is not so blind as not to want to ward off these dangers. But it is likewise certain that in spite of the relaxation produced in the interior by the stabilization of the ruble, the government's unpopularity among the thinking elements of the population is too profound for it to be able to show itself really liberal. At all events, the bureaucratic machine will endeavour to reduce to nought or to pure formality the legal measures that might give back to the citizens a modicum of security. Nothing would be easier at the present moment than to abolish deportation and replace it profitably with certain applications of the passport custom. Nine-tenths of the political prisoners could be ostentatiously amnestied, and it would be enough to keep *one-tenth* of them in the prisons—the 10 per cent of real oppositionists—for all the shades of socialist and communist opinion to remain stifled. Having become by far too odious, the administrative sanctions may be abrogated and replaced by the activity of the tribunals—which are, moreover, entirely administrative—meeting behind closed doors, admitting no defence counsel and consequently offering no guarantee whatsoever to the accused.

# 3.

# *The Fate of the Socialists—The Fate of the Anarchists*

IN ORDER TO BE COMPLETE, IT WOULD BE NECESSARY TO devote a volume to this chapter alone, as well as to the two or three that follow, and no volume could be sadder. All the representatives of all the shades of revolutionary opinion, without exception, are prisoners or deportees. All have behind them long years of persecution. I know them well enough to know that they all consider themselves doomed to perpetual persecution. A socialist deportee told me with a bitter smile, at the moment of the negotiations on the united front between the socialist and communist Internationals: "Our comrades in the West don't really give a damn about us. You will see that if it is to their interests, they won't hesitate to let us be trampled in the dust. . . ." I do not take upon myself the responsibility for these remarks; I report them as the index of a state of mind. They came back to me when I was able to observe the complete silence that gripped the socialist press of France and of Belgium with regard to the anti-labour repression in the U.S.S.R.

Of the Social Revolutionaries, Abraham Gotz is deported to Central Asia, under what are said to be tolerable conditions. At Orenburg I saw Leo Gerstein die, a member of the Central Committee, an old idealist of the left wing of the party. His term of deportation was regularly renewed every three years. Gravely ill, he worked up to his last days in a Soviet bank. Finding it impossible to cure himself in Orenburg, he had asked for authorization to go to the Kazan hospital, and he received it on the morning of the day he died. So it cannot be said that it was refused him! I learned in 1934 of the death of the son of the former president of the Constituent Assembly, Boris Chernov. Imprisoned for many years, primarily because of his name, he ended by being deported to Central Asia where a tropical fever soon carried him off. He was a trained agronomist, a convinced socialist, and a fine character, whose cellmates often spoke of him to me with a good deal of emotion. I do not know where Timofeyev and Donskoy are; not at liberty, that is certain.

An old Social Revolutionary militant, Volkenstein, former collaborator of the Soviet Military Academy, hence one who had joined up some time ago, was subjected for years to absolute isolation in the secret prison of Yaroslav where she practically lost her speech. She is now in Verkhne-Uralsk prison.

Of the social democrats, in Orenburg I met George Kuchin, deported for the third or fourth time. He gave the socialist régime its just due, but, attached to workers' democracy, he had declared himself in his private correspondence a partisan of "silent opposition." An Estonian political refugee, Sommer, came to us after leaving prison. He was arrested at the beginning of 1936, for some imprudent remarks, and he must now be in a concentration camp. I also saw at great intervals a Muscovite socialist comrade, Goldenberg, and a solid old Georgian, Ramishvili, whom privations had not succeeded in finishing.

Eva Broido, an old socialist militant, came illegally to

Russia in 1927, was speedily arrested, naturally, spent three years of imprisonment in Suzdal, and was then deported for five years to Tashkent. At the expiration of this term, in 1935, she was again deported for five years, but this time to Ulala, that is, to a village of the Oyrat territory, 77 kilometres from the nearest railroad station. This courageous woman went through a term of hard labour under the old régime.

Braunstein, who was sent to Russia by his party in 1927–1928, spent years in the Suzdal prison. I do not know his whereabouts today. Lieber and Zederbaum (the brother of Martov), other old Mensheviks, were deported in 1934 to the Volga region, in Kazan and Ulianovsk. After the Kirov affair they were imprisoned and again deported to more remote places. Many socialists were sentenced for having declared themselves, in a message to *l'Humanité* and *Le Populaire*, partisans of the People's Front in France, or for having discussed it among themselves.

What has become of old Bazarov who, in 1930, flatly refused to lend himself to the monstrous comedy of the famous trial of the alleged Mensheviks of Moscow? (They declared that they had prepared, under the direction of the Socialist International, a foreign intervention against the U.S.S.R. in agreement with the French General Staff!) They did not dare to try either Bazarov or Cherevanin, another veteran of Russian socialism whose attitude was similar, so the former was sent to a concentration camp for ten years and the latter was deported. Former collaborators of Gorky in the *Novaya Zhizn* (*New Age*) of 1917–1918, the historian Sukhanov who gave us several volumes of memoirs of unique interest concerning the early days of the revolution, the economists Groman, Finn-Yenotayevsky, Ginsburg, Sher, old socialists who had long ago rallied to the government, influential functionaries of the Planning Commissions, falsely accused themselves of everything that was wanted of them and were condemned to ten years of imprisonment, not without having risked their necks. (Gorky did not flinch.) Ikov, an authentic member of the Social Democratic party—the only one in the whole affair—was sentenced together with them. A reputable young scholar, Rubin, absurdly accused his master and protector, Riazanov, of having concealed the "directives of the Second International on the intervention." The truth seems to be much more simple: Riazanov raised vehement protests among the ruling circles against the concocting of this trial. All the more embarrassing because he was irreproachable, he disappeared. In order the better to show what kind of men are being eliminated in this way, I dwell for a moment on his biography. Arrested in 1891, young Riazanov, who is one of the earliest Russian Marxists, spent five years in prison. In the revolution of 1905 he became one of the first organizers of the Russian trade-unions. Later he was founder of the Communist Academy, founder and guiding spirit of the Marx-Engels Institute, one of the rare scientific institutions of Moscow that honestly measured up to the requirements of its task. . . . He was first deported to Saratov. What have they done to this scholar who belongs to the international proletariat?

In the Verkhne-Uralsk "solitary," the condemned of this trial were boycotted by the communists as traitors and by the socialists as impostors. I do not know what became of them, but they have not regained their freedom. They know too many things and they were made the actors of too revolting a comedy for it to be possible to grant them their freedom. Sukhanov demanded it in 1934, by means of long hunger strikes, at the end of which he was removed from the prison.

Vladimir Skazin, having gone through the Soviet prisons, assembled an impressive documentation on the anti-labour repression, tried to send it abroad by approaching a Scandinavian socialist on an official mission in Moscow. He addressed to the Soviet Congress in 1934 a written protest, impressively motivated, at the end of which he declared that he renounced his Soviet nationality as incompatible with a socialist conviction, and demanded the possibility of emigrating. He himself went to give this document to the Secretariat of the congress, where he was arrested. A secret tribunal sentenced him to capital punishment for high treason. He spent two months in a death cell, waiting for his brains to be shot out. When he was apprised that his penalty had been commuted to ten years of forced labour, he summoned the government to have the courage of a more complete crime. He refused to go digging up the ground in some northern waste, carried on a long hunger strike, and succeeded in having himself sent to a "solitary."

What has become of the left-wing Social Revolutionaries who collaborated vigorously in the October Revolution, giving it such energetic fighters as Sablin and Kivkidze, and who then formed a turbulent opposition in the Soviet republic, which perished in 1918 by its own mistakes? Maria Spiridonova, terrorist, hard-labour prisoner, martyred by the gendarmes under the old régime, leader of the party until its defeat; Irina Kakhovskaya, terrorist and hard-labour prisoner under the autocracy, she who, under the occupation of the Ukraine, also organized terroristic attacks upon the heads of the German General Staff and escaped the rack only by a miracle; all of them, together with Kamkov,

Mayorov, Trutovsky, have not recovered their freedom since 1920–1921.

Fate of the anarchists:

Nicolas Rogdayev, after having gone through three revolutions as a combatant, from 1905 to 1917, died in deportation in Tashkent in 1932, in the same Turkestan which he helped to sovietize. Alexis Borovoy, professor of the University of Moscow, deported in 1929 for having corresponded with friends abroad, had his penalty prolonged in 1932 by three years by administrative measure. He died in Vologda 1936.

Aaron Baron left prison in 1920, for a few hours, and I heard him shoot out his fiery words over Kropotkin's grave, not yet filled with earth. I had the impression, at one and the same time, of a redoubtable foe and yet of a great comrade. Since that time he has been in the prisons of Moscow, Orel, Kharkov, Yenisseisk; in the concentration camps of Pertominsk and of the Solovietsky Islands; deported to Byisk, in the Altai, to Korosino, in the tundras of the Siberian North, to Tashkent, to Voronezh, a mild zone; then he disappeared, arrested once more. Where is he? His life is hard and his ideas are firmly fixed in his soul. Why was there not applied to him the decision of banishment abroad that had been adopted against him in 1922? It is true that he did fight the Reds in the Ukraine in the name of the free communes, in the chaos of the civil war. But the Blacks of that epoch fought the Whites still harder and they amounted to something in the débâcles of Denikin and Wrangel. And hasn't the civil war been finished for fifteen years now? [1]

Vladimir Barmash, arrested in 1929, served in the prisons

[1] An agent provocateur of the Cheka had his wife, Fanny Baron, and the theoretician, Leo Chorny, shot in 1922.

of Suzdal and Butirky; ill, he was deported to Yenisseisk and finally again imprisoned in Verkhne-Uralsk. He has a proud and tough rebel's character that they will not succeed in breaking.

Also in the Verkhne-Uralsk prison is Gerassimchik, the indefatigable editor of the *Voice of Labour* (*Golos Truda*), the syndicalist organ from the first years of the revolution, very much for the soviets at various times.

In Orenburg I met Albert Inaun, a solid Georgian who could say with his fine, prepossessing smile: "In ten years I have passed through all the concentration camps of a sixth of the world or pretty near all of them." When I left, his morale was perfect, but his lungs seemed to be finished.[1] Khudolay and Askarov, the latter once the theoretician of universalist anarchism who came over to the dictatorship of the proletariat, are in prison or deported. How are we to know the fate of those men whom the Secret Service has covertly scattered in the prisoners, the penitentiaries, the filthy corners of the vast country? What has become of Kolabushkin who rendered such great services in foodstuffs provisioning during the civil war? Where are Maria Vegger, Ivan Tarasuk-Kabass (arrested in 1920 in Kharkov and sent from one concentration camp to another, from Kholmogori to Pertominsk, imprisoned in Briansk and in Petropavlovsk, then in Kazakstan, then deported to Tashkent), Nicolas Tumanov, Shkolnikov, Nicolas Bielayev? I name only the known militants, the prominent ones. Before me lies a list of a hundred anarchists and syndicalists drawn up in 1934. It is quite incomplete and we know that the Stal-

[1] Met in the same town: Pavel Sokolov, building painter of Leningrad; Alexander Smoliukov, Alexandra Andina, and Kornilov, all three of whom had settled there in spite of themselves after many years of tribulations, being unable to go anywhere with their passports as persecuted persons.

inist reaction raged systematically in 1935 in a manner calculated to purge the whole country of the slightest leaven of nonconformism. On that occasion they even recalled old anarchists who had ceased activity for years back and inflicted implacable penalties on them. Herman Sandomirsky, former terrorist, condemned to death, escaped from the Warsaw Fortress, hard-labour prisoner; since the revolution, director of the Balkans Division of the Commissariat of Foreign Affairs, member of the Soviet Writers' Union, author of interesting memoirs and useful monographs on Italian fascism, was deported to Yenisseisk for five years without any known or imaginable reason. Novomirsky, terrorist, hard-labour prisoner, fugitive under the old régime, came over to the party under the personal influence of Lenin in 1919 but left it at the beginning of the N.E.P., initiator of the first Soviet encyclopædia, was sent to a penitentiary for ten years. His wife was given five years of the same penalty.

Sometimes foreign refugees, hounded by fascism in their own country, only succeed in changing prisons upon arrival in the U.S.S.R. I learn, while writing this, that the wife of Erich Mühsam, the fine militant of the Bavarian soviets in 1918, the prisoner (for eight years!), the anarchist poet assassinated recently in a German concentration camp–I learn that his wife, Zeinl Mühsam, has been imprisoned for several months in Moscow. From Yaransk, where he was dying of hunger, Otello Gaggi has just been transferred to a hamlet in Kazakstan. . . . Gaggi: a Tuscanese worker, condemned by the Arezzo Court of Assizes to twenty-five years' imprisonment for having valiantly defended his village of San Giovanni di Valdamo against the Black Shirts in 1921, a fugitive to Moscow with his wife and little girl, is one of a number of anarchists [1] arrested after the Kirov affair. His wife has also been deported, but separately. What has become of their child?

One sees, for example, socialists and anarchists whom neither the services they have rendered, their courage in adversity, their firmness of conviction, their age as veterans, their scientific merit, their withdrawal into private life, their personal misfortunes, the great name of men who had sacrificed, the persecutions suffered elsewhere, nor the courage displayed in the international struggles—whom none of these considerations insured against a repression which drives cruelty to the point of absurdity. For it is certain that Gaggi and Zeinl Mühsam, known abroad, are more dangerous to the régime while in prison than at large in Moscow; that way they make people reflect more deeply. Nothing counts save an obscure reason of state, the enemy of all genuine reason. The simplest common sense would dictate a different treatment of the representatives of revolutionary generations who have survived so many battles.

We shall see this even better in connection with the communist opposition.

It is true that the Social Revolutionaries [2] were the irreconcilable opponents of the October Revolution; that they supported the counter-revolution, encouraged the Czechoslo-

---

[1] Gustave Bouley, French ex-anarchist, arrived in Russia in 1920 after having participated in the disturbances in Germany. He was a visionary who wanted nothing more than to live in peace and he ended by settling in the Commissariat of Foreign Affairs, where he was an esteemed collaborator for more than ten years. From there, he went over to the editorship of the *Journal de Moscou*. Mysteriously arrested in 1935 and condemned to five years in a concentration camp. Sent to Kamchatka.

[2] The name "Social Revolutionaries" creates a big misunderstanding. In reality they formed a peasant party led by radical intellectuals who were supporters of a bourgeois republic.

vakian intervention in 1918, formed governments in Samara and Ufa, killed Volodarsky, planned the assassination of Trotsky, wounded Lenin, belonged to the Omsk Directorate that bore Admiral Kolchak to power. But the Third Republic amnestied the Communards in 1879, eight years after the battle of the barricades. Is it fitting that a socialist régime should show itself more vindictive towards completely vanquished adversaries of whom so many—and that is very well known—had in reality come over to it some time ago? And if they are still deemed too dangerous, if they are still feared, would it not be simpler to banish them than to inflict upon them perpetual captivity?

With respect to the social democrats (Mensheviks), the left-wing Social Revolutionaries, and the anarchists, the matter stands differently. The first experienced many hesitations during the revolution and committed not a few mistakes. Their conception, which had matured over a period of twenty years, was fundamentally hostile to the seizure of power; and thinking that the "experiment" that was taking place was doomed to failure, they prepared the failure. However, they did clearly pronounce themselves, and in time, for the defence of the soviets, not without severely criticizing the government at home, which was strictly within their rights. The legend which makes them accomplices of the foreign intervention rests upon miserable confusions or is only an imposture. They took their place, together with the left-wing Social Revolutionaries, the Maximalists, and the anarchists, among the dissidents of the revolution. The difference—extremely serious because it relates to the philosophy of action, labour's strategy, tactics, in a word, to socialism in all its aspects—which separates them from the Bolsheviks is about the same as that which separated for so long a time the socialist left in the West from the communists.

And here is a vital problem. Every revolution will have its dissidents, its minorities, all the more annoying at certain hours because they will be more attached to the social transformation. Every revolution will have to deal with a proletariat that is divided or that bears the mark of its old divisions. One will see minorities become majorities and dissidence changing camps. The Bolsheviks did not in general commit the mistake, despite the sharpness of the sometimes bloody struggles, of confounding the dissidents with the counter-revolutionists; exaggerations of this sort became increasingly frequent in proportion to the bureaucratization of the régime, and finished by constituting a system. If it is true that dissidence and differences of opinion can, in time of revolution, play the game of the enemy, it is just as true to state that the errors of the leaders and of the majorities play the game of the enemy to no lesser degree. On both sides it is a facile argument, double edged, which contains its part of the dialectical truth, but which it is always a mistake to abuse. For the absence of a thoroughly alive critical thought also plays the game of the enemy!

In Russia the civil war and the encirclement created an atmosphere of mortal peril in which were dictated measures of public safety, sometimes terrible ones, but no less terrible for the party in power (*alone* in power because of the defection of certain dissidents) than for its adversaries in the ranks of the revolution. If the dictatorship of the proletariat refused the Mensheviks and the anarchists the right to sabotage, even with the best intentions, the defence of a commune threatened at every moment with the worst fate, it showed itself no less severe towards the deficiencies of the members, of the Communist party. It never refused the right of criticism to its dissidents, it never thought of refusing them the right to existence. It can, moreover, be asserted that if the Bolshevik party had declared at the beginning that it meant to build up a totalitarian régime excluding all freedom of opinion to the workers it would not have triumphed—the masses do not battle in order to go to prison; we know that, on the contrary, it announced the broadest labour democracy. On the morrow of the disarming of the anarchist Black Guards in Moscow (1918) the anarchist-syndicalist daily newspaper continued to appear; the anarchist-syndicalist publishing house of the *Voice of Labour* (*Golos Truda*) disappeared only in 1925 or 1926; at the same time, that is, after the victory of the bureaucratic reaction, there also disappeared the organ of the left-wing Social Revolutionaries, *The Banner of Labour* (*Znamia Truda*). The anarchist paper *Pochin* (*The Beginning*) and *The Maximalist* succumbed a little earlier. The Menshevik party had a daily newspaper in Moscow in 1919, *Vperyod* (*Forward*). Its fractions maintained themselves in the soviets until 1923. The year 1927 must first be reached, at the moment when the bureaucracy consummates its victory in the party by the expulsion of the Trotskyists, before one can hear Tomsky and Bukharin proclaim with a single voice: "Under the dictatorship of the proletariat, two, three or four parties may exist, but on the single condition that one of them is in power and the others in prison." [1]

We are quite familiar with the antipode of this theory of the prison-state; it is Lenin's conception of the commune-state. The socialists know that they are not insured against

[1] Bukharin in *Trud* of November 13, 1927, and Tomsky in *Pravda* of November 19, 1927. The corollary of this monstrous theory is: a single opinion in the single party and it soon becomes the opinion of a single one. Tomsky, Bukharin, and their friends did not have long to wait before experiencing at their own expense the virtues of the prison-state.

mistakes, against defects, against deviations, against dissidence or even against treason. But they are not founding a theocracy, they are emancipating the world. They cannot abandon the rigorous discipline of action without which no victory is possible, or the advantages of collective thought, any more than they can renounce imposing within the toiling classes the will of the majority and, at certain turning points, the will of the vanguard upon that of the rearguard which is at once fearful, disabled, corrupted, and manœuvred by the bourgeoisie. They also know that socialism cannot live and grow without living thought, that is, without freedom of opinion, divergences, criticism by the masses, active public opinion, contrast of ideas. . . . On these points Stalinism has done immense damage to the working-class world, which the proletariat of the West alone can remedy. In theory and practice, the prison-state has nothing in common with the measures of public safety of the commune-state in the period of the battles: it is the work of the triumphant bureaucrats who, in order to impose their usurpation, are forced to break with the essential principles of socialism and to refuse the workers any freedom at all.

# 4.

# *The Fate of the Communists—The Death of the Oppositionists*

FOR MUCH SMALLER DIVERGENCES—IN APPEARANCE—THAN those which formerly separated the Bolsheviks from the other socialist parties, the oppositionists have quickly become the most persecuted. That is so because they constituted the greatest danger to the bureaucracy, invoking against it a patrimony of common ideas—and invoking them better—and constantly putting it in contradiction to itself. In a word, the oppositionists enjoyed a clear moral and political superiority over the bureaucracy. Besides, they formed a veritable mass movement within the communist vanguard. And the further removed governmental morals were from the early days of the revolution, from those days when the commune-state, the great workers' democracy, was the program and the ideal of the dictatorship of the proletariat, the more brutally reactionary these morals became.

It is not yet sufficiently known how many assassinations, legal (but is it permissible to speak here of legality?) and otherwise, imparted to this struggle its fierce character, showing that one side would stop at nothing and that the other side would consent to any sacrifice rather than surrender.

Albert Heinrichsen was one of our first dead. I was in

Leningrad when he was killed. He was a worker in a large factory in the suburb of Narva—the Putilov factories, if I am not mistaken—and the former commissar of a Red battalion at the front. When they came to arrest him (and the arrest of communists was then still an innovation which aroused lively indignation), he flew into a passion against the agents of the G.P.U.: "Ah, you have come to the point of locking up the Leninists! And you aren't ashamed of yourselves! Thermidorians!" He was taken off almost by force without being allowed to kiss his wife, who later told us the story. The next day this workingwoman, called by the chief of the preventive prison, was received by him with embarrassed looks. He ended by announcing the suicide of her husband and offering her the aid of 100 rubles. The woman wanted to see the body of the deceased; no opposition was offered to that. Yet she had difficulty in finding him, until finally, thanks to active sympathies, she saw him in the morgue from which they were preparing to remove him. His mouth was torn, and his face and torso were covered with bruises. The autopsy recorded it without stating precisely the causes of the death. . . . A request for investigation addressed by the widow and his comrades to the Central Control Commission of the party remained without reply. Our personal investigation led us to conclude that Heinrichsen had been killed in his cell. We discovered by accident that agents provocateurs of the G.P.U. were operating among us. This happened at the end of 1927 or at the beginning of 1928.

My friend, Vassili Nikiforovich Chadev, was assassinated on August 26, 1928. Entering the party and the revolution in 1917, he had become an excellent journalist. His articles in the *Krasnaya Gazeta* of Leningrad on the new morals, housing, the tribunals, collected in a book, still retain their documentary interest. He was, among us, the author of a sort of agrarian program advocating an effort at collectivization in the country. We were expelled together from the party, for we belonged to the same cell where, alone among four hundred members who did not dare to commit themselves (although many of them were sympathetic to us), we frequently took the floor. He did six months in prison, in secret, before consenting to engage himself not to be active, even though he kept his convictions. At this price he recovered his freedom and his job as correspondent of the *Krasnaya Gazeta*. But it was now out of the question to allow him to pursue the abuses in the workers' quarters. He was sent to report the first *colkhozes* of the Kuban, where he was assassinated on the highway, with the evident complicity of the local authorities, by bandits who remained unknown. We were refused authorization to bring his body back to Leningrad. We were refused authorization to dedicate a plaque to him.

About this time there died in prison, after an atrocious struggle, one of Trotsky's secretaries, George Valentinovich Butov. Already disquieting intrigues were being hatched around the Old Man.[1] Butov, collaborator of the Præsidium of the Supreme Council of the Army, was charged with espionage. It was the intention to extort from him declarations capable of compromising Trotsky, after which he would have been sent for ten years to the Solovietsky Islands. He spurned this infamous accusation, turned from accused into accuser, and died exhausted, after having carried on a hunger strike for half a hundred days. The similar death of the Lord Mayor of Cork shocked the civilized world on the morrow of the war. That of the upright

---

[1] Leon Trotsky is meant.—*Trans.*

revolutionist Butov remained unknown for a long time to his closest friends.

Our great comrade, Yakov Gregorievich Blumkin, was assassinated—shot—in December 1929. We shall see to it that this mighty figure of a fighter is not forgotten. He had lived an epic life. A terrorist of the left-wing Social Revolutionaries, he executed, by order of his party, Count Mirbach, ambassador from Germany to Moscow in 1918. Joining the Communist party a year later, he fulfilled the most perilous missions in the Ukraine, from which he returned riddled with wounds. In Persia, at the beginning of 1919, he directed the revolutionary attempt of Kuchuk Khan in Ghilan. Later, organizer of the army of the Republic of Mongolia, collaborator of *Izvestia* for which he wrote noteworthy articles on Joffre and Foch, charged with secret missions in the Indies, in Egypt, in Constantinople. In Constantinople he saw the banished Trotsky and offered to transmit a message from him to comrades in Moscow. (This letter explained the tendencies among the Opposition abroad and asked that efforts be made to distribute in Russia the *Bulletin* published in Paris.) Betrayed upon his return to Moscow, he had an interview with Radek who, according to my personal information, is supposed to have advised him to turn to Ordjonikidze, "the only man who might save you, for the Georgian [Stalin] won't spare you." From Radek's place Blumkin telephoned to Ordjonikidze and made an appointment with him in the Kremlin, but the telephones were tapped, he was arrested as he came out, and then shot on the personal order of Stalin. He had lived courageously, he died the same way. I was assured that he asked and obtained from the G.P.U. a stay of execution of fifteen days to write his memoirs. The G.P.U. is now suppressing a magnificent book. One of Blumkin's collaborators, a young Frenchman, was executed in the South. The formal justification of the execution of Blumkin was that he had committed, in his capacity as counter-espionage agent, an act of high treason in communicating with Trotsky. But the authorities did not dare to make public this execution in the U.S.S.R., where it was known to the public only through a dispatch of the *Berliner Tageblatt.* The communist organ of Vienna, *Rote Fahne*, denied it as an "infamous counter-revolutionary lie." In Moscow, however, there was circulated in the leading spheres of the party a version of an impudence hard to characterize: "Blumkin, feeling the gravity of his mistake, himself asked to be shot." It was also affirmed that he had committed suicide. The assassins, embarrassed, began to exaggerate. . . . I note here that Blumkin left a wife and a child. What has become of them?

The still more mysterious execution of Silov and Rabinovich dates from the same time (the winter of 1929–1930). According to my recollections, the affair stands thus: Rabinovich, a young communist, collaborator of the G.P.U., had communicated to his oppositional comrades information on the repression. He had just been married when he was arrested. He was shot for high treason. Silov, a non-party man, journalist or collaborator of a publishing service, was shot for having rendered him a service. An old Chekist of the civil war, Yoselevich, former member of the College of the Petrograd Cheka, was condemned to ten years in the penitentiary. A former member of the Executive Committee of the Communist International of Youth, Blumenfeld, was given the same penalty. Blumenfeld had shifted several times from the Opposition to Stalinism and back again, and his rôle in this drama has not been made clear.

From a protest addressed by the oppositional deportees

of Tomsk to the Central Committee of the Communist Party, I extract the following lines which seem to refer to Comrade Pitersky, sent to the Solovietsky Islands in 1927: "One of our comrades incarcerated in Solovky carried on a longer hunger strike in order to obtain the status of a political. He was shoved into the black hole. Coming out of it, he wrote a document on the monstrous rule of the camp and tried to get it to the authorities in Moscow. The message was intercepted. A short time later this comrade was led away and we never saw him again. The administration officially informed us that he had been killed in the course of an attempt to escape." Like Liebknecht and so many others in the world! The Spaniards call this the "ley de fuga"—the law of flight—by analogy, no doubt, with the law of retaliation.

In 1930 a guardian of the Tomsk prison consented to pass through illegally to the outside a letter from the oppositionist Sosnovsky (since converted to the "general line"). He was arrested for this infraction of the regulations and was shot. We are not even aware of the name of this obscure victim.

These executions are certainly not the only ones. I cannot overemphasize here the necessarily incomplete and fragmentary character of my documentation. In 1929–1930, there was a German oppositional comrade in the Leningrad sailors' club who soon disappeared, accused of having established illegal contact with countries abroad. I heard it stated that he had been shot. Since everything happens in absolute secrecy, fortuitous circumstances are needed in order to learn, long months or years afterward, that a militant whom one has known has mysteriously perished. Finally, one may die a more or less natural death in the prisons and places of deportation, like Leon Papermeister, Red fighter in Siberia, who made a search for his mother in all the Central Homes of the U.S.S.R. and who died in one of them—I don't know which! There were four brothers, oppositional communists, all four of them in prison—on December 8, 1934.

Helen Tsulukidze, an old Georgian militant, member of the Bolshevik party since the first revolution (1905), deported to Arkhangelsk and its cold climate, then to Khokand in the burning sands, beaten by her guardians in the course of a transfer—died for lack of medical care in Akmolinsk, in the sands of Kazakstan, at the beginning of 1932.

Kote Tsintsadze had preceded her to the grave at the beginning of 1931. He was one of the most esteemed of the Old Bolsheviks of the old groups in the Caucasus. Stalin could not forgive him either his inflexible resistance or his past, his legendary record or his authority. With Stalin himself (Koba), Krassin, Kamo, Djorjiashvili, he had belonged since 1906 to the Bolshevik fighting organization which committed several famous assaults, such as the execution of General Griaznov, who repressed the revolutionary movement in Georgia (this terroristic act was organized by Stalin), and the attack upon a treasury wagon in Tiflis where the revolutionists "expropriated" 341,000 rubles (June 26, 1907). In August 1911 Tsintsadze helped in the escape to a sort of eagle's nest of Kamo, who had been extradited from Germany and imprisoned in the fortess of Metekh in Tiflis. The following year the Bolshevik terrorists tried an expropriation on the road to Kodja. Tsintsadze and another gave battle to the Cossacks in order to save Kamo; they killed seven of them, were taken alive together with Kamo and were condemned to death. In Boris Souvarine's *Staline* will be found the detailed recital of these exploits, taken from the soviet works formerly published in

Moscow and now withdrawn, no doubt, from circulation. After the expropriation of Tiflis, Litvinov was charged with transporting the funds abroad. He was arrested in Paris in 1908 and was found carrying a big sum of notes coming from the assault in the Erivan Square. On the morrow of the sovietization of Georgia, Tsintsadze became the president of its Cheka. From 1923 onward he fought against the bureaucratization of the régime. He was deported to the Crimea in 1928. From his prisons he had carried away an advanced case of tuberculosis. He could live a short while longer but only in Abkhasia, in the invigorating and warm climate of the mountains. His relatives vainly solicited his transfer to these regions. Stalin seemed to want to hasten the end of his former companion-in-struggle. Tsintsadze died persecuted, isolated, his mail confiscated, in the midst of the arrests of deportees, of brutalities, of raids. His death remains unknown to most people. A few of his last letters have been published. They are human documents of a tragic power.

I met Eleazar Solntsev in Moscow when he returned from America to offer himself to the blows of the repression. He had been sent on a mission, in the capacity of expert in economic questions. Friends advised him to remain abroad, seeing in him an economist and theoretician of a calibre seldom found in the young generation. I see him again, slender, grey-eyed, the elongated face, the serious expression with an ironical half-smile at the corner of his lips. He was incarcerated for three years in 1928, without the trouble of a formulated accusation against him—his communist convictions sufficed. At the expiration of the three years, two more were added by administrative measure, as was the case with most of the oppositionists. At the expiration of their five years these prisoners were finally liberated because all the detained Trotskyists (who were joined by the militants of the Sapronov tendency and the anarchists) had demanded, by means of a hard-fought hunger strike, the cessation of the automatic doubling of sentences pronounced without trial. . . . . In deportation, I met a young woman who had known Solntsev in the Verkhne-Uralsk prison. She was still under the influence of his spiritual power and of his great mind. He looked incontestably like a leader, in the good sense of the word. He was deported to a village of the Urals or of Western Siberia, whence he wrote us of his absolute solitude and his material poverty, because for several months he was unable to find any work. His wife and his child had been deported *elsewhere*. Two-thirds of his letters were "lost" upon arrival or upon departure, lost in the vast files of the black cabinet, of course. After the Kirov affair, a black silence covered him up; then we learned, by fragments, the story of his end. Arrested again, and again sentenced without trial to five years' imprisonment, he had categorically refused to allow the continuation of this cat-and-mouse game, declaring that he preferred to fling his cadaver to the stranglers of the revolution. That would have been of some use too. The eighteenth day of his hunger strike, when the doctors observed the aggravation of his condition, the G.P.U. yielded. He was informed that he would be maintained in the status of a deportee; and this time he could even rejoin his wife and his son in Minussinsk. He insisted upon leaving immediately, even though he was at the end of his strength. On the way, his exhausted organism failed him, an inflammation of the interior ear broke out and necessited an immediate surgical operation. Solntsev died on a hospital cot in Novosibirsk in January 1936.

# 5.

## *The Life of the Oppositionists*

THE TROTSKYIST OPPOSITION—WHICH, IN ORDER THE BETTER to assert its attachment to the tradition of the October Revolution, calls itself Bolshevik-Leninist—is today virtually alone at the point of combat against the bureaucratic régime. The old parties do not renew themselves. Those who represent them leave the scene one after the other without being replaced, no propaganda being allowed them. The communist oppositional movement, on the other hand, renews itself within the ranks of the ruling party, whose living conscience it is and which it is constantly showing to be in conflict with the principles of Bolshevism. Just as the French bourgeoisie, trembling at the memory of the red banners of the Faubourg Saint-Antoine, lived for a long time, after 1848, haunted by the spectre of socialism, so do the *parvenus* of Russia fall asleep every evening, perturbed by the spectre of Trotskyism. No three months pass by without violent press campaigns denouncing the evil all over again, or without *hundreds* of communists, official only yesterday, designated as Trotskyists despite themselves, perhaps simply for having manifested some intellectual bent, starting on the road to prison.

Many of the original Trotskyists have finished by yielding to the pressure of the totalitarian state. We have known, on the part of men who are incontestably worthy of better than the destiny to which they are resigned, amazing recantations, others that were ridiculous, and still others that were neither amazing nor ridiculous because they only attested the impossibility of resisting further. Old Rakovsky, the man of the Rumanian revolution of 1917, the president of the Council of People's Commissars of the Ukraine for many heroic years, later on ambassador of the U.S.S.R. in Paris, held out for six years in the suffocating exile of Barnaul. For months on end, his friends failed to learn if he were dead or alive; more than once he was thought dead. In Barnaul he wrote irrefutably correct pages on the bureaucratic régime and the decay of the party. Abruptly, in 1934, he made his apology, disavowed himself, and kneeled before Stalin. We thought that he had been blackmailed by reference to the imminent war and to the need of a sacred union of all the communists around the real power. In Moscow he obtained a subordinate position in the Commissariat of Public Health. . . . Sosnovsky, of the first troop of the party, capitulated in the same period, after six years of imprisonment. Kasparova, deported in 1928, and her son in a penitentiary, did the same. . . . Piatakov, who played a big rôle in the sovietization of the Ukraine, oppositionist from 1923 to 1928, had abandoned the struggle at an early hour, saying that there was nothing that could be done: the reaction was triumphing all along the line, the proletariat was tired and depressed. Stalinism was, after all, the fruit of this situation; there was nothing more to be done save to bow before the strongest and to make oneself useful, like an honest specialist. He was made a director of the State Bank. Radek reasoned in the same way.

The process of selection, nevertheless, shaped up men in the prisons who were ready to make a complete sacrifice and, what is more, who were sufficiently clear-sighted not to abdicate their reason in the absence of any objective information, of any intellectual intercourse, of any freedom. The persecution came down upon their heads with tenacity and increasing fury and, as in the religious wars of old, it spared neither women nor children and did not recoil from the employment of any means.

Leon Davidovich Trotsky has not only been outrageously calumniated, vilified, excluded from the museums, from literature, from history—he who, more than anyone else, has entered into true history as the organizer of the revolutionary victory—deported, banished, deprived of Soviet nationality: he has also been systematically struck at through his family. His wife, Natalia Ivanovna Sedova, his son Leon Lvovich, his daughter, Zinaida Lvovna, because of their attachment to husband and father, have been treated as public enemies and have forfeited their Soviet nationality. His daughter Zinaida was unable to withstand this atmosphere of persecution. She committed suicide in 1933 in Berlin. His older daughter had died of tuberculosis in Moscow a short time earlier, in a state of penury. I know where her tuberculosis came from, having seen her, still an adolescent, actively working in Petrograd—the imperilled city—in the difficult moments. His two sons-in-law, Man Nevelson and Platon Volkov, have lived only in prison and in deportation since 1928. At the end of 1935 Volkov was in Semipalatinsk. His younger son, Sergey, who remained in Russia, was not interested in politics. An engineer and professor of technology in Moscow, he disappeared in 1935, as did his young wife. They are said to have been seen deported or imprisoned in Krasnoyarsk (Siberia).[1] Of his four secretaries, one,

[1] Natalia Sedova wrote in an appeal to the workers dated July 1935: "It is only out of a base instinct of vengeance that the ruling bureaucracy strangles and tortures a highly qualified and incontestably loyal Soviet worker: for it is quite plain that the blows struck at the son cannot exercise the slightest influence on the political activity of the father, an activity in which our Sergey never took any part. That is why I permit myself to believe that the case of my son deserves to be brought before public opinion. Silence and impunity make us fear that the vindictiveness of Stalin will soon reach the point of the irremediable."

Glazman, committed suicide in 1923; we already know that another, Butov, died in prison of a hunger strike lasting fifty days; the two survivors, Poznansky and Sermux, have been in captivity since 1928. Finally, the first wife of Trotsky, divorced for some thirty years, but who remained his friend and comrade, Alexandra Lvovna Bronstein, a pedagogue esteemed in Leningrad, who has behind her more than forty years of devotion to the working class, has been deported for years to the Tobolsk region. She had charge of Trotsky's grandchildren. What has become of them?

Most of the oppositionists were expelled from the party in 1928 and immediately imprisoned: they still were in 1936. The G.P.U. disdained to seek any legal pretexts to motivate the three years of imprisonment that it inflicted upon them by administrative measure—to begin with. Ordjonikidze, then chairman of the Control Commission of the party—charged with guarding over the execution of the laws!—replied to an oppositionist who observed to him that nothing was left of Soviet legality for us: "Don't be astonished, you are outlaws." These first three years terminated, their penalties were prolonged two years when they rejected apostasy. Let us note this new custom which is so very happily unknown to civilized countries. It must be excoriated sufficiently before the conscience of the masses so that no reaction shall dare, now or tomorrow, to avail itself of the example of Stalin. The prisoners of 1928 finished their five years in 1933–1934, were deported, *arrested again* without any special reason after the Kirov affair, and *once more imprisoned for five years.* This was and this is, with few variations, the fate of a young Leningrad professor who distinguished himself both by a book on Germany and by his activity as a militant, Gregory Yakovin; of Vassily Fedorovich Pankratov, former Kronstadt sailor, civil war fighter, Chekist, subchief of the G.P.U. of Transcaucasia, a man with a balanced mind, the temperament of a calm hero, capable of accepting all eventualities with a firm smile; of Shanan Markovich Pevzner, collaborator of the Commissariat of Finance in Moscow, wounded in the war of the Far East, deported for nearly two years, then imprisoned for four years, then deported to Orenburg for a year, then imprisoned in Cheliabinsk for five years; of Eleazar Solntsev, whose death I have related; of Socrates Gayvorkian, publicist from Baku; of the young worker Dvinsky, of Leningrad (he was in Semipalatinsk in 1935); of Man Nevelson, already named, former head of the Fifth Red Army that won the decisive victories over Kolchak; of the old Bolshevik and hard labour prisoner under the old régime, Grinstein; of the writer Nicolas Gorlov, editor in 1917 of the *Pravda of the Trenches;* of the brothers Aaron, Paul, and Samuel Papermeister, former Red Partisans of Siberia; of Anna Yankovskaya; of Marie Ivanovna, Siberian militant who directed the illegal actions against the Whites; of Ida Lemelman—and of many others. . . .

Most of those persecuted are hit at through their near ones. Deported are the wife and the child of Solntsev (in Minussinsk); the sister of Pevzner (Arkhangelsk); the sister of Zinoviev, the sister of Kuklin, an old Leningrad militant, the wife of Shaktsky, who was shot—are deported in a village of the Yenissei, not far from the Arctic Circle. . . . At Orenburg I knew the wife of Pankratov, Elisa Senatskaya, deported for her fidelity to her husband. She was pregnant when Pankratov, who had recently come out of prison, was again arrested. She remained without news from him for six months, then she was deported to Astrakhan together with her newly-born infant. . . .

In the fate of others, the proportion between deportation,

imprisonment, incarcerations of all sorts and forced labour varies still more. I do not know the stages passed through by Fedor Dingelstedt, one of the organizers of the Baltic Fleet in 1917, author of a work on the *Agrarian Question in India*. I only know that he went through several deportations, prisons, the Solovietsky Islands, before being deported to the environs of Alma-Ata. Boris Mikhailovich Eltsin, one of the old comrades of Lenin, fighter of the revolution in the Urals, member of the All-Russian Executive of the Soviets, has done nothing for the last eight years but go from prison to deportation, sicker every time, yet raising his black mane as soon as you speak of Hegel, of Marx, or of the international proletariat; his son Sergey died in deportation; his son Victor Eltsin was recently deported to Arkhangelsk, without being permitted to work. Where is Maria Mikhailovna Yoffe? Her husband, Adolf Yoffe, who gave proof of his merit as a revolutionist under the old régime, represented the Soviet in Berlin on the eve of and during the revolution of 1918 to which he was no stranger, then in Japan and in China where he succeeded in winning the sympathy of Sun-Yat-sen. He signed the peace treaty of Riga. Sick and cunningly hounded, he committed suicide in 1927; in his last letter he gave his action the sense of a supreme protest against the Stalinist régime. Shortly afterward his widow was deported to Kazakstan. Years later I learned that their only son had died of privations.[1] Then, at the expiration

[1] On the fate of children in deportation, Dr. Ciliga writes: "In Yenisseisk, where I spent a year, the children of Belov who had recently arrived from a concentration camp, fell ill of undernourishment. They literally died of hunger before our eyes."

From a letter from Siberia: "Katya Kh. is in Chardyn with a twelve-month-old baby. She is not given any work. Her husband is in prison. She asks but one thing of the comrades: that they should not let her baby die." At the moment that this is being written, newspaper dispatches announce, on the morrow of the Zinoviev trial, the suicide of Maria Yoffe.

of her term, Maria Yoffe, accused of having tried to organize an action of solidarity for the comrades who had become destitute, was imprisoned and finally deported I know not where. . . .

Lado Dumbadze, old Georgian Bolshevik, former president of the Tiflis Soviet, suffering from progressive paralysis of the limbs as a result of a concussion received at the front during the civil war and so sick that his cellmates have to dress and feed him, has been transferred from prison to prison since 1934, in search of a treatment that they do not want to grant him; he was finally deported to Sarapul, alone, absolutely alone, without resources or the possibility of work. . . . Lado Yenukidze spent five years in prison, after which he was sent to the Oost-Pechorsk concentration camp, together with Belov, Boiko, and others. Forced labour behind barbed wires, in a frozen desert land.

Joseph Krasskin, after imprisonment, was deported to Turukhansk. Does this name mean nothing to you? It is on the Yenissei, 62° N. latitude, a thousand kilometres from the nearest railroad station, a straggling village of a few dwellings in which the tourists and the writer-friends of the U.S.S.R. will never set foot. Aurora borealis. . . . I remember a remark made by Smilga, himself imprisoned in 1933 in Verkhne-Uralsk: "When you have such vast polar regions and so many steppes at your disposal, you really do not need the guillotine." That was true only for a time. . . .

In the spring of 1936, Vladimir Kossior, one of the founders of the Russian trade-unions and of the Bolshevik party, was deported to Minussinsk; Musya Magid was in the same town after six months of illness on a prison cot; Mikhail Andreyevich Polevoy had just been arrested in Kursk after his fourth year of deportation; Trukhanov, former Red fighter, a Leningrad millinery worker, was in

Byisk (Siberia). Nicolai Muralov, who played a great rôle in the street battles of Moscow in 1917, has been deported for the past eight years in the region of Novosibirsk; Mikhail Bodrov has just been sent to a concentration camp after the usual vicissitudes. I do not know the whereabouts of Dora Zack, fighter of 1905, who came out of General Denikin's torture chamber a sick woman. Ida Shumskaya is alone and without bread in a village of Siberia. Where are the three Yugoslavian militants, Stenka Dragič, Stephan Haeberling, Mustapha Dedič, arrested in 1933?

In Orenburg, in addition to the comrades already named, I knew Boris Ilych Lakhovitsky, a tailor from Minsk, a maimed civil war fighter, who was driven by unemployment to the point of misery before being sent to a concentration camp; Alexis Semenovich Santalov, lather from Leningrad, participant in both 1917 revolutions, deported and then sent for five years to the Karaganda concentration camp; Lyda Svalova, a Perm worker, machine lather, whose whole youth has been spent in deportation; Yakov Belenky, history professor, deported after three years' imprisonment; Yakov Byk, tannery worker, Red fighter of the Ukraine, deported after years in prison and a sojourn in Solovky; Fanya Upstein, young militant from Odessa, deported for three years after her imprisonment; Leonid Girchek, former chargé of the commercial mission in Persia, imprisoned several times; Vassily Mikhailovich Chernykh, former commissar at the front, head of a Ural Cheka, in his eighth year of peregrinations between prison and deportation. . . . The accident of a common captivity brought me the acquaintance of these communists so exemplary in the firmness of their convictions and the seriousness of their devotion. I address to them here the respects of a loyal memory. What is to become of them now that they are the object, day in and day out, of the demand of the Soviet press that the oppositionists be shot "like dirty dogs"? This is the approved formula.

May I be permited tq dwell here for a moment on my own experience? It is not lacking in a certain interest. I was expelled from the party in 1928 and immediately imprisoned. I owe the recovery of my freedom to the efforts of my Parisian friends, but from that moment onward it became impossible for me to publish a single line in the U.S.S.R. and increasingly difficult to make my living. The persecution soon descended on the heads of my near relatives. My father-in-law, an old dye-worker and political émigré, founder of a trade-union of Russian sailors in Marseilles, expelled from France in 1919 for having organized a strike on a Russian boat loaded with ammunition for the Whites, was driven from the factory and the union, doomed to unemployment, threatened with capital punishment after a sordid quarrel which was provoked by a G.P.U. spy who was charged with watching my domicile. Without the intervention of Panait Istrati, of myself, and of several others, poor old Russakov would surely have been put to death! My wife could not endure this atmosphere; she contracted a serious malady of the nerves which we found it impossible to cure, the good health establishments being reserved, it goes without saying, to the right-thinkers. This lasted for five years.

In 1932, the persecution was resumed with a new fury, because we were right in the midst of the famine and of the terror. The old man was refused bread cards and internal passports. They thought better of it later, it is true, but he died—his heart. . . . I was arrested and deported in 1933. Deported for three years, at the same time with me, were two valiant communists of Moscow, guilty of knowing me:

Sheva Ghenkina, secretary of the Red International of Miners, whose husband was already in Central Asia, and Nadyezhda Moisseyevna Almaz, fighter in the Urals in 1918, secretary to Losovsky, sent to Astrakhan where she was doomed to unemployment. My sister-in-law, Anita Russakova, who worked as my typist, did three months in the secret prison and was then released. Imprisoned again at the beginning of 1936. . . . Nothing is clearer in my mind than the reasons behind this all-too-common affair. Right after my arrival in the West, I wrote on this point to my friend, Magdeleine Paz: "They finished [at the magistrate's examination] by presenting me with a forgery—a flagrant, unmistakable forgery signed, apparently, by my sister-in-law. . . . When I grew angry, it was withdrawn and the young woman was given back her freedom. But last December, when my departure abroad and consequently my passage through Moscow became imminent, she was arrested; after three months of secret examination, she has just been deported to Viatka for five years. She is a minor employee, entirely apolitical, of a skittish and timid nature, The game is odiously clear: it had to be made impossible for me, meeting her in Moscow, to have any light thrown on the dirty trick that had failed against me. Inquisitors who, in spite of everything, may be called upon to answer for their conduct—above all when they fail!—defend their careers." I name the principal one among them: Rutkovsky. He attempted, by making use of this forgery, to dictate to me, I repeat it, *entirely false* confessions. . . . I declare that no definite charge was brought to my attention. The first interrogation began with these words: "Well, what do you think of the general line?" Then the question was raised of my books published in Paris, of an appraisal I had formulated on the poet Selvinsky in a letter to the *Journal des*

*Poètes* of Brussels, of my relatives. . . . I understand that agents provocateurs had been sent to me, without success, however. It is plain that without the struggle that was carried on for my liberation by a few old friends and a number of French comrades, my independence of thought alone would have condemned me to perpetual captivity, not free from other risks. . . . An old oppositionist, a translator known in the literary circles of Moscow, Jean Renaud, had the courage to come to visit me in Orenburg; he disappeared on the way back and it has been impossible for me to find a trace of him. When I was finally able, thanks to the campaign of protest conducted abroad, to leave the U.S.S.R., the Soviet censor illegally retained all the personal papers that I wanted to take along and all my unpublished manuscripts, three completed works, the fruit of years of labour. Everything is under lock and key. I left behind many who are dear to me. It is impossible for me to know what has become of them, impossible to know if they are paying for their affection for me with iniquitous sufferings. The black cabinet has cut me off from all correspondence. Three months after my departure, a decree that they did not trouble to motivate—and for which no legal motivation can be found, unless they resort to inventions that would not stand up under the slightest critical examination—deprived us, me and mine, of Soviet nationality. I had the following brief colloquy with the Soviet functionary who informed me of it: "Don't I have the right to be heard before a decision of such importance is made against me?"—"It doesn't seem like it."—"Might I not know the reasons?"—"It doesn't seem like it."—"Don't I have the right of defence?"—"It doesn't seem like it."—"Or of appeal?"—"You can write to Moscow."—"And this measure applies also to my eighteen-month-old baby girl who cannot, I think, be reproached for subversive ideas? Does this measure also affect my sick grown-up girl?"—"That's it exactly."

And I haven't said everything about the persecution of those near to me. . . .

* * *

There is an old group of oppositionists that advocates democratic centralization in the party. These militants differ from the Trotskyists in the fact that they long ago denied that the bureaucratic régime has any socialist character. The two leaders of this tendency, like all its supporters, have been in captivity since 1928. Both of them, Vladimir Mikhailovich Smirnov and Timothey Sapronov, took a direct part in the October Revolution. Vladimir Smirnov was one of the leaders of the insurrection in Moscow. Incarcerated for a long time, he almost lost his sight in the Suzdal prison. At the end of his five years of imprisonment, he was deported to Ulala, in Oyratia, where he had two weeks of comparative liberty before being thrown into prison again for five years. Sapronov was recently in the Verkhne-Uralsk "solitary." Both men are worn down, sick and intractable. . . .

Thousands of names would be needed here, totalling tens of thousands of years of proscription for the Opposition, and nobody knows how many hidden dramas. Here are some data on the arrests: At the beginning of 1928, from 3,000 to 4,000; October 1929, about 1,000 in the large centres; January 1930, 300 in Moscow; May 1930, on the occasion of the Sixteenth Congress of the party, from 400 to 500 in Moscow; August 1930, several hundreds. In 1931–1932 there were no more oppositionists at large. At the end of 1932, hundreds of former oppositionists, readmitted into the party, were again arrested.

None of these men committed any crime save that of expressing his opinion and of demanding, inside the party, the right of criticism and of discussion. Those who tried to resort to "illegal" action, like an Eltsin or a Yakovin, came together among themselves, clandestinely, and at most published a few multi-copied tracts. . . . These men made the workers' revolution. They were the builders of the Soviet Republics. They spilled their blood for them, lived for them, accepted all the tasks for them. They are carrying on! These pages, I feel, are depressingly monotonous. All these dismal destinies seem to repeat themselves, all these men move about in a hopeless greyness. Prisons, "solitaries," Verkhne-Uralsk, Suzdal, Tobolsk, Yaroslavl, Cheliabinsk, hunger strikes, S.O.S. that nobody hears, bullyings, muted struggles in the dungeons, futile heroism and stoicism, deportation, deportation, deportation; and over again, prison, prison, indefinitely. . . . The year 1936 rang in the ears of the prisoners with the noise of the shootings that approached. Yes, this struggle of revolutionists against the machine that grinds down everything has about it something depressing when you think of it in that way, in the abstract, without seeing the simple and shrewd faces, without being well acquainted with their lives, seeing the Russian land, the walls, the windows. I would like to efface this impression. Every one of these men has his true grandeur. They are not vanquished, they are resisters, and they often have victorious souls. All of them have done a good stint of work from the first hours of the transformation of the world. They know it and they know that they are right. What is best and clearest in the conscience of the masses which, tomorrow, sooner or later, will awaken, lives in them. They stand up, and they stand up alone in this country, solid and faithful. You can count on them.

# 6.

## *The Capitulators*

A NUMBER OF FIGHTERS OF THE REVOLUTION, AFTER HAVING tried to resist the bureaucratization of the party and the personal politics of Stalin, soon begged for mercy under the blows of the repression, forswore their convictions of yesterday, multiplied their demonstrations of servility to the Leader. . . . That began in 1928. Some capitulated as a tactic, others out of weakness or self-interest. With all of them, the attachment to the old party was a decisive psychological factor. The demoralization that resulted from these disavowals ended by making the atmosphere of the party unbearable.

Let us point out, at the outset, that physical resistance has its limits. A man resists for five years, eight, ten; then he begins to weaken, for he can do no more. He writes to the Central Committee that he abjures his mistakes, condemns his comrades of yesterday, admires above all the gifted Leader who . . . Other guarantees are often asked of him: become an informer.[1] Then he is given a small job. Peace. (Not for long, as we shall see.) Here are a few lines from a letter of a deported oppositionist. "T. capitulated at the end of two years of deportation. He says that he was driven to the end of his tether. He writes: I am an invalid, I have sick

[1] My comrade Yurgens, of Leningrad, who had bowed to the general line of the party although she refused to become an informer, was the object of such persistent persecution that, her nerves completely shattered, she put an end to her life (1932).

nerves, an ulcer of the stomach, scurvy to boot (acquired in prison), and these are the main causes of my retreat, although I am also pessimistic about the future of our struggle."

I remember a Leningrad worker who came to ask my advice before capitulating. He had children; his hand mutilated, there was only one enterprise where he could work and he knew that he would be turned out if he persisted in asserting his convictions. Finally, every oppositionist being condemned to enforced inaction, many men, accustomed to intensive work in an epoch when it was a matter of building up in order to continue the revolution, have recanted so that they might be permitted to work. The fear of fascism and war has forced others to sacrifice their thoughts so as to remain with the great historical force which—they hope—embodies the socialist revolution despite the worst mistakes.[1] The maintenance of a conviction in a totalitarian state is a daily feat that implies a genuine stoicism and a tenacious clear-sightedness, in addition to a spirit of sacrifice. No aid to expect from anywhere, no escape possible, no perspective of relief—keep that well in mind.

Many oppositionists would not, however, have arrived at that point if they had demonstrated more civic courage from the very beginning. There were revolutionists who made a tactic out of capitulation, duplicity, mental reservations, even treason. Their devotion assumed this monstrous form under the pressure of the despotism. Heavy indeed are the responsibilities of the Zinoviev-Kamenev tendency in this respect. In order to maintain themselves regardless of

---

[1] The oppositionists do not have the monopoly of these capitulations. Thus, the anarchist Arshinov, companion-in-struggle of Makhno, bowed before Stalinism in 1935, at a time when precious few illusions were permitted a libertarian spirit.

cost in the Stalinist party—where it had been definitely decided not to let them live—the militants of this group did not recoil from the worst debasement. Three times in less than five years they were expelled, three times they renewed their submission under the most humiliating conditions, three times Stalin, who needed now them and now their humiliation, had them readmitted before flinging them into prison for ten years, inflicting upon them a supreme degradation, and finally having them massacred. Their tactic of "going back into the party on your belly," according to a phrase of Zinoviev's, ended in political suicide. I have known some of them who, under the blows of the persecution, in the courtyards of the prisons, continued to declare themselves "100 per cent" Stalinists; but who, in intimate conversation with the reliable oppositionist from whom one need fear no denunciation, unburdened themselves with boundless bitterness. In effect, they thought thus: "There is nothing to do outside the party. Remain there at all costs, waiting for the hour when we will finally be able to try making a change. Whoever separates himself from the party is automatically playing the game of the counter-revolution. We will submit to all the affronts, all the iniquities, in order to stay in it, the essential thing being to find yourself there on the day when the inevitable hour of the crisis of the régime strikes."

The Opposition, called "Leningrad" because it was crystallized in the former capital where all the old cadres were devoted to the ex-president of the Soviet, Zinoviev, was itself basically bureaucratic. Formed by functionaries who had been the first to apply the methods of constraint and corruption in the party, it was in large measure a coterie turned out of power, fighting to regain it and thereupon brought around to raising the great questions of principle.

Its momentary merit was to do it in an internationalist and proletarian spirit. For many of the old Bolsheviks the bureaucratic system was not an evil in itself; the evil was that it carried on a false policy. As if it could have carried on any other policy but one of self-preservation! Their narrowly intolerant minds pictured a state confounded with the party apparatus, and the party ruled by the Old Guard, as something far superior to a commune-state and workers' democracy. In this sense they differed from the Stalinists only by their more faithful and clearer socialist conceptions. The intense press campaigns, the phraseology of the congresses, the implacable repression, disturbed their minds sufficiently to make their capitulations always half sincere.

Let us also take into consideration the obscurity of the problems. Today we see that these struggles brought to grips the working class and a new social stratum of *parvenus;* they appeared far less clearly a few years ago to the militants engaged in action. They tore apart a party once strongly cemented, separated old companions-in-struggle. On both sides the same phrases were employed, on both sides there was the claim of supporting the same ideas. The very formula of socialism in a single country, so characteristic of Stalinism, was enveloped in such billowy contexts that it might appear to be an expression of internationalism. The official thesis was that socialism could be built up in a single country, but that the construction would not be completed by the passage to communism without the support of the international revolution. Only, the accent put on the first proposition really annihilates the second. The obscurity of the debates, an often exaggerated feeling of external dangers, the attachment to the unity of the party, the basically healthy even if not clairvoyant feeling that brothers were rending each other apart, the bureaucratic spirit of many of the best men—these are the factors that explain the defeat of a large part of the Oppositions. Fear, material privations, the physical difficulty of resisting are certainly secondary factors.

Beginning with 1928, Zinoviev and Kamenev drew many thousands of communists along the road of capitulations of conscience. They obviously could not rally to Stalin except with tongue in cheek; nobody had any illusions on that score. Would they be allowed, while keeping silent in the ranks, to retain their private opinion of the Leader and his policy? Stalin could not allow it, his credit was too weak. The speeches of the former Oppositionists who mounted the tribunes of the congresses to flagellate themselves before him no longer carried conviction. Their value was known, everybody had gone through that, and those who had always kept quiet knew that they themselves were no better—on the contrary—than the vanquished who were so zealous in dishonoring themselves upon command. They also knew that tomorrow they might be commanded to do the same thing. There was no longer, in reality, either credit or discredit—everything was false except force itself. There remained the fact that certain men had been the companions and the confidants of Lenin, that they had recognized capacities, and more impressive biographies than those of the Leader. There remained also the fact that those who had once raised their voices against him would never appear to him to be sufficiently reliable, sufficiently muzzled, sufficiently outraged. The dictator felt that, at bottom, no matter what was said, they *could not* rally to him. He knew that, having arrived at the zenith of power, he could not tolerate comparison with anybody. In December 1932, everything that remained of an opposition being in prison, he turned inexplicably upon his strangled party, and arrests began by the hundreds. Ex-Trotskyists were the first to go to the inner prison of Dzerzhinsky Square, formerly the Lubianka, situated behind the figured façade of the old building of an insurance company.

Ivan Nikitich Smirnov, one of the finest figures of the old party, an oppositionist of 1923, who rallied to Stalin in 1928, was arrested and mysteriously sentenced to ten years of imprisonment. We will speak of him again, and of his fate. . . . Ivar Theunissovich Smilga, member of the Central Committee that carried through the October 1917, charged by Lenin with directing the operations of the Baltic Fleet, later a member of the Supreme War Council, one of the men who marched on Warsaw in 1920, member of Planning Commissions, oppositionist of 1927 who rallied in 1928, was imprisoned for five years in Verkhne-Uralsk. Mrachkovsky, one of the greatest soldiers of the Red Army, born in prison, riddled with wounds in the Urals, later the builder of a strategic railway in the Far East, who also rallied, lands in the same "solitary." (He is the one to whom, a short time earlier, Stalin had complained in the course of a private conversation that he was surrounded only by imbeciles.)

The batch taken in the winter of 1932–1933 comprised several hundred communists who could, strictly speaking, be accused of hidden sympathy for Trotsky. In the same period hundreds of party functionaries, many members of the government, a whole mass of Marxian professors belonging to a right-wing tendency which did not proclaim itself but, on the contrary, constantly disavowed itself, are thrown into prison. Among them were: Eismont, Vice-

Commissar of the People for Agriculture, and Tolmachev, representative of this Commissariat in the Northern Caucasus. Both were influential old Bolsheviks. Both had spoken in private against the abuses of the forced collectivization. Since their arrest in 1932 nobody knows exactly what has become of them. A recent rumour said that they had been stood up against the wall and shot. In prison also are the professors of the Communist Academy, disciples of Bukharin—who hastens to disavow them according to the custom: Sliepkov, Astrov, Maretsky, Eikhenwald. . . . In prison also is the former secretary of the Moscow organization, Riutin, guilty of having compared the Leader to the agent provocateur Azev and of having rendered belated justice to Trotsky—all this in a document which circulated from hand to hand. Since he is supposed to have written that the Leader had to be "removed from power at all costs," an allusion to terrorism is seen in the phrase and he is sentenced to capital punishment. But they dared not execute him, and all traces of him have been lost in the prisons.

In prison are the old worker-Bolshevik Kayurov, esteemed by Lenin, and almost his entire family. In prison is Nesterov, collaborator of Rykov in the presidency of the Council of People's Commissars. In prison is the historian Nevsky, who never belonged to any opposition.

1935. On the morrow of the Kirov affair a categorical instruction sent to the party committees and to the G.P.U. ordered the arrest of anybody who once belonged, no matter to what extent, to an opposition. . . . Zinoviev, Kamenev, Bakayev, former president of the Petrograd Cheka, Yevdokimov, former secretary of the Central Committee, Gertik, Fedorov, Safarov, and others, are sentenced after a secret trial to long terms of imprisonment for moral complicity in the assassination. Official communiqués announce the sending to concentration camps or to deportation of a hundred communists of the same tendency. In reality, several thousands suffer the same fate. Among them are: Kostina, former secretary of the Petrograd Soviet, Vuyo Vuyovich, a Yugoslavian militant, former secretary of the Communist International of Youth, his wife Budzinskaya, Zosia Unschlicht (the sister of the government official of the same name), Rotskan, Nathanson, Olga Ravich, who shared Lenin's exile in Switzerland, Hessen, the literary critics Lelevich, Gorbachev, Ilya Vardyn, the historian Anishev.[1]

In prison are the veterans of the Workers' Opposition of 1921, Shliapnikov, of the metal workers' union, one of those rare Bolsheviks who took an active part in the whole revolution, beginning with the fall of Nikolai II, and his friend Medvedyev, both sick and discouraged. . . . "Solitary" of Verkhne-Uralsk.

In prison. . . .

In prison. . . .

---

[1] In Orenburg I met many communists suspected of lukewarmness towards the Leader, although they called themselves Stalinists: Mdineradze, professor of philosophy in Moscow; Dimitriev, professor of history in Ivanovo-Voznessensk (he was soon interned in a concentration camp); Boris Prozorov, professor of history in Dniepropetrovsk; Maria Sorkina, wife of a suspect of Trotskyism (Konstantinov, of Moscow, imprisoned and then deported to Arkhangelsk); Radyn, former member of the regional committee of Samara; Ivan Bocharov, former regional secretary; Russin, teacher in Irkutsk; Chervonoborodov and his wife; Solovian Jr. and his wife (Solovian Sr. had been deported to Krasnoyarsk); Tsuladze, former member of the Tiflis government; Yudin, a Moscow functionary; Kaznatcheyev, former Kronstadt sailor, sent to a concentration camp for the second time; and many others.

# 7·

# *The Cult of the Leader*

THE REPRESSION HAS THUS DECIMATED THE COMMUNIST party. Its oldest cadres have disappeared. The principal survivors of the illegal struggles against the old régime and of the heroic times are in prison. Tens of thousands of minor functionaries of the party, made responsible at every turn for the disastrous effects of the internal policy, have experienced the inquisition. To voice an opinion, a judgment, a vote, to take an initiative, has long been out of the question in this party, which is, actually, anything but a party. Appointed from top to bottom, beginning with the General-Secretary, the hierarchy of secretaries wants docile and zealous executants, never docile enough, never zealous enough, and always kept under suspicion themselves. No matter how submissive they may be, these executants have no real security. Dark blows are periodically struck among them. When the order comes from Moscow to disclose the Trotskyists who are surely hidden in the heart of the organization, every committee knows how matters stand. If it replies: But we haven't any! it will be upbraided, at the very least, for its lack of vigilance, more probably for sabotaging the defence of the party against the internal enemy, and perhaps for itself falling into Trotskyist counter-revolution. It must find victims in its midst and invent crimes for them. The unfortunates who are picked, by intrigue or chance, to enact this rôle will protest in vain their devotion to the Leader, their right-thinking faith, but they will not escape either prison or concentration camp. I have met hundreds of these Trotskyists-in-spite-of-themselves who continue, under implacable sentences, to affirm their undeviating fidelity to Stalin, to spy upon each other, to accept any situation and any dirty job in the hope of being restored to grace.

The life of the party is reduced to the life, very intense, of the bureaux. They name the administrators of production and of commerce, the holders of the power; nothing escapes their supervision. There is no position, no matter how slight in importance, that is not watched by a party member, who is himself watched by others and whose dossier is in the local committee. This system, far from preventing corruption and abuses, really necessitates them. What haven't we seen! One of the directors of the economic institutions of Leningrad, Kolgushkin, turned out to be, a few years ago, a former agent provocateur or informer. They confined themselves to displacing him. Oppositionists deported to Siberia discover that the authorities are constituted out of former functionaries and non-commissioned officers of Admiral Kolchak; they denounce this fact and they are the ones to be imprisoned. Somewhere in Siberia, it is learned that prostitutes have been shot as "incorrigible" and, moreover, as "incurably sick." An inquiry is launched, but a member of the Central Committee, Kubyak, who was all-powerful in Vladivostok for a long time, covers up the shooters. (The story is an old one, Kubyak having since been run out.) In 1929 four presidents of the regional tribunal of Leningrad, Tomashevsky, Okudjava, Derzybashev—the fourth name escapes me—were shot: the first two were convicted of connections with bandits, a third was a former agent provocateur. Derzybashev, my neighbour, a fairly honest man, was the victim of his intractable character, having refused to play the rôle of scapegoat. Periodically discoveries are made of "centres of corruption" almost everywhere, and men are sabred and men are shot. Since they are discovered by command, there are not a few innocent victims, and since nothing is changed in the system, corruption continues to exist in the midst of the terror.

Apart from its administrative functions, the party has no political life. For many years now the large meetings of "active members" where discussions took place are no longer held. The functionaries are convoked several times a year to hear the reports commenting on the words of the Leader and to vote unanimously, after the customary ovations, their enthusiastic approbation. That is all. These resolutions are always adopted after the fact. Formal though these consultations of the party are, they never deal with anything but accomplished facts. You are invited, for example, to approve the entry of the U.S.S.R. into the League of Nations; you were not invited, even as a matter of form, to debate it in advance. In the ranks the cells of the party come together to study the speeches of the leaders, that is, to hear them read (for nobody takes the chance of expounding them in his own way), and to repeat, everyone in his turn, a few passages from them. The fear of heresy is such that the repetition, word by word, of the official terms has become the custom. If *Pravda* has labelled the oppositionists as "miserable social dregs," nobody will say differently. At the Seventh Congress of the Communist International the spokesman of Stalin presented Dimitroff from the tribune in these words: "Long live the pilot of the Communist International, our comrade Dimitroff!" For the entire press, for all the orators, Dimitroff became *the pilot* from that moment on. Nobody allowed himself to say the leader, the chief, the guide, the animator, the conductor. No, it's the pilot. Any variation from the vocabulary itself becomes a crime. Not a breath of thought passes through the party that has been turned over to idolatry of the Leader.

Open up the press of the party: since there is no other, this means the press as a whole. *Not a single article* of a journal or a review that does not begin and end with quotations from the words of the Leader. Let us open up any chance number of a newspaper, the Moscow *Izvestia* or *Pravda*, big papers circulated throughout the U.S.S.R. Here is *Izvestia* of August 2, 1936. The editorial, entitled "Towards New Victories," invokes the "wise thought of Stalin" four times in two columns. The peroration of a speech of the People's Commissar of Transportation, Kaganovich, in two columns, carries this subheading: "Let Us Learn from the Great Locomotive Engineer of the Revolution, Comrade Stalin." In two hundred lines "our great Stalin" is quoted seventeen times and almost every time with several lines of eulogy. "By his Leninist firmness, his wisdom, his stoicism, his great and gifted mind, his perspicacity, his practical work, by the education and organization of men, Comrade Stalin is assuring us the victory over the enemies of our country! (*Thunderous acclamations, cries: Hurrah!*)" Thus the fifth paragraph: "Let us persevere in the Stalinist course of our international policy! (*Applause.*)"—"The greatest document in history, the Stalinist Constitution! (*Applause.*)"—"Stalin has incorporated into the Constitution his Leninist love of the people. . . ." And here, translated word for word, are the last lines of this report: "Let us gather still more closely around the Central Committee and the government and, under the leadership of Stalin, let us win new victories! Hurrah for our great Stalin! (*Thunderous applause. The ovations follow without interruption. Cries: Hurrah! Long live the great Stalin! Long live the organizer of our victories, Comrade Stalin! Long live the creator of the Soviet Constitution, our dear Stalin! Long live our beloved People's Commissar, Comrade Kaganovich! The unanimous audience rises and sings the 'International.'*)"

All the speeches at all the congresses are of the same type. On important occasions the hurrahs, the applause, the epithets bestowed upon the gifted Leader, father of the country, leader of the world proletariat, "the greatest man of all times," "the greatest man of the greatest epoch in history," run to twenty lines and those twenty lines are begun all over again four or five times in the same number of the paper. To finish my description of a typical number of *Izvestia*, I add that the one I have just quoted devotes, on four pages, ten full large columns to the enumeration, which is obviously devoid of any interest, of the 248 food workers decorated with the Order of Lenin. Twelve large columns are occupied by the speech of Kaganovich (plus a large-size portrait). On the events in Spain, where the destiny of the Western proletariat is at stake, there are three brief dispatches.

Another number of *Izvestia* picked out quite by chance offers us a bit of the style, characteristic in the sense that thousands just like it have appeared and do appear. The coal miners of the Karaganda desert (Kazakstan) address "to the great leader of the peoples, our dear and beloved comrade Stalin" a message of thanksgiving (how should they express themselves otherwise if they want to be exact?), in which the personal pronouns and the possessive adjectives, when they refer to the Leader, are printed in capital letters as is usually done in addressing monarchs. It is a new trait and I underscore it. "It is [the miners write] Your great love that warms us and inspires us. . . . Inspired by You, our wise teacher. . . . We promise You to multiply the number of shock workers and Stakhanovists." In substance, they thank him for having created the mining basin of Karaganda. They do not say, naturally, that this basin is the centre of an immense concentration camp, that the work in the mines is done, in largest measure, by condemned men, that perhaps a number of the signatories to this document are themselves condemned men, that the Karaganda is one of the most dreaded camps for the hunger that rages there, for its remoteness from all civilization, for the harshness of its inner rule. Many of these miners are Turkmen, Tadjiks, Uzbeks, Sarts from Central Asia, and everybody in Russia knows that these nomad peoples, accustomed to the open air, adapt themselves with difficulty to industrial labour, and hardest of all to labour in the mines; their mortality rate is very high, their productivity is often derisory. The message closes this way:

"Under the leadership of our great and glorious communist party, under Your leadership, Comrade Stalin, we are successfully building up a new mechanized basin, we are building up a new, free, happy, and civilized life. We shall make of Karaganda the city of coal, of coke, of verdure, of flowers, one of the fortresses of the defence of our socialist fatherland. The hearts of all the workers of these mines overflow with a burning love for the fatherland, with a great pride in the socialist victories, with a boundless love and devotion for our dear communist party and for You, our dear teacher and leader, Comrade Stalin.

"The bard Kazak Djambul has expressed our feelings in these words:

"*Stalin! Thou hast annihilated the fortress of our enemies!*

"*Beloved! Thou art the dweller of my soul!*

"*The tellers of tales no longer know with whom to compare thee,*

"*The poets have not enough pearls with which to describe thee!*

"Long live the triumph of the Leninist-Stalinist national policy! Long live our socialist fatherland! Long live the great party of Lenin and Stalin!"

Right after this, the same issue gives a brief message from the sailors of the cruiser *Marat* "to Comrade Stalin, teacher and leader of the world proletariat." Let us quote:

"Our dear and beloved Josef Vissarionich! Sailors, officers, and political collaborators of the vessel of the line, *Marat*, we send you the militant salute of the Red Fleet. Object of Your tenderness, animated by Your fatherly love and Your fatherly solicitude, the men of our magnificent fatherland are accomplishing miracles such as the world has never seen and are multiplying exploits on land, in the air, on the water and under the water." (There follow ten lines of the same type.) "We shall not spare our efforts and we shall, if need be, give our lives for the happiness of our country and the great work of Lenin-Stalin! Long live the wise and beloved Leader of the toilers of the universe, the great Stalin!" (*Izvestia*, August 15, 1936.) In another number of *Izvestia* I find this declaration by the aviator Chkalov who has just been decorated: "Where Stalin appears, the shadows are dispelled and the sun shines." In a word, the Sun-Leader. . . .

The cult of the Leader leads to the deification of the Leader. . . . An editorial in *Izvestia* (August 23, 1936) says textually: "Stalin, our sun and his genius which . . ." *Pravda* of August 28, 1936, publishes the translation of an Uzbek poem which attributes to the Leader the creation of the world:

*O great Stalin, O leader of the peoples,*
*Thou who broughtest man to birth,*
*Thou who fructifiest the earth,*
*Thou who restorest the centuries,*
*Thou who makest bloom the spring,*
*Thou who makest vibrate the musical cords.*

. . . . . . . .

*Thou, splendour of my spring, O Thou,*
*Sun reflected by millions of hearts. . . .*

The reader will excuse these tedious quotations if he only remembers that a people of 170,000,000 has had no other spiritual nourishment for many years; that this people finds these texts again and again, every day, in every periodical; that they are shown in large letters in the cinemas, the theatres, the hospitals, the prisons, the stores, the clubs, the schools, the barracks, the streets. It would be wrong to conclude, as do certain travellers who are, in reality, not very conscientious, that this shows a widespread mysticism among the masses. Messages of this sort are written by the local secretaries of the party on the precise instructions of the propaganda section of the Central Committee. They are manufactured, the audience raises its hand (woe to him who would shrug his shoulders!), and everybody goes home, happy at not having to think about it any more. A directive says that the texts emanating from the Caucasus or from Asia ought to end with a few verses from a national poet. Thousands of messages contain these few verses, because a bard like Djambul is always to be found; he is, moreover, rather well paid for these rhymes. The style reminds one of the Assyrian inscriptions and of the manner of the poets at the court of ancient Persia. King of Kings, Chieftain of Chieftains, Beloved, Sun: servility has never found other words with which to speak to despotism.

The invariable portrait of the Leader in a jacket or a uniformed greatcoat, with a sort of military bearing that makes him look like a non-commissioned cavalry officer, appears almost every day in all the periodicals of the U.S.S.R.; at least three days out of four. You find him in all the magazines. Open *Soviet Photo*, *Soviet Sports*, *Soviet Medicine*, *Soviet Philately*, any one of these small weeklies that nobody thumbs through outside of the barber's or the dentist's; portrait of the Leader, quotations from the Leader, commentaries on his luminous thought as applied to philately, to photography, to sports, to hygiene. Works of philosophy, history, literary criticism, sociology, are set up the same way. The writer Avdeyenko, in a speech delivered at the Writers' Congress in 1935, broadcast by wireless and reprinted by the entire Soviet press, repeats with every phrase: "Thanks, Stalin!"—"Thanks, for I feel well, thanks, for I am joyous, thanks, for . . ." and ends by saying: "My wife expects a child, the first word that our child shall pronounce will be the name of Stalin!" And the writers applaud, thunderous applause! In the hall are André Malraux, Ehrenburg, Jean-Richard Bloch, Aragon. They also applaud, I have no doubt. It is only ludicrous and the writers in question have sufficient reasons for endorsing a little of the ludicrous with good will. But here is something heart-rending: Peasants of *colkhozes* where the famine has just ended—the government having finally decided to leave them something to eat this year—write to the beloved Leader to thank him for such good living. As I read it, I see the dismal destitution in which the peasants live. I see a troop of emaciated Cossacks stop before a cinema, in an odour of rancid boots. They are delegates to a local conference. A new film is to be shown for them and it just happens to be *The Peasants*, in which the members of a *colkhoz* guzzle until they are gorged. And the screen shows this to members of *colkhozes* who, themselves, fill up on food only on state occasions, three or four times a year. You also see a lovely young peasant girl, sleeping and dreaming of happiness: she is quietly crossing a park, pushing her baby carriage, and the gifted Leader, in his long military greatcoat, accompanies her at a vigorous pace. . . . O felicity! to have a child by him!

And here is something that becomes odious. On the occasion of a congress meeting in Moscow in midwinter, in 1934–1935, it was decided to make an ascent into the stratosphere, in order to beat the American and Belgian records and, from the depths of the azure, to send a wireless message of devotion to the gifted Leader. It was sheer madness. The cold of 60° produced the inevitable catastrophe. The stratonauts suffered a frightful death, for they fell for almost a quarter of an hour. . . . The Leader himself brought their urns to the Red Square, and he had 10,000 rubles given to the families. And the press published a letter signed by the widows, the orphans, and the relatives which thanked him for *his great kindness*. From that time on, it became a custom. The survivors of catastrophes thanked him on all occasions for the kindness which his love heaps upon the people.

The gifted Leader enjoys, it goes without saying, power over life. It is up to him, it likewise goes without saying, to choose his eventual successor. Should it please him, tomorrow, to proclaim his power and his genius hereditary in his family, who will oppose it? An evolution is thus taking place before our eyes that permits us better to understand how the Roman republic of Brutus became the empire of the divine Augustus and the republic of the Phrygian bonnet the Napoleonic Empire.

*We want no condescending saviours*
*To rule us from a judgment hall;*
*We workers ask not for their favors,*
*Let us consult for all.*

These words of the "International," inspired by the rightful distrust of the workers towards great personages who, as a rule, serve the working class only in order to be served by it and to betray it, are in profound harmony with socialist thought on one of the points where its scientific contribution is incontestable. Marxism has greatly reduced the rôle of the individual in history. We know today that there are no saviours; we readily leave to the apologists of the old régime the history of the "forty kings who made France in a thousand years." We know that the destiny of communities is dominated by their conditions of existence, dependent, in the last analysis, upon economic factors. This new idea of the interdependent relations of the individual, of masses, of interests, of events, is just as important an element of the modern mind, in short, as the idea of the sphericity of the earth. To abandon it deliberately, as the bureaucratic reaction does, is to turn European thought several centuries backward—and morals just as much!

This should be the moment to evoke once more the exemplary simplicity of Lenin. I see him scribbling notes on his knee, at the foot of a tribune at the congress. Crossing the Kremlin court, dressed in his well-brushed coat with its mended sleeves. . . . Mingling with the foreign delegates in a hall of Smolny. . . . And I think of how any hare-brained person who took it into his head to give him any "gifted Leader" would have appeared mad to us and would have made him burst out with that great jovial laugh that was perhaps his best defence against imbeciles and knaves.

# Part Three

# THE POLITICAL EVOLUTION
## (1917–1936)

# I.

# *From Soviet Democracy to . . .*
# *1917–1923*

LET US RECALL THE GREAT DATES AND THE GREAT IDEAS. At the beginning, the dictatorship of the proletariat announces itself to the world as "a superior type of democracy." In place of bourgeois democracy, purely formal because it rests upon the economic subjection and exploitation of the workers, the régime of the Soviets or of the Council of Workers' Deputies freely elected in the factories, sets up a genuine democracy, because economic privilege no longer exists. Deprived of political rights are only the expropriated owners, to whose manifest interest it is to provoke the subversion of a still poorly assured régime.

That is the ideal charter of the October Revolution, time and again proclaimed by Lenin, consecrated by congresses, made organic law by the Constitution of 1918. The revolution summons to political life, in a state such as never existed before, the masses themselves, only yesterday oppressed and deprived of all power.

It is worth while tracing to their roots the causes of the defeat of Soviet democracy. Neither the Russian people's lack of preparation in liberty nor its ignorance appears to me to have been of decisive importance. In many circumstances the workers and the peasants, sometimes illiterate, proved to be amply capable of organizing and governing themselves. The absence of workers' organizations, primarily of trade-unions, was certainly a negative factor. But the principal causes of the defeat lay outside the new system. "The normal functioning of an ensemble of institutions of vast scope and complexity—soviets, executive committees of soviets, congresses, All-Russian Executive Committee, factory committees, etc. (the problem was to facilitate the political activity of thousands of workers), presupposed, in the absence of a revolutionary upsurge, the existence of peace, of security, of a level of well-being that would permit a free, variegated, rich, constant political life at home, translated into countless initiatives. But it was precisely in this hour that mortal danger imposed upon the republic the régime of an entrenched camp, defended—in the front line—by a phalanx of conscious and resolute revolutionists in whose hands the dictatorship was to be the decisive weapon. Let us note that until that moment nobody had formulated the theory which was to acquire the force of law later on, according to which the dictatorship of the proletariat is naturally exercised by the Communist party. As to the theory—life will impose it." [1] Far from that, the Soviet Constitution implied no monopoly of power. "The Soviet power alone," Lenin had said from 1917 on, "would assure the broad and steady development of the revolution and the peaceful competition of the parties within the soviets." [2] The Bolsheviks did indeed intend to retain political hegemony, but this was to be the result primarily of the correctness of their policy. Lenin defined as follows the characteristics of the commune-state, a profoundly

---

[1] Victor Serge, *L'An I de la Révolution*, p. 331. Paris, 1930.
[2] V. I. Lenin, *Collected Works*, Vol. XXI, p. 171, Fr. ed.

new proletarian state, inspired by the example of the Paris Commune:

"1. The source of power does not lie in law, deliberated and promulgated by parliament, but in the direct initiative of the popular masses, a local initiative taken from below. . . .

"2. The police and the army, institutions distinct from the people and opposed to the people, are replaced by the arming of the people. . . .

"3. The functionaries are replaced by the people itself or are, at the very least, under its control; they are named by election and may be recalled at any moment by their constituents. . . ." [1]

Without leaving the shop, subject to recall at any time, the deputies to the soviets debated general policy, applied the laws and the decrees, administered in their commissions the town or the district, designated the delegates to the congresses which, thanks to a somewhat complicated system, it is true, formed the All-Russian Executive Committee of the Soviets and of the Government. In the All-Russian Congress of the Soviets, the representation of the workers was five times larger than that of the peasants (1 deputy for 25,000 city inhabitants or 125,000 rural inhabitants; in reality the hegemony of the proletariat was complete). Refuting his adversaries, Lenin exclaimed: "Yes, we do not admit equality between the workers and the peasants, and you who defend such equality are the partisans of Kolchak. . . ." (Kolchak was then organizing the counter-revolution in Siberia.) "The vote of a single worker is worth several peasant votes. You will say that this is unjust?—No, it is just, just for the epoch in which

[1] V. I. Lenin, *The Duality of Power*, April 1917. See Victor Serge, *Lenine 1917*. Paris, 1924.

the question is to crush capital. I do not know where you take your notions of justice. From your capitalist experiences of yesterday, no doubt! The proprietor, his equality, his freedom—there are your notions of justice. They are the remnants of your petty bourgeois prejudices; all our justice, our equality, are subordinated to the interests of the destruction of capitalism. . . ." These interests demanded the hegemony of the working class in relation to the peasants attached to private property.

In the midst of the proletarian revolution, the civil war brings about little by little the disappearance of democratic liberties. It would be necessary to sketch here a picture of those terrible years, to show the revolution hemmed in by its foes, undermined at home by Vendées, by conspiracies, by sabotage, by famine, by the disorganization of transports, by epidemics, by schisms, to show the conflict between the battling vanguard of the working class and its backward elements, the least conscious and most selfish, those least inclined to sacrifices demanded by the general interest. The misfortune of the dissident parties or groups in those times is that their opposition runs the risk of rallying these discouraged rearguards who are ready unconsciously to second a counter-revolution. In 1919, the social democrats (Mensheviks) and Left Social Revolutionaries attempt a general strike in famished Petrograd, threatened from two sides by the Whites, in the factories which all the revolutionists have left! It may be that there was some justice in their criticisms, but in those circumstances their policy was suicidal. Suicide for the revolution if a general strike of backward workers paralyzes it, suicide for the party which has undertaken this criminal enterprise, if it fails. By virtue of similar struggles, the social democrats lose the benefit of legality, which is nevertheless rendered to them a little later when they seem to orient themselves with a little more revolutionary common sense. It was necessary in 1918 to disarm the anarchist Black Guards in Moscow, whom their own general staff was no longer responsible for. . . . The Right Social Revolutionaries had fomented the counter-revolution, together with the Czechoslovakian troops, in the Volga region. The Left Social Revolutionaries, in July 1918, had attempted—and failed in—a coup de force in order to seize the power and reopen the war against Germany.

These are the struggles which bring about the suppression of the parties in the Soviet régime and this suppression will become complete only with the advent of the bureaucratic régime. In the years of the greatest peril, the soviets and the Central Executive Committee of the Soviets include Left Social Revolutionaries (who were part of the government during the first nine months), Maximalists, anarchists, Menshevik social democrats, and even Right Social Revolutionaries—the latter unalterable enemies of the new power. Far from fearing discussion, Lenin seeks after it, having Martov and Dan, who had been expelled from the All-Russian Executive, invited to come there to take the floor. He feels that he has something to learn from their merciless criticism.

The Bolshevik party, known for the firmness of its discipline, owed it more to the unity of its doctrine than to constraint. Democratic centralization, that is, a strongly centralized leadership, democratically elected and supported by a party democratic at its base, implied a wide freedom of discussion and the strictest discipline in action. At the time of the Brest-Litovsk negotiations, Lenin was in a minority in the Central Committee. In the moments when the leadership of the party escaped him, Lenin threatened to resign from the Central Committee, in order to resume his freedom of agitation in the ranks, among the militants. In 1918, the Left Communists, led by Bukharin and Radek, could be seen forming an opposition which prepared openly for a split and negotiated secretly with certain Left Social Revolutionaries over the arrest of Lenin. This opposition published periodicals and held meetings. Since it was animated by good faith, there was neither a split nor sanctions, the events having modified the policy and the situation of the party. The opposition was reabsorbed. The democratic customs of the party will give way in 1919 and in the years to follow to the state of mobilization necessitated by war communism. In order to strengthen itself and to find men, the party recruits without having the time to educate; the civil war does not leave it an hour of respite and everything must be organized in an entrenched camp gripped by famine. The conflict between the advanced and the backward elements of the proletariat also finds its expression within the party and it must be purged incessantly of adventurers and profiteers; it is harder to clean out the petty parvenus who are neither ostentatious adventurers nor profiteers, who are often good labour fighters and whose number begins to grow apace. They begin the conquest of the state without knowing it. The routines of the old régime, abolished in the institutions, are still very powerful in their minds; and so they bring along little of the socialist spirit into the offices that are called upon to direct everything. . . .

From 1920 on, the bureaucratic evil makes itself felt. The defeat of the commune-state can be clearly perceived. The *Workers' Opposition* (Shliapnikov and Alexandra Kollontay) denounces the peril at the time, at about the same period as does Miaznikov and the group of the *Workers' Truth*, as well as the Paniushkin group which will endeavour to found a new Communist party in Moscow (1922). These oppositions come to grief. Their protests coincide with waves of uprisings in the country, with the peak of the famine, with the terrible episode of Kronstadt, with the crisis—in a word, with war communism which is no longer lifeworthy. It rests upon requisitions in the country, the complete handling of production and distribution by the state, feeding by categories, in the cities, so as to be able to provide first for the needs of the workers. In nationalizing everything in order to shatter all resistance, too much has been nationalized. All this is well known, for they had wanted to follow other paths. By misfortune, Lenin's clear-sightedness is defective this time, he doesn't see the possibility of quitting the road of war communism without surrendering to the rural counter-revolution. Trotsky, crossing the country in every direction, has more contact with the masses, especially in the countryside, and beginning with February 1920, upon returning from the Urals, he proposes replacing the requisitioning system with a sort of tax in kind, that is, the pacification of the countryside by means of a new economic policy.[1] Faced with the defeat of his proposal in the Central Committee, he will seek other solutions, not quite so happy. The uprisings of Kronstadt and Tambov bring the republic to the brink of ruin at the beginning of 1921, and Lenin, the evidence before him, has adopted the tax in kind for the peasants and the totality of the measures which were called the N.E.P.—the New Economic Policy: freedom of small trade (monopoly of grain), concessions to foreign capitalists, encouragement to arti-

[1] See Trotsky, *My Life*, p. 464.

sans; in a word: compromise with the agrarians.

The question of political freedom is raised from two different aspects. It is not a question of giving the counter-revolution facilities of agitation on the shifting terrain of the N.E.P., but of curbing the growing bureaucratization of the state and of giving the floor to the revolutionary proletariat organized in the party, the only party that powerfully survived the tests of the civil war, the only party to which, despite its errors, the revolution owes both victory and life. The last years of Lenin are to be tragically haunted by these preoccupations. "Our state," he says, "is a workers' and peasants' state with bureaucratic deformations." How reform it? How cure it? Lenin, ill, exerts his expiring strength in seeking means of reform. A sort of anguish pierces through his last declarations. "The machine is slipping out of your hands, one would say that somebody else is steering it, it runs in a different direction from the one set for it . . ." (Speech of March 29, 1922, at the Eleventh Congress of the Communist Party.) "If we consider Moscow with its 4,700 responsible communists and the whole bureaucratic machine, which of the two leads the other? The truth is that the communists do not lead, they are led." He proposes to Trotsky to join hands in order to combat at the top of the party the bureaucratic core already crystallized around Stalin. He proposed the expulsion for two years of Ordjonikidze, who distinguished himself in the Caucasus by his dictatorial behaviour. He writes his study on the Workers' Inspection, called upon to become an organ of permanent struggle against the bureaucracy—but at the head of which is immediately placed a proper bureaucrat who resorts to base stratagems to deceive Lenin, glued to his invalid's chair, going to the point of proposing not to print his articles but to publish for his eyes alone an issue of *Pravda* containing them. In the document which has been called his Testament, Lenin urges that Stalin, "rude and disloyal," be relieved of his functions as General-Secretary. The last letter he writes is a letter of rupture with Stalin, who thenceforth becomes the master of the party apparatus, in other words, the most representative personage of the rising bureaucracy.[1]

The Opposition of 1923 reawakens the party for a moment. Trotsky gives it a charter in demanding in his articles a "new course" within the ranks of the party. Let us translate: the return to democratic morals, the freedom of tendencies in order to avert the formation of factions, the floor to the youth. The youth of the universities, the communist cadres of the Red Army and of the Cheka support this program. The Central Committee, led by a secret faction at whose head stand Zinoviev, Kamenev, Stalin—"the unshakable triumvirate," Zinoviev will soon say—manœuvres, publishes a very democratic resolution which will never be applied, brutally purges the universities and even dangles the spectre of a military plot, for Trotsky is still the head of the Supreme War Council. The death of Lenin on January 21, 1924, seems to soften the debate by a vast mourning. In reality, the Opposition is already beaten, the bureaucratic coterie is consolidating all its positions.

There has been no little retrospective comment on this defeat. Some go so far as to reproach Trotsky for not having resorted at the time to a coup de force, the success

[1] In addition to Trotsky's autobiography, fruitful consultation can be made of Boris Souvarine's *Staline* and Max Eastman's *Since Lenin Died.* A Russian counter-revolutionary savant has made an honest choice and translation of Lenin's works from 1917 to 1923: *Lenine, La Révolution bolchéviste, traduit par Serge Oldenbourg,* Paris, 1931.

of which would have been likely, given his popularity and the attitude of the military circles. This means forgetting that socialism and workers' democracy cannot be born out of pronunciamentos. It is to the merit of the revolutionist that he refuses to take to this road, so tempting to all the ambitious. However, the explanation of the defeat of the Opposition of 1923 is to be sought neither in the indisposition of Trotsky, who was out of the fighting in the most critical days, nor in his repugnance for the coup de force. The Marxist discerns it without difficulty in deeper and more general causes.

At no point in its history can the socialist revolution which unfolded in Russia be considered apart from the international labour movement. The Russian party and the Third International were already very much dulled and stiffened at the joints in 1923, not sufficiently, however, for the Russian proletariat not to be roused to boundless hope during the revolutionary crisis through which Germany was passing. The Russians were ready to support the German Revolution. Without much secrecy, Trotsky saw to the adoption of preparatory measures necessary for an entirely effective supporting action. Russian militants took part in the preparation of the abortive insurrection in Saxony. They noted at the Chemnitz conference that the Communist Party of Germany was not prepared in the technical sense. The vanguard of the German proletariat asked only to fight for socialism against a bourgeoisie whose bankruptcy was striking; the masses would have followed, the general situation seemed clearly favourable, but there was a lack of arms and the cadres of the party weren't worth much. In point of fact, the bureaucratization of the International compromised everything. The social democratic president, Ebert, gave full dictatorial powers to General von Seeckt, the Communist party was dissolved without resistance. There was nothing more than a short street battle in Hamburg, where the countermanding order did not arrive in time. Since the end of the World War, this was the third defeat, conclusive for a whole epoch, of the European revolution. (The German proletariat had been vanquished by arms in 1918–1919; in Italy the preventive counter-revolution had just brought Mussolini to power a year ago.) In Russia the repercussions of this defeat were to be very grave. The hope of breaking the iron circle within which the soviets were suffocating, had galvanized the last efforts of the generation of October. The defeat of Chemnitz-Hamburg signified for it a lasting isolation, increased economic difficulties, a moral depression, the weakening of the internationalist revolutionary tendencies, the strengthening of bureaucratic nationalistic, moderating tendencies. . . .

The conquest of the socialist state by the bureaucracy is to be explained above all else by the defeat of the workers' revolution in Central Europe.

# 2.

# ...*The Advent of the Bureaucracy*

## *1924–1927*

UPON THE DEATH OF LENIN, THE BUREAUX CARRY OUT A stroke worthy of a genius. A publicity campaign, turning to profit the deep emotion evoked by the disappearance of Old Ilych, brings into the party 240,000 workers, which raises its membership from 351,000 to 591,000. What are these new communists worth? They had not come to Lenin during his lifetime. They had stayed on the outside of the party during the civil war. Now they were coming to the embalmed Lenin, to the strong power, to a restored, stable order which no longer required sacrifices and which even promised benefits. The spiritual atmosphere of Russia changes at a single stroke in 1924, while a mausoleum is built at the foot of the Kremlin wall for the mummy of Lenin. Marxian thought congeals into verbal repetitions; formulæ must be stereotyped so that their content vanishes, and Leninism, invented yesterday, solemnly substitutes for the revolutionary Marxism of Lenin its grubbing into texts—presently bowdlerized—its verbal violence, its oaths, its deformations, its bigotry.

A short time ago the party numbered 50,000 workers and 300,000 functionaries in its total of 350,000 members. It was no longer a workers' party but a party of workers-turned-functionary. A quarter of a million backward workers have just been admitted. The appearance of the statistics is altered and it can now be asserted that the party is once more a workers' party. In any case, it is no longer a party of the vanguard, but rather that of the rearguard. Since the functionaries retain all the commanding levers in it, we are obliged to define it: a mass party of backward workers led by *parvenu* bureaucrats.[1] In the rank-and-file organizations, the militants who have passed through the period of illegal action under the old régime, the true guardians of the Bolshevik tradition, are now reduced to such an infinitesimal number that they no longer count numerically; those who participated actively in the revolution now constitute only a tiny percentage.[2]

---

[1] Stalin and his leading gang know this so well that they denounce as criminal Trotsky's proposal to institute the secret ballot for the selection of the organizations' bureaux. "You would like," they reply, "to accord the counter-revolution an easy victory in the party."

[2] Some time later, in 1928, I described the situation as follows, in a letter to Jacques Mesnil:

"Basically, what is happening—leaving aside the economic roots of the problem (they are clearly visible, I believe, even from afar)—boils down to this: the elimination of one generation by another. Those who made the revolution are removed by those who are rising. The new generation did not know the class struggle in its clear and direct forms, nor the yoke of the old régime. On the contrary, it has been told time and again that it was victorious and it ends by believing it, without the slightest way of getting the idea that it thus renders itself incapable of gaining a victory over itself—the condition of all progress. Nor did it go through the civil war and it knows nothing about the heroism of the war or about its leaders. Everything we went through before, the difficult and perilous working out of convictions, the tempering of the militant by devotion and individual effort, the courage of being in a minority, scrupulous theoretical intelligence, revolutionary lyricism—all these things are alien to it. It is fed an official science, it has an oversimplified, avid, and practical mentality of the *parvenu* on the make. It naturally distorts the clearest ideas as its interests dictate, ready to retain the old prestige-labels so long as they cover something new. Since heredity weighs down, since the country is one of small peasant property, since the pressure of the capitalist encirclement is enormous—the attempts to deny it are ludicrous—you now have a whole new potential bourgeoisism, latent but already pushing upward and even flourishing in places, and infinitely skilful in

Now the question of Lenin's succession stands before this sick party. Naturally it is a question of a purely spiritual succession. Lenin was neither a party president, a General-Secretary, nor a proclaimed leader: just a member of the Central Committee, and chairman of the Council of People's Commissars, prime minister of the revolution, his personal influence was that of a moral and intellectual superiority, so well acknowledged that there was no need of imposing it. His simplicity as a militant, the rectitude of his socialist spirit made him ever intolerant of the slightest sycophancy.—One single person could, by virtue of the magnificence of services rendered and of an incontestable superiority, lay claim to his succession: Trotsky. Lenin had, so to speak, recommended him before his own departure. But he did not belong to the coterie of the Old Bolsheviks, which had been discussing Lenin's ideas for fourteen years, from 1903 to 1917; in addition—and this was the most serious point—he had made himself the promoter of the new course against the bureaucracy. When the passive and wearied masses are silent, personal intrigues can acquire capital importance. Two men solicit —against Trotsky—the succession of Lenin: Zinoviev, in

---

its disguises. I am intimately acquainted with writers, with intellectuals, who are, at bottom, our mortal enemies, whose anti-socialist convictions have the firmness of rock: their professions are made in Marxian terms, they remove heretics from editorial staffs. . . . And they understand quite well what they are doing. Their whole problem lies in staying on for a few years and then the game is theirs.

"This process has overtaken the party. Here is the membership proportion of a cell that I know well: 400 members, 20 of whom go back to August 1921, and 3 or 4 to August 1917. Consequently, 380 against 20 came over not to the militant or the painful revolution, but to the power, and after the N.E.P. Two elements must be discerned there: men of mature age—they deliberately refrained from joining before the N.E.P. That's clear enough. And the young: they know neither capitalism nor the civil war and the creator of a Red Army built out of nothing has less prestige in their eyes than the minister of the hour."

the front ranks, aloud, and Stalin, half concealed, behind the scenes. Zinoviev, the closest of Lenin's collaborators since the beginnings of the party, president of the Petrograd Soviet, chairman of the Communist International, a remarkable agitator, somewhat vulgar in tone, of whom it may be said that he was Lenin's greatest mistake. Stalin, an old Georgian militant, little known to the party, unknown to the masses, firm in character, Oriental in mind, limited, alert, and tricky, had long been boring from within the army and had converted the General-Secretariat of the party, once the post for carrying out decisions, into a secret post of command. His tireless activity consisted in placing his creatures everywhere. His political flair lay in translating with great practical skill the aspirations of the *parvenus* of the revolution.

To impair the popularity of Trotsky it was necessary to invent a whole idealogy—Trotskyism—the baneful antipode of Leninism. One of the Old Bolsheviks who did this melancholy job of falsifying history and ideas, Kamenev, was later to speak of it to Trotsky with the most unrestrained cynicism. The totalitarian state put in operation all its means of repression. The press was inundated with anti-Trotskyist copy. The libraries filled up with works dishonestly or untalentedly written to suit the occasion, but overwhelming and misleading by virtue of the power of sheer mass, impudence, and monotony. Editions were printed by the millions. The communist parties abroad were broken if they showed any hesitation to condemn Trotskyism. The destruction of the first cadres of the Communist International began with the most important party, the French, from which its earliest militants, like Souvarine, Monatte, and Rosmer, were eliminated by the worst kind of measures. It was the epoch of the "rapid and complete" Bolshevization of the parties of the C.I. (theses of Bela Kun); of the extreme concentration of the C.I. as the "single world party" (Zinoviev); and inside the parties, of the totalitarian régime. The officially sanctified phrases were "monolithic" organizational structure and "one hundred per cent approval" by the members of the policy of the leaders. The bureaucratic machine was approaching perfection.

Towards 1926 the situation clears up; Trotskyism is beaten. Trotsky, ousted from the leading organs, is silent. The International vegetates after the bloody defeats in Estonia and Bulgaria. Zinoviev, the first personage of the Political Bureau, flattered by the periodicals, welcomed at functionaries' meetings with frenzied ovations, appears to be thrusting himself into Lenin's place. He is neither a great political mind nor a genuine leader, nor even a scrupulous militant in his relations with the masses and the party—far, indeed, from that. Nevertheless, he is a Bolshevik bureaucrat sincerely attached to revolutionary internationalism. The gradual conquest of the party apparatus having been achieved by his coterie, Stalin lies in wait for Zinoviev there, at the turning-point of the latent crisis of the régime.

In 1926–1927 production reaches approximately the prewar level, with an increased population. A fine achievement, when you bear in mind that it was attained after terrible ravages, and by a new class, only yesterday exploited and ignorant and suddenly called upon to manage the whole economic life of a vast country. Industry, very weak, only imperfectly assures the supply of manufactured articles to the country. The peasants begin to enrich themselves, after paying their taxes, by accumulating grain reserves. There are almost a million registered unemployed, and almost a billion poods of grain—worth about a billion gold rubles—in the granaries of the wealthy peasants. Themselves responsible for the difficulties of the internal policy, Zinoviev and Kamenev discover that an embryonic bourgeoisie is in the process of formation: wealthy peasants, traders, speculators, functionaries and well-remunerated specialists. At the Fourteenth Congress of the party, a struggle, as sudden as it is bewildering, starts raging between the Leningrad organization (Zinoviev) and the rest of the congress, prepared by the General-Secretariat. Stalin wins hands down, reorganizes the Central Committee and the Political Bureau and, while he allows his now impotent opponents to remain in these bodies, he installs himself strongly in power. "It is the equivalent of the lifetime Consulate—the irremovable secretariat. In five years Stalin has carried out his molecular *coup d'état*" (B. Souvarine). From now on, a Soviet witticism well explains the chain of victories of the bureaucratic apparatus. A worker asks his shopmate if it is true that the latter, a party member, sympathizes with the Opposition. "Says you," replies the other, "I've got a wife and kids!" Burdened with a family, the average communist has no desire whatsoever to be dispatched suddenly, after the slightest manifestation of opinion, to the cold regions of Northern Russia or the hot ones of Central Asia (on an assigned mission, of course). He learns to keep his mouth closed.

The party is virtually finished. The old directors of the revolution should not have been unaware of it. But some, like Zinoviev, are caught in their own phrases before being strangled by the bureaucratic machine which they have set up, and others, like Trotsky, think that even if there is only one chance in a hundred of obtaining an internal rectification, it ought to be tried. From the point of view of the superior interests of the proletariat, the latter are undeniably correct. What a demoralizing effect it would have had on the labour movement of every country to see a bureaucratic degeneration of the Soviet régime, without a struggle taking place against it, without opposition, without the sacrifice of the best?

In 1927 an unexpected regrouping is observed which would be incomprehensible anywhere else, except as denoting the sorriest lack of political scruples. Yesterday's inventors and the persecutors of Trotskyism, Zinoviev and Kamenev, turn to Trotsky, offer him their alliance, acknowledge that he was right against them, eulogize his revolutionary probity and, together with him, demand the new course in the party. A common platform of the new Opposition is signed by Trotsky, Zinoviev, Kamenev, Piatakov, Bakayev, Yevdokimov, Smilga, Preobrazhensky. The document denounces the danger which the revolution risks from the formation of a new bourgeoisie (the *kulak*, the Nepman, and the bureaucrat: the wealthy peasant, the tradesman, and the functionary). It criticizes the moderate pace of industrialization which deepens the gulf between the proletarian cities and the country—industry, too weak, being unable to satisfy the needs of the agrarians. It advocates the revision of the ridiculously curtailed Five-Year Plans proposed by the bureaucracy. It denounces the capture of the party by the bureaux and of the bureaux by the Stalin faction, and demands the return to internal democracy. In the realm of doctrine, a big debate is opened between the nationalist conception of socialism (Stalin, "socialism in a single country") and socialist internationalism, which assumes its clearest form in the theory of the permanent revolution formulated by Trotsky. This theory regards the socialist revolution, even when it triumphs for the time being in an isolated country, as essentially international and constituting a continuous process, whose forms may be modified, which may know periods of calm, but which cannot interrupt itself until the international victory of the proletariat.[1]

It would have been proper, in this connection, to recall that clear phrase of Lenin's: "Our salvation lies in the

---

[1] From Trotsky's book, *The Permanent Revolution:* "Marxism proceeds from world economy, not as a sum of national parts, but as a mighty, independent reality, which is created by the international division of labour and the world market, and, in the present epoch, predominates over the national markets. The productive forces of capitalist society have long ago grown beyond the national frontier. . . . To attempt, regardless of the geographic, cultural, and historical conditions of the country's development, which constitutes a part of the world whole, to realize a fenced-in proportionality of all the branches of economy within national limits, means to pursue a reactionary utopia" (p. ix). "The permanent revolution, in the sense which Marx attached to the conception, means a revolution which makes no compromise with any form of class rule, which does not stop at the democratic stage, which goes over to socialist measures and to war against the reaction from without, that is, a revolution whose every next stage is anchored in the preceding one and which can only end in the complete liquidation of all class society" (p. xxxii). "The maintenance of the proletarian revolution within a national framework can only be a provisional state of affairs, even though, as the experience of the Soviet Union shows, one of long duration. In an isolated proletarian dictatorship, the internal and external contradictions grow inevitably, together with the growing successes. Remaining isolated, the proletarian state must finally become a victim of these contradictions. The way out for it lies only in the victory of the proletariat of the advanced countries. Viewed from this standpoint, a national revolution is not a self-sufficient whole; it is only a link in the international chain. The international revolution presents a permanent process, in spite of all fleeting rises and falls" (p. xxxv). "Internationalism is no abstract principle but a theoretical and political reflection of the character of world economy, of the world development of productive forces, and the world scale of the class struggle" (*ibid.*). (New York, 1931.)

European revolution." (Speech at the Seventh Congress of the Soviets, in 1918.) If the German Revolution, that is, the socialist revolution in a country provided with a more advanced industrial basis and a more numerous proletariat, had required the sacrifice of the Russian Revolution, Lenin judged that this sacrifice would have had to be consented to.[1] An honest glance backward would suffice to convince one that the Soviet Federated Republics owed everything to the Western proletariat, hence to the permanence and the international character of the workers' action, and that its vicissitudes reflected at once the world economic conjuncture and the situation of the workers in the other countries. Was it not in Berlin, Vienna, Glasgow, Paris, Toulon, *throughout the world*, that the military intervention had collapsed because the proletarians refused to fight against their Russian brothers?

But from the dominant side in the debate, honesty of any kind, either intellectual or otherwise, is inadmissable. Whoever has lived through those moments will never forget the nightmare: It is inexpressibly dejecting to breathe lies, to see all reason perverted, to hear every word pronounced distorted, in brief, to witness the beclouding of the social consciousness. The fact that it was deliberate is a sign of tragic gravity. The truth was not at all in question. It was power alone that was involved, and the more unluckily false the position of those who held the power, the greater the conflict between their policy and their own declarations, the more violently they had to distort the image of all things. In order to complete the conquest of

[1] Victor Serge, *L'An I de la Révolution russe*, pp. 388 *et seq.*, also p. 235.

the workers' state, the bureaucracy first had to impose its national socialism, its new conventional lies, its falsifications of doctrine.

The Chinese Revolution complicated the debate by making it absolutely necessary for the revolutionary tendency to raise clearly, regardless of what it might cost it, all the questions of principles and tactics. Without the events of Canton-Shanghai-Hankow, the Opposition would have been able to temporize a while, perhaps until the moment when, a few months thence, the grain crisis would compel the rulers to recognize the existence of the wealthy peasant and the seriousness of the problem of industrialization. But the Chinese Revolution was moving towards tremendous victories, calculated to counterbalance by their international consequences the subsiding of the European proletariat. The taking of Shanghai by the trade-unions, the occupation of the concessions and the factories of Hankow after the amazing campaign from the South to the North, directed in reality by the former head of the Urals partisans, Blücher, the movement of the peasants—all testified that inestimable possibilities were opened up. . . . We knew, however, that Chiang Kai-shek was personally allied with Stalin—Stalin whom he duped—and that the Kuomintang was preparing the disarmament, if not the slaughter, of its communist members (it is always on the pretext of disarming that there is a slaughter). For the first time, in broad daylight, the bureaucratic régime stubbornly sabotaged a prodigious revolutionary movement, because its own (national) interests, contrary to those of the proletariat, forced it to. A revolution of the Chinese workers and peasants, triumphing with the support of the U.S.S.R., would have come into conflict immediately with the imperialist powers. But the Political Bureau did not want any trouble. It did want prestige and for the sake of prestige it spilled torrents of coolie blood, as in the senseless and magnificent (magnificent for the courage of the victims) insurrection of Canton, concocted by unscrupulous agents—a Lominadse, a Heinz Neumann—in the criminal hope of celebrating a ringing success on the opening day of the Fifteenth Congress of the Soviet Union Communist Party. While heads were falling by the thousands in China, the congress pronounced the expulsion of the Opposition. The Communist International untiringly approved everything, without having to overcome the slightest nausea when it stood before the deepest pools of blood, the most enormous or the most pettifogging knavery.[1]

From now on, it becomes known that expulsion means arrest, prison, deportation. Remember the date when the party ceases to be a voluntary organization, since one must stay in it—in silence—under pain of prison. The Soviet jails will now fill up with October fighters. Trotsky, carried off by force in Moscow, leaves at night for Alma-Ata, sentenced by administrative measure to three years of deportation. Only yesterday, the press and the T.A.S.S. agency had sent out an official communiqué denying the rumours about

---

[1] Throughout the black hours, series of enthusiastic telegrams came to the Soviet journals from the Central Committees of the various parties. Now that the past has congealed, you must reread the stupefying prose of the Cachins, the Sémards, and the Doriots on the Chinese Revolution in order to plumb the abyss of their servility or ignorance, reread them while thinking of how much blood every line of these communiqués cost the workers there! I followed those events day by day in a lengthy study published at the time by *Clarté:* "The Class Struggle in the Chinese Revolution." In order to spare me a premature departure for some Central Home, a Parisian comrade had to put his signature in place of mine under the article devoted to the Canton Commune.

deportations. . . . Zinoviev tries to duck responsibility by manœuvring. He submits, together with Kamenev and their whole crew, not without piling up all imaginable mental reservations. This Jesuitry will become a demoralizing leaven of the worst sort for the last of the Bolsheviks.

Tomorrow, the leading coterie of the Political Bureau will rend itself apart again. "Never," declares Stalin, "has the leadership of the party been as united as it is today. . . ." It doesn't matter much, the party will remain silent. Tomorrow will begin the drama of the collectivization, when all the strength of the country will be strained to the breaking point by vast and needless sufferings. The party will remain silent. What has happened, after all? I do not mention secondary episodes, in order the better to delineate the physiognomy of the event. One thing: the bureaucracy, separating itself from the working class, has just liquidated the Bolshevik party. It has retained only the sign-board and a few hostages. It installs itself in power for its own benefit. Rakovsky will be right when he writes from the depths of his exile in Barnaul, paraphrasing Lenin's words, "We have a bureaucratic state, with worker and peasant survivals."[1] The doctrine of national socialism—"in a single country"—becomes official. Whoever objects to it disappears between midnight and three in the morning in a G.P.U. Ford. Let us summarize:

The defeat of the Opposition is the defeat of the party and the working class, overcome by a caste or a class of *parvenus*. It can be explained only from the international angle, by the two defeats of the revolution in Europe and

---

[1] Remember that Lenin's phrase was: "We have a workers' and peasants' state with bureaucratic deformations."

in Asia, to which it is directly linked: Germany in 1923, China in 1927.[1]

---

[1] The most probing recital of these events, so far as they relate to the U.S.S.R., will be found in Boris Souvarine's *Staline*, Chap. IX. "The Opposition succumbed primarily under the weight of its own mistakes. . . ." writes the author (p. 436). I do not think of denying that the Opposition committed a number of secondary mistakes and no doubt some capital errors, above all from the standpoint of the detached observer judging after the fact. . . . But it is enough to consider from a little height, that is, without lending an exaggerated importance to individual attitudes and to details, the unchaining of the facts, in order to get an idea of the injustice and the lack of justice of this evaluation. Comparing the attitude of Trotsky towards the party which exiles him and the "deference of Robespierre for the Convention of Thermidor," our comrade concludes: "In both cases, the actual power of empirical politicians triumphed, by a cynical combination of force and astuteness, over doctrinaires poorly equipped with a practical sense." Isn't it plain that the practical sense of revolutionists is basically different from that of the empirical politicians *who represent other social formations?* The practical sense of Liebknecht has little in common with that of Noske. The practical sense of revolutionists who deem it necessary to fling themselves under the chariot wheels because it is in the higher interests of the proletariat, is just as different from that of the *parvenus* to whom the morrows of the great defeats of the working class offer invaluable opportunities for better installing themselves in power. Souvarine ought to know this, after all, for he, too, was a "doctrinary" vanquished by the "empiricists" because of his devotion to the International of the great years.

On the state of mind of the oppositional communists and the situation in the U.S.S.R. at that time, see Panait Istrati, *Vers l'autre Flamme*, above all Vol. II, *Soviets 1929*. (Paris, 1929.)

# 3.

# *Industrialization and Collectivization (1928-1934)*

TWO MONTHS AFTER CONSUMMATING THE DEFEAT OF HIS adversaries by political-police methods, Stalin, in a blind alley, will have to apply in all haste their program, soon to be crudely expanded and disfigured.[1] In February 1928 *Pravda* declares that the grain is not coming in, the peasants, their taxes paid, refusing to sell it to the state, whose printed engravings do not have sufficient commodity-equivalents. The weakness of industry sets the agrarians against the collectivist state. The theses of yesterday are so much idle talk. The bureaucracy takes a radically new direction: an abrupt turn-about-face. It must be acknowledged that, dominated by the instinct of preservation, it will display an extraordinary power.

It had refused to foresee and it had deported those who did foresee, because the question of power took priority over everything else. Now there is going to be a scarcity of grain for the cities and the army. Instead of applying a political pattern, Stalin is reduced to improvisations. Had he entertained the idea, up to now, of encouraging the enrichment of the peasants and a backsliding towards a régime

1 "This shows," writes Trotsky, "how a correct policy makes it possible for the Marxian tendency to fecundate developments." (*The Workers' State, Thermidor and Bonapartism.*) Even when it is overpowered and hounded!

of bourgeois small property, as advocated by Bukharin, Rykov, Tomsky—the right wing? It is not hard to believe, in view of the zeal he displayed in defending the N.E.P., that is, the compromise with the agrarians, against an opposition which only demanded its correction. But in order to beat the Opposition, the leading coterie was obliged to defend itself constantly against the unbearable accusation of being Thermidorian. And since it has a bad conscience on this point, it has begun to outbid its opponents. Impossible to retreat now. All of Stalin's ideas will look like caricatures, six months or a few years late, of Trotsky's ideas. Special commissions hastily revise the variants of the first Five-Year Plan and the battle starts in the countryside.

For several years the bureaucratic régime will go from exploit to exploit, piling up difficulties only to overcome them, mobilizing all its resources in men and natural wealth, drawing draughts on the future that are senseless at first sight. The collectivization seems at times to be a prodigious second stage of the revolution: the conquest and transformation of the countryside. Sympathetic intellectuals, too far removed from the working class, and too foreign to Marxism to make the necessary discrimination between violence and revolutionary action—not all violence is revolutionary and not only revolutionary action is necessarily violent—will admire at leisure the reservoirs of strength in the case.

This ought, perhaps, to be the moment to reflect on the nature of this state, the most virile in existence at the moment. Forged by a new class which has just acceded to power, its cadres of functionaries are composed of rugged *arrivistes* of a new kind. Many of them fought well, had their hours of true grandeur and heroism, learned to remove obstacles, to make light of suffering and of privation, and are sincerely inclined to think that "the revolution, it is we." To be sure, they have become wise, bloated, they have settled down; but that which they are no longer capable of doing *for* and with the proletariat, they are quite able to do for their own benefit. They recoiled before the vast difficulties of the industrialization when they were asked to face them for the revolution. Now that it is a matter of defending their own privileges, their position in the state, their power, they no longer fall back. The possible conflict with the peasants frightened them, and yesterday they clung to the N.E.P. But now that their unintelligence has imparted to this latent conflict an exceptional gravity, they declare war upon the peasantry. Yesterday it was a matter of continuing the socialist revolution; today it is a question of their own salvation. Yesterday, moreover, all the questions were bound up with the democratization of the party and the trade-unions, that is, with their abdication. No longer capable of the slightest exploit in favour of the International, and above all incapable of the slightest abdication, they will display a fine energy in order that they themselves may endure. Let us render them this much justice, and let us leave the mediocre pleasure of admiring them to the littérateurs smitten with conformism.

The bureaucracy disposes of still immeasurable moral resources. The masses have been stirred to their depths, the ideas, the promises, the phrases of the ardent years have not yet lost their effectiveness. The dim socialist consciousness of millions of men, the great memories, the tradition of October, can be mobilized. The skill of the Stalinists will consist in combining these spiritual forces with others that are plainly retrogressive, with the old bourgeois individualism, dressed in the proletarian apparel of the new *arrivisme*, the national spirit, the servile instincts of peoples who never knew freedom, the harshness of military men trained in the school of terror, the amoralism of vulgar Marxists. . . .

A paradoxical thing, but setbacks that would bring to ruin any other ruling caste, will consolidate this one. The more unpopular and the more responsible for the calamities inflicted upon the country it feels itself to be, the more resolute it will prove to be in defending itself by all means. A vast misery will spring from its policy, but in this misery the tiniest material benefits become precious. It will now suffice to offer a worker a plate of soup the least bit nourishing and a shelter the least bit habitable in the winter for him to attach himself to the privileged amid the general destitution. . . . In that way a stratum of subordinate bureaucrats will be formed in the enterprises, in the party cells, and in the villages where the collectivization is to result in a new differentiation between leaders and led. Around the former will gravitate a clientele eager to serve. The misery will consolidate those who conjured it up.

The industrialization is directed like a march through conquered territory. The propaganda department thinks up a whole vocabulary of communiqués: firing lines, shock brigades, assaults on fortresses, impregnable positions, breaches, Order of the Red Flag of Labour, Order of Lenin, insignia of honour. The collectivization is like installing an army in a conquered land, according to the worst rigours of war. . . .

Let us return to the facts.

At the end of 1927 Stalin reproaches the Trotskyists for advocating industrialization "with a vengeance" because they condemn the industrialization at a slackened pace. He denounces their project of a forced loan to be floated in the country, as likely to violate the N.E.P. and to embroil the party with the peasants. The Opposition is expelled.

January–February 1928. Stalin declares war on the *kulaks*, that is, the rich peasants, and begins the liquidation of the N.E.P. Labour detachments spread throughout the country in order to constrain the peasants to surrender their grain to the state and the nationalized co-operatives at ridiculous prices. It is the return to requisitioning. Since a fierce resistance is encountered, all the greater because the requisitions are illegal and run contrary to the often-repeated promises to the agrarians, and since nobody presumes to predict the end of this resistance, a solution is dictated: dispossess the agriculturist by making him enter a collective farm, the *colkhoz*, to which he will bring all his goods and in which he will find himself under the control of an administration appointed by the party. But if he refuses? We will force him. From requisitions,[1] the shift is made in 1929–1930 to forced collectivization.

At the outset the idea of a complete collectivization does not occur to anyone. Much more reasonably, the government thinks of creating collective farms only to the extent that it is able to provide the *colkhozes* with the agricultural machinery necessary for large-scale motoculture. This would have been the only, the genuine socialist policy and the peasants would have promptly convinced themselves of the benefits of the new mode of production over small-scale and primitive cultivation. Only, we know the margin between the socialist intentions of the bureaucratic government and its real action, dictated by interests which are no

[1] The original procedure was to take an inventory of the stocks of grain, flax, etc., in the possession of the peasants. The proprietors were summoned to make known their reserves and to sell them to the state at the legal price. These measures having yielded no satisfactory results, confiscation was resorted to.

longer those of the community. It now turns out that the agriculturists who were most tenacious in their resistance to collectivization, who remained individual proprietors in spite of the persecution, are obviously better off than the dispossessed of the *colkhozes*, who no longer even dispose freely of their arms. Stalin declares that the co-existence in the same villages of free agriculturists and collectivized agriculturists threatens the very existence of the *colkhozes*. The collectivization must therefore be complete, and he orders it. The resisters will be called *kulaks*, designated as enemies of the people and be "liquidated as a class." The well-off peasants, or those so labelled for the needs of the case (and many of them once fought well for the soviets), are suddenly driven from their homes by the thousands, packed together in cattle cars and sent in trainloads to the subarctic tundras, the forests of Siberia, the marshes of Narym, the sandy wastes of Kazakstan. All the deserts of the vast Russias are going to swarm with little white crosses. Several million peasants will undergo this fate. It will be the greatest transplantation of populations that history has ever known and its concrete details are atrocious. I still hear a comrade recount the resistance of the women of a Kuban Cossack village. They had undressed, thinking that nobody would dare to take them, nude, from their dwellings and lead them to the train by force. The young communists, the party and G.P.U. men, surrounded the village in which all the men had previously been arrested, dragged from their homes the dishevelled women and their kids, crazed with fear and rage, and brutally drove this naked flock to the station. . . . The children, the old folk, and the feeble succumed en masse. The newspapers, however, overflowed with copy on the collectivist enthusiasm of the agrarians. In *Monde* I read the shocking prose of Barbusse on the miracle of the collectivization. Oh, the abominable wretchedness of obsequious intellectuals! What can be imagined that is more contrary to the socialist spirit than these falsehoods and these atrocities? Must we recall the opinion of Engels on the socialist attitude towards the middle classes and more specifically towards small peasant property? or the constant recommendations of Lenin: to fight the well-to-do agriculturist who is becoming a small capitalist, but not to coerce the peasant masses, to make an ally out of the middle peasant?

In his day, Lenin's policy towards the peasants, in spite of mistakes and abuses, assured the victory of the Reds in the civil war. The policy of Stalin led to a disaster in 1930–1931. Fallow fields, crops rotting on the ground, the reduction of corn-sown land, the disappearance of the emaciated cattle, abandoned or surrendered to *colkhozes*, which are organized by circular letter amid general ill will, and which allow the cattle to perish.... When the uprisings are counted by the hundreds, when throngs of agriculturists are seen carrying off their belongings and their urchins, trying to cross the frontiers at the risk of being massacred—and at times they are massacred—in order to take refuge in Chinese Turkestan, in Rumania, in Poland, Stalin understands and calls a halt to the manœuvre. Enough! *The dizziness from success*—he writes—is making subordinate bureaucrats lose their heads (for the policy of the Central Committee itself, it goes without saying, is, was, and will be correct), they have abused constraint. There is not much success to be seen in all this. Henceforth, the collectivization must be strictly voluntary and considered complete when it reaches 68 per cent, and that is just where they are. There is no point in continuing the demolition of churches.

Hesitant concessions to the peasants will follow, granted

reluctantly, more on paper than in reality. Considering the point that has been reached, moreover, the misery is so great that no measure can have an immediate effect. The power hesitates between the system of *sovkhozes*, large nationalized agricultural enterprises where the workers get wages, the *colkhozes* and the *artels*, which have more liberal statutes, more like those of a co-operative, in reality. Its choice will finally fall on the *artel*, in which it will seek to interest the peasant. . . . *Colkhoz* markets are opened in 1932, where the agriculturist can sell for his private benefit under certain conditions. The members of the *artels* and the *colkhozes* are authorized little by little to keep as their private property their dwellings, a kitchen garden, poultry, small cattle, a cow. . . . In 1935 the slogan of the enrichment of the *colkhozniki* is launched. The state solemnly gives the land to the *colkhozes* in perpetuity.

In 1931 the scarcity has become a famine. In 1932–1933 the famine is general in the countryside of Russia which was once and ought to be today the bursting granary of Europe. People tell each other in whispers of cases of cannibalism. A famine organized by the state, it must be said. The harvests, appreciably reduced by the disorganization and by the resistance of the peasants, have not been so bad; but sometimes the state takes everything—to feed the cities, to give reserves to the army, to export. For several years the country will not consume the fruits it produces in abundance because they will be sold below cost in the West.

It goes without saying that the industrialization according to the successive, increasingly ample plans is completely distorted. The quasi-complete collectivization was not foreseen in the plans. It necessitates the creation of gigantic factories for agricultural machinery and it undermines the very foundation of Soviet industry by producing a scarcity of raw materials. The industrial cultures, flax, cotton, hemp, the oleaginous plants, are in a no less grievous condition than are the grain cultures. Yet it is impossible to go into reverse gear without avowing the bankruptcy of a policy and changing the leading group. There is nothing left but to persevere, by giving the press the order to proclaim every day economic victories that are the envy of the universe. . . . The actual solution adopted: constrain the workers to work more and to consume less, as little as possible. Since the forcibly proletarianized rural masses offer vast reserves of labour, there is no need to respect any iron law of wages, or to take into account any physical wear and tear.[1] The food ration of the worker will often fall well below what is strictly necessary. No matter, the exhausted will be speedily replaced. The first Five-Year Plan announced an increase in real wages of 71 per cent at the end of the fifth year. In actuality, nominal wages almost doubled, but the ruble fell on the market to exactly one-fortieth of its purchasing power in 1926, and the co-operatives granted only famine rations to the workers. A precision-machinist working in Moscow told me in 1933: "I get 270 rubles but I live much worse than I lived in 1926 with an unemployment allotment of 27 rubles." In fact, he was boney and pale. The shock brigades tied the worker to his crew, obliging him, at the end of his working day, to sacrifice half of his leisure hours in good-will work in the shop. The socialist emulation made the shock brigades compete with each other. The distribution of products to the workers took place in secrecy in the reserved stores where a multitude of privileged or unfavoured categories was created. People

---

[1] Doctors who permitted themselves to show the connection between rest, working conditions, food, and industrial accidents were denounced as public enemies.

lived on petty favouritism, on combinations, on petty speculation, on pilfering, on clandestine work at home for the open market. At the first opportunity the worker fled the factory or changed jobs in the hope of gaining by the exchange. . . . According to official statistics, there was a complete turnover in the personnel of the big Ukrainian factories in three months.

The party demanded of the workers a solemn commitment not to quit the plant before the end of the Five-Year Plan. The workers voted unanimously, of course, for the resolutions and deserted the following morning. Administrative measures intervened more effectively in the same direction.

The law of August 7, 1932, declaring collective property to be sacred, makes thieves liable to capital punishment. Some poor devils of peasants will be shot for a few kilograms of grain. The fields will be put in a state of siege, flown over by inspection airplanes, and traversed by mounted guards! The death penalty for any kind of sabotage. The death penalty for serious negligence in the railroad service. One railroad catastrophe following the other at an augmented rate, the switchman, the engineer, or the stationmaster will be shot, as the case may be, without succeeding in remedying the disorganization of transports. In November 1932 a new law prescribes immediate discharge for any unjustified absence, and discharge means depriving the worker and his family of bread cards, as well as the loss of lodgings, if the lodgings are attached to the enterprise. The famine is at its peak, these Draconian measures do not check the evil, it is impossible to keep the personnel of the factories at a stable point. At the end of 1932 the Council of People's Commissars re-establishes—in a much more aggravated form—the régime of internal passports abolished by the revolution as "a police instrument of oppression of the masses" (*Small Soviet Encyclopædia*). The passports will be delivered in the factories and the worker, deprived of the right to move about as he pleases, for the passports are subject to strict registration formalities, will be fixed for good in his place of work. . . .

The terror, the ultimate method of coercion when men have nothing more than their lives to lose, is aimed just as directly at the technicians and the intellectuals. Some, honest men, contest the value of hastily recast and militarily applied plans. They foresee disastrous results, and sometimes they even refuse to comply with demands which they consider absurd but which are in reality only demagogic, whether it be for the purpose of bluffing foreign opinion, of duping domestic opinion, or in the case of zealous administrators, of pulling the wool over the eyes of the government. Others follow the course of the-worse-the-better, thinking that "this can't last." Some of them sabotage, thinking that the hour has finally struck for the long awaited catastrophe of Bolshevism. And, indeed, never has the situation been so bad since the worst moments of the civil war and the blockade. Some engineers are subsidized by émigrés whom they keep informed or by spies who flatter them. Above all, scapegoats are needed. The policy of the Central Committee has provoked the destruction of the cattle by the peasants who preferred to slaughter them rather than turn them over to the *colkhozes;* there is no more meat, there will be no more leather. Professor Karatygin is shot, accused of sabotage, together with forty-seven other specialists and administrators of the Department of Meats and Canned Foods. The unfortunates confessed to infinitely more than can be believed, undoubtedly because they were threatened with shooting unless they did confess. Five Shakhty engineers are shot, almost convicted of intelligence with foreign legations. The Industrial party of the engineer Ramzin, who has just the appearance of an agent provocateur, is tried.[1] Tried and sentenced to long terms of imprisonment are old socialists, preposterously accused of having fomented intervention against the U.S.S.R. upon instructions from the Second International. They are strange trials, in which the accused accuse each other more than they are themselves accused, going to the point of flagrant enormities in their self-flagellatory zeal. There are no few doubts about what is at the bottom of them. That will not be known, however, until later, in part when certain of the condemned will disclose in prison the behind-the-scenes story of these sinister comedies concocted out of whole cloth. Those who do not lend themselves to the game also disappear, like old Bazarov, one of the founders of Russian socialism, and the erudite Riazanov. The whole directing personnel of the Commissariat of Agriculture is arrested, composed of men from the right, advocates of a return to small peasant property (Kondratiev, Makarov). Two years later, in March 1933, their successors are shot, two Under-Commissars of the People, several influential communists (Connor-Poleschuk, Wolfe, Kovarsky), thirty-five persons in all, on vague accusations of sabotage and of intelligence with countries abroad. Historians, physicists, geologists, bacteriologists fill the prisons. The historian Platonov dies there, the historian Kareyev is set free a

[1] Condemned to death, pardoned with all his fellow accused, Ramzin never stopped teaching and working for Soviet industry up to the moment when, in 1936, he was rehabilitated because of services rendered. The treatment which this organizer of treason, sabotage, and intervention—according to his own confessions—together with his accomplices, benefited by, is in singular contrast to that which was inflicted upon so many socialists and communists. . . .

dying man, the historian Tarlé is sent to Alma-Ata after long months of secrecy; the physicist Lazarev has a similar fate, one of the greatest Russian bacteriologists dies in a Leningrad prison hospital.[1] Then it is noticed that the G.P.U. has exaggerated and new instructions demand that the intellectuals be reassured. Now it is overly clever examining magistrates who are arrested, now it is they who are shot—all this in the dark, in secret—while the engineers who were incarcerated yesterday, in the anguish of an execution suspended over their heads, receive premiums and decorations. . . .

The Five-Year Plan is finished in three years here, in four years there, in five years elsewhere, in six or seven years in still another place, as in river transport—in brief, without any plan! Reports, not written by humorists, point to the prodigious development of passenger transportation by railroad. A fever of moving has gripped the disturbed and famished population. You travel in order to find shoes, tea, bread, soap, to flee excessive exploitation; you travel because wherever you are you feel bad. And all the forecasts of the transportation economists are exceeded, there is more travelling done than there was in California during the great gold rush! How you travel is another matter. . . . The cities grow before your very eyes, at least so far as population is concerned, faster than Chicago not long ago, faster than San Francisco: for the villages have become uninhabitable.

In the party the dry guillotine functions without let-up. Not always dry. . . . In 1930 the president of the Council of People's Commissars of the R.S.F.S.R., Syrtsov, together with a group of left-wing Stalinists, is denounced as a

[1] Lazarev and Tarlé have since been rehabilitated just as arbitrarily as they were condemned.

counter-revolutionist and removed. In 1932 two Old Bolsheviks, directors of the Commissariat of Agriculture, Eismont and Tolmachev, disappear in prison. The former secretary of the Moscow party organization, Riutin, the family of the old communist worker, Kayurov, intellectuals of the Bukharin school, the Sliepkovs, Astrovs, Maretskys, Eikhenwalds, are expelled and imprisoned. The right-wing tendency, which secretly advocates peace with the peasants and a moderate policy (Rykov, Tomsky, Bukharin, Smirnov), is driven out of the Political Bureau, persecuted in in turn, reduced to reiterated recantations. Nationalist tendencies come to light among the communists of the federated republics, in the Ukraine, in Central Asia. The G.P.U. is on guard and there are expulsions, imprisonments, and deportations of whole governments. . . . Thousands of Ukrainian communists and intellectuals are arrested in 1933. Skrypnik, an old member of the Central Committee, October fighter, Stalinist from the outset, People's Commissar of Education in the Kharkov cabinet, blows his brains out so as not to see several of his protégés shot. Shumsky, leader of the Ukrainian communists, is sent to Solovietsky Islands.

Giant factories rise from the ground, Moscow will have its subway, the G.P.U. builds itself veritable dungeons in the heart of almost every town, new cities rise in the boreal steppes, like Kirovsk (formerly Khibinogorsk), near the apatite beds of Northern Russia, dammed rivers operate powerful electrical stations, an automobile industry is created out of nothing, the aviation of the U.S.S.R. becomes perhaps the most formidable in the world. The plan has been executed chaotically. Upon analysis, all its forecasts, retail prices, intervals, results, prove to be false, distorted, or erroneous. But what remains is that the country has given itself a new and powerful industrial equipment. At the cost of blood, built literally upon bones, like Tsar Peter built his capital of Petersburg and began the construction of the port of Rogerwick. . . .

Fighting a rebellious peasantry in its entirety, whose passive resistance seemed constantly on the verge of turning into active resistance, unpopular among the overworked proletarians and among the bullied intellectuals, the government felt at certain times the chill of death pass over its face. A thrust on one of the frontiers might have provoked the fall of the régime. Stalin brought the U.S.S.R. to the brink of the abyss. Dominated by the fear of the war, he subjected the Five-Year Plan to a new transformation, discreet and expensive, and it became an armaments plan unique in the world. The resources that might have left the Russian people a bit of well-being went into that plan. But in exchange for that, the Italian general Graziani, confidant and envoy of Mussolini, was the first to marvel at the sight of the results obtained, truly grandiose. . . .

Who can fail to recall, with this picture before him, the pages of *Capital* where Marx describes the relentless mechanism of primitive capitalist accumulation? One is tempted to speak of a primitive socialist accumulation, just as cruel as the other, just as anti-socialist in its methods and in the treatment inflicted upon man. But we are still far from concluding.

# 4.

# *The Great Wretchedness (1931-1934)*

---

BEGINNING WITH 1929–1930, THE FAMINE SPREADS OVER THE immense country like leprosy. People learn to make bread of oilcakes, to eat herbs and bark.

Little children have swollen bellies, epidemics perpetuate themselves: typhoid, exanthematic typhus carried by lice (soap is a rare product), dysentery, cholera. Public rumour announces cases of the plague in Stavropol (Northern Caucasus) during the winter of 1932–1933. Whole regions —I have lived in them—are sapped by malaria. There is a shortage of medicaments. The nomadic populations of Central Asia are decimated by hunger and maladies. Build, build, build, export, shoot, build. This is what was called the epopee of the great plan.

What characterizes the conditions of the people in these years?

1. In the countryside the expropriation and the deportation of anybody who gives the appearance of resisting, even passively, any one of the instructions of the authorities—and God knows that there are plenty of them, that they vary, that they contradict each other! The forced collectivization and its consequences.

2. In the industrial centres, overexploitation. The working day is no longer limited in fact, the shock brigades, the brigades of enthusiasts, the young communists make the day limitless. The rest days become days of voluntary labour,

imposed in reality, in order to outstrip the production plan, to make up statistics, to meet a deficit, to publish a fine communiqué. . . .

3. In the provisioning of the cities, the system of reserved stores. Every category of workers, every factory—and within each factory the ordinary workers, the shock workers, the technical men, the bureaucrats—has its private store, closed to the other categories, with special rations and prices, confidential or secret. No displays, just a card that is open-sesame. As a rule, the reserved stores of the foreigners, the high functionaries, the G.P.U., the well-paid specialists, are sufficiently supplied with merchandise. Those of the ordinary workers and of the population at large are dirty and virtually empty. The government intervenes in order to fix the minimum rations of the workers and fixes them at a level appreciably below requirements. A meat card is created in the large centres in 1932, for workers doing especially hard work, and it entitles the bearer to two kilograms of beef per month. The rations vary greatly and can often be delivered only on paper. The housewife arrives at the store only to learn that there is no sugar left. She is promised that the sugar due in January will be available in February, but in February the January sugar coupon is annulled. Nothing is simpler. In the large cities the worker receives, as a rule: 400 to 600 grams of black bread a day, 200 to 300 for the wife and for each child; a kilogram of sugar per month on a co-operator's card; monthly: a half-litre of sunflower-seed oil, 50 grams of tea, a kilogram of salted herring, a piece of laundry soap, 800 grams of food pastes. The rations were substantially smaller in the provinces where the women, children, and old folk usually had food cards refused them. I saw this placard in a bureau: "Grandparents have no right

to food cards." Bread is suppressed for certain days. There isn't any on the market, trading in bread is forbidden. Food grains like millet are sold by the glass and the glass costs as high as 2 to 3 rubles.

4. Inflation everywhere. Silver money, withdrawn from circulation, not without some unlucky hoarders being shot by a firing squad, the currency gradually depreciates in value, since there is no real exchange except on the semi-clandestine market where it is worth one-fortieth of the 1926 value. In the reserved stores, the purchasing power of the ruble varies according to the status of the purchaser. A stenographer of the G.P.U., with a monthly wage of 100 rubles, provided with an admission card to the stores of the political police, obtains for her 100 rubles products worth 2,500 to 3,000 rubles on the market. In another reserved store, the 100 rubles of the stenographer of a technicians' office are worth practically 1,200 rubles. The 100 rubles of the stenographer of a Soviet bureau are worth a maximum of 300 merchandise rubles of the moment. Finally, the 100 rubles of the stenographer of a school, a co-operative, a hospital, a small artisans' enterprise are worth exactly . . . 100 paper rubles. This system rested upon the division of the exploited, secret privilege, combinations.

The economists are forbidden to speak of inflation. The compulsory rate of a purely theoretical exchange, since foreigners make their purchases in Torgsin and pay their hotels in valuta, remains unalterable. A theory of socialist money is elaborated, according to which it no longer needs a coverage of gold or commodities, but serves in the hands of the party for the distribution of the products in a class spirit. . . . Of what class?

5. Everywhere, the extortion of gold, and the Torgsin.

The possession by private persons of precious metals, in

the form of jewels, watches, silver plate, was and remains permitted. The possession of foreign valuta was also permitted and was never legally prohibited. The banks leased strongboxes to citizens and guaranteed them the secrecy of deposits. No press campaign invited the citizens to part with their gold and their valuta. The extortion of gold, entirely illegal, not clandestine at the beginning, probably denied abroad, therefore betokened, in its arbitrariness, a complete contempt for the indivudal and the law. The state stores, like Mostorg of Moscow, continued to sell gold jewels. . . .[1]

The extortions began in 1930–1931 with nocturnal domiciliary visits to the homes of people enjoying a certain ease —doctors, dentists, lawyers, former watchmakers (it is curious that the writers, although richer as a rule, were not touched). They continued in the form of systematic searches of the homes of all persons supposed to be in possession of jewellery or valuta. As the gold disappeared into hiding places, the G.P.U., which was also executing a plan providing a certain return from every locality within a fixed period, turned to sequestrations. It was, indeed, made clear to the persons taken from their homes that they were neither under arrest nor charged with a crime. Men and women remained for weeks or months behind bars, insulted, threatened, forced to live standing up, packed in like herrings, thirty, forty, fifty to a small room, deprived of drinks, of air, deprived of the possibility of satisfying their wants, brutalized, submitted to treatment that I prefer not to describe. I have known many victims of these ex-

[1] In this way the extortions are dependent upon a sort of state banditry which is absolutely contrary to revolutionary expropriations, whose great honesty may be brutal or painful; expropriations, carried on in broad daylight, invoke and create a new law.

tortions and they were neither capitalists nor former capitalists. Those who had hidden a watch, a wedding ring, a bracelet, a twenty-dollar bill, finished by handing it over; those who had nothing, finished by convincing the extortionists that there was nothing to get. . . . One of my Leningrad neighbours was thus sequestered three times in one year.

In the same period, in addition to the empty co-operatives and the reserved stores with private entrances, the richly furnished stores of the Torgsin, "State Society for Trading with Foreigners," are opened. There Soviet citizens are able, in exchange for gold—jewellery, gold fillings, gold dust, moneys, all of it taken in by weight regardless of artistic or numismatic value!—and foreign valuta, are able to obtain products unobtainable anywhere else. The Torgsin would demonstrate if necessary that the possession of gold and of valuta is legal, but who cares about that? A new scandalous privilege is established in broad daylight for the benefit of possessors of a few bits of gold, foreigners, relatives of émigrés. . . . The Torgsin stores naturally become centres of speculation, where the G.P.U. multiplies its raids. They were the only stores where medicaments, cloth, shoes, soap, food of good quality, all "articles of export" could be obtained. . . . Crimes committed for the sake of gold multiplied considerably.[1]

The enormity of it all, besides the challenge to the public conscience, is that the Soviet worker, unless he has an émigré aunt who is able to send him a few dollars, cannot procure the products which he himself manufactures.

---

[1] A prominent doctor of Saratov, known for his learning and his devotion, was killed in 1932 by bandits who stole his gold teeth. The communist director and subdirector of the Astrakhan Torgsin were shot in 1935. Acts of this kind were extremely numerous.

6. Everywhere: the atrociously widespread application of the death penalty by administrative and secret measure. The execution of peasants, who are often called terrorists, for having spoiled the looks of a functionary, or embezzlers, for having stolen a sack of grain. The execution of habitual criminal offenders and of prostitutes who are declared incorrigible. The execution of priests guilty of having protested against the demolition of churches. The execution of hoarders of small silver money. The execution of technical men accused of sabotage. The execution of depraved functionaries. The execution of persons of various sorts accused of espionage. The execution of hostages in the concentration camps after attempts at escape. The execution of former officers. The execution of agents of the G.P.U. . . .

No statistics have been published, none are publishable. Anybody who is acquainted with Russian life knows that the death penalty has entered into the morals of the country and that innocent blood has flowed in streams.

7. Everywhere the bureaucratic state increasingly accentuates its police-state aspect. The G.P.U. meddles in everything. There is not a scientific or industrial establishment, there is not a bureau, which does not have its Secret Service and its informers. They are in the dwellings, in the hospitals, in the co-operatives; they are among the writers, the artists, the priests [1]—they are everywhere. Party members are obliged to become informers at the first summons. In 1933 *Political Services* are created in transportation and in

[1] In Leningrad I was astonished at the election to the Academy of Sciences of a professor with no discernible merit. "Now look here," I was told, "don't you understand? He's one of them!" The G.P.U. pushed its impudence to the point of convoking the savants, who were not disposed to vote for this candidate, in order to deliver a lecture to them. The Autocephalic Church of the Ukraine had an informer at its head for a certain period of time.

the *colkhozes*. Agents of the G.P.U. can be seen substituting in actuality for the rural soviets and for the lower committees of the party. On this basis they do such bad work and the police organization of work in the fields reveals itself to be so utopian, that the *Political Services of the Countryside* are abolished in 1935, at the moment when the G.P.U. becomes a state within the state. At the end of 1933 the restoration of internal passports places the entire population under the meticulous control of the political police.

In order to get an idea of the life of the Soviet citizen during these years one must picture the worker preoccupied with obtaining, stamping, checking, and re-registering a bread card, which is refused to half the workers on various pretexts; the housewife, running from one empty store to another, and registering in a queue at the doors of a fish-stall early in the evening, pauper No. 758, in order to wrangle the next morning over a ration of salt fish; the worker exposed to spying in the shop, coming home to comment at the table on the arrests made the night before; finding rhymed apologies for the death penalty in his paper; not knowing where he can get a spare shirt; fearing to be driven out of the big city by being refused a passport, because his son has married the daughter of a former small merchant; wondering what risky combination to resort to in order to get hold of a dollar and buy some precious medicament at the Torgsin. . . . Hemmed in by the police, by poverty, by lies.

In the political order the soviets, the trade-unions, the co-operatives, the Communist party disappear together. Nothing remains of them but expensive and fairly cumbersome sign-boards, an army of red-tape functionaries, and words. You go to vote in the elections to the soviets in a cortège, music at the head, hands raised in unanimity; or else the vote takes place in the factory during working time, with all doors closed. Certain soviets never meet. Nobody knows whom he has elected, nobody is interested. The trade-unions collect dues and distribute among the active, that is, the right-thinking, elements special tickets for trips to the country and the theatres. They support a numerous bureaucracy in the plant and they build workers' clubs, which are unnecessary palaces, amid the hovels where the workers live. The co-operatives deliver to their members the mediocre rations we know of, and sell small quantities of low-quality calico prints at high prices. They exhort the co-operators to be good enough to increase their annual dues payments which cannot be less than the monthly wage of the person involved and which are raised every year. Ways are thought of by which the consumers grant them a credit. Do you want to buy an overcoat? Then you obtain, through your factory committee, in your capacity as shock worker, the favour of being inscribed on an order blank, you pay the price of the article in advance, for ten months, and maybe, although it is by no means sure, you will end by getting an overcoat next year. . . . The party is exceedingly powerful, but it is no longer a workers' party in the traditional sense of the term. At one and the same time, it resembles a religious order in the Jesuitical sense, a militia, and a career army. Its bureaux distribute the promotions, the jobs, the sinecures, the pensions, the passports, the food rations, the clothing, the lodgings, the theses, the professorships, the insults, the years in prison, the death sentences, the pardons. . . .

# 5.
## *The Laws*

LET US CONSIDER FOR A MOMENT THE EVOLUTION OF SOVIET legislation in the course of these last years. The law of a country reflect its social condition. We already know the law of August 7, 1932, which declares socialist property to be sacred. For the first time in our epoch, in a civilized country, the death penalty will be applied for theft, sometimes for insignificant thefts, and that under conditions where theft is accounted for by the deepest poverty.[1]

A law on high treason had been promulgated some time earlier as a result of numerous defections that had taken place in the diplomatic, military, and commercial personnel of the missions abroad. Numerous functionaries, dreading the terror, remained abroad. Some of them betrayed, like the first secretary of the legation in Paris, Bessedovsky, the G.P.U. agent in Istanbul, charged with watching Trotsky,

[1] In Moscow in 1932 I saw a worker sentenced to ten years' imprisonment for having stolen a package of pencils in the factory. I borrow from Comrade Yvon, of the *Révolution Prolétarienne* the following examples taken from the Russian press: "For having made unauthorized use of things belonging to the *colkhoz* (horse, fishing boat), *colkhoz* members were sentenced to death in accordance with the decree of August 7. . . ." —"Paraskeva, 28 years old, mother of three young children, and Pashtchenko, Anna, 40 years old, illiterate, poor *colkhoz* members, were sentenced, in virtue of the decree of August 7, by the judge of the Eysk region, to ten years in prison for having stolen 4 kilograms of grain. Upon protest of the prosecutor, the Supreme Court reversed the decision and, applying another law, reduced the penalty to one year of obligatory labour. . . ." (*Pravda*, April 28, 1934.)

Agabekov, and the military attaché in Stockholm. Defections and betrayals ran into the hundreds. The director of the State Bank deserted in Berlin, a personal secretary of Stalin's ran away. These episodes disclosed the profound uneasiness of the bureaucracy and the low quality of the personnel called upon to replace the eliminated October generation. (The scandals that took place within the country demonstrated the same thing.) Henceforward, any functionary who refused to return from abroad would be outlawed; in case of arrest on Soviet territory, he would be executed by a firing squad upon the establishment of his identity. For Soviet citizens on a private trip the penalty might be reduced a degree.

A law of March 30, 1935, punishes with five years of imprisonment the carrying, the manufacture, or the possession of a knife or a side-arm. It is a confession that the number of murders has become disquieting.

A law of April 8, 1935, extends all the penalties for ordinary crime to children twelve years old, including, of course, capital punishment. Adults who shall have encouraged criminality, mendicancy, or infantile prostitution will incur five years in prison. For the first time in a civilized country children are liable to the death penalty. It is a confession of the tremendous misery, a confession that they are losing their heads in face of this misery, that they do not know how to combat it, that for the legislator with a Browning the old socialist ideas on the responsibility of society towards a criminal, on the education and the re-education of delinquents, and finally on the death penalty solemnly condemned by the International Socialist Congress of Copenhagen (1910)—are old ideas that no longer have any importance. Even before this law the death penalty was applied by administrative measure to young former offenders. And the life of a twelve-year-old gamin sent to the northern labour camps doesn't amount to very much.[1]

On June 9, 1935, *Pravda* published the text of a Draconian law on the punishment of crimes against the fatherland. Espionage, passing over to the enemy, *the crossing of the frontier to another country without a passport*, are punishable by death and the confiscation of all property; no attenuating circumstance may be allowed if a military man is involved. The adult members of the culprit's family, if they knew his intentions without reporting them, shall be punished with from two to five years in prison and the confiscation of property. If completely ignorant of his designs, they shall be deported for five years to the remote regions of Siberia. For the first time in a civilized country, the law dictates informing in the midst of families, pitilessly chastises innocents and punishes by death the simple crossing of the frontier! (And I underscore the fact that the worker has no possibility of obtaining a passport for abroad.) What necessity does this monstrous law correspond to? The text provides against flight abroad in an aeroplane. Aviators had

[1] In the Orenburg region, where I was deported, there were several crimes committed in 1934–1935 by children. If the papers are to be believed, some Pioneers who were defending socialist property were killed by young counter-revolutionists of their own age. Motions were put through in the schools demanding that the death penalty be applied to the guilty. Then, the campaign ceased on command. I do not know the epilogue of these affairs. The law of which I am speaking having provoked lively protest at the congress of the Unitary Federation of Education (Angoulême, August 1935), pedagogues of the Stalinist tendency sought to defend it by arguing that the excellence of Soviet pedagogy makes children adults at the age of twelve. These singular educators, obviously poorly informed on the psychology of growth, did not dream for a moment of explaining how it happens that the precocius maturity of the young people is translated primarily into an increase of criminality. If the case were otherwise, would not the Soviet legislator have to grant the twelve-year-old children the right to vote, to be elected to office, and to occupy what are called responsible posts? One blushes at having to discuss remarks that only denote the decay of an ideology.

deserted in the Far East. The press, however, justifies the new law only by "the increasing love of the fatherland among the Soviet workers, a love which brings them to show themselves merciless towards traitors. . . ." Krylenko, Prosecutor of the Republic, will speak this language at the Central Executive Committee of the Soviets. It is necessary, literally, to take the reverse of this official gibberish in order to explain a law which could correspond, in reality, only to the most alarming wave of disaffection and defeatism.

A 1935 law punishes homosexuality with three years in prison. Krylenko justifies it by saying that sexual inversion is the tare of degenerated bourgeois classes. Prison treatment for degenerates, therefore, seems to him to be indicated.[1] And how can it be admitted that the tares of the bourgeoisie, vanquished almost twenty years ago, should still be deep-rooted? You do not know, really, what to be more amazed at: the vapidity of this argumentation or the ignorance of the legislator, contemporary of Freud and of Havelock Ellis, who deliberately ignores the scientific attainments of half a century of sexology.

A law punishes with three years in prison the production and dissemination of pornographic works, pornography not being defined therein. It will suffice for me to recall that the application of a text of this kind in France would have lodged in prison for many years such men as Flaubert, Baudelaire, Richepin, Zola, Descaves, and in our time Jules Romains, André Gide, Victor Margueritte, Céline, and many others. . . .

It would be no more than right to expect a power which

---

[1] The Soviet diplomat, Florinsky, Chief of Protocol of the Commissariat of Foreign Affairs, was one of the first to be sentenced in virtue of this law.

invokes the name of socialism to set the example of human respect, some scientific intelligence, the application of the principles for which the socialists of all countries have fought since the dawn of the First International. What we see is, on the contrary, a clearly retrogressive legislation, in comparison with that of the advanced capitalist countries, one which does not bear up under comparison with that of the fascist countries. All reactions resemble each other.

# 6.

# *A Turn: The Stabilization of the Ruble (1934-1935)*

IN 1934 A TURN APPEARS IN THE OFFING. THE PEASANTS ARE broken down, the power has come to understand.[1] The concessions it has made to the collectivized agriculturists enable them to live from hand to mouth. They adapt themselves. By unexpected luck, the harvests have been good for several years in succession. The gold production, intensified in the placers of Siberia, has permitted the reconstitution of a treasury, exhausted at the beginning of the industrialization by purchases abroad and by the losses incurred on the fall of the dollar and the pound sterling. It becomes possible to cease the disastrous exportation of food to the foreign market. The government has restored the grain reserves. It is perceived that despite a skilful admixture of pitiless chastisement and trifling compensation, undernourished labour

[1] It was certainly high time that it did understand, in view of the fact that half the livestock had been destroyed in four years.

Stock (in millions of heads)

| | Horses | Horned Cattle | Sheep and Goats | Swine |
|---|---|---|---|---|
| In 1929 | 34.0 | 65.1 | 147.2 | 20.3 |
| In 1933 | 16.6 | 38.6 | 50.6 | 12.2 |

The destruction of horses continued in 1935. These official statistics seem to me to understate the truth.

is clearly unprofitable. It slows down on the job by every means, so that at bottom it resembles a vast strike-on-the-job. Productivity is very low. The new equipment requires a greater effort on the part of the worker, which he can contribute only if he receives in exchange for it a wage representing a fairly adequate food equivalent. The Political Bureau decides, towards this end, on the stabilization of the ruble on a par with bread.[1] It does not want a financial reform and it denies the rumours that are circulating on this subject for, obviously a reform would involve a much more general stabilization of wages and a readjustment of wages to prices. . . . Beginning with January 1, 1935, bread cards are abolished. Bread will be sold openly in the state stores and on the markets, but its price will be greatly increased. The kilogram of brown bread becomes the commodity-equivalent of a paper ruble.

Let us examine this operation more closely. At first blush the reform appears to be a blow to the worker because the price of bread, recently doubled, undergoes still another increase. The state allots, it is true, a general increase of wages of 10 per cent, made public with a great to-do and aimed to cover up the price increase. What the newspapers do not explain is that the increase applies not to the wage as a whole but to the sum expended on purchases of bread by the card. Thus, the worker earning 100 rubles per month will not get an additional 10 rubles. She will be told: according to your bread card, which gives you the right to 400 grams per day, at 60 kopecks the kilogram, you spend 18 rubles per month for bread; 10 per cent of that gives you an increase in your monthly wage of 1.80 rubles. Here

---

[1] On inflation: According to the official documents, the circulation of paper money increased from 2,028 million rubles in 1929 to 7,734 million rubles in 1935.

they are. Now, the bread ration of this worker was well below her needs and henceforth she will buy not less than 800 grams of brown bread per day at 1 ruble the kilogram, which will mean a monthly expenditure of 24 rubles; hence, an actual reduction in wages of 4.20 rubles! Only, she doesn't care a fig for a paper wage whose fluctuations upset or enrapture naïve economists abroad. What matters to her is to be able to buy bread freely at an accessible price. Before the reform, her 100 rubles in wages represented 12 kilograms of black bread at the co-operative's price and—at the outside—20 kilograms of bread at 4 rubles on the clandestine market. Hence, she really earned 32 kilograms of black bread per month and she was doomed to permanent inanition. From now on, her 100 rubles are worth 100 kilograms of bread. She will eat her fill. I am blueprinting these calculations a little. They remain literally exact. The vast majority of the Soviet women workers still earn less than 100 rubles. On the clandestine market the price of a kilogram of black bread varied between 3 and 8 rubles; the main thing was to find it.

The pegging of the ruble to bread was therefore an immense relief to the workers: they emerged from a state of hunger. The observer living in the country has the feeling of seeing a bared economic organism throbbing. Where are the mysteries of money? One of the effects of the stabilization of the ruble is the rebirth of Soviet trading in the form of stores opened by the state in increasing number, and an activization of the free market. Where are the mysteries of the exploitation of labour? At one stroke you perceive one of the great advantages of the bureaucratic mechanism and of managed economy: exploitation there is visible at first glance. Not to discern it, you must have the boundless ingenuousness of a bourgeois guided around by the Intourist, or the subtle good will of a left-wing writer who has come over to the revolution a dozen years after the embalming of Lenin. It is better to follow the commercial operation that occurred in 1935. The government decrees the shutting down of reserved stores—those centres of corruption, demoralization, squandering, and privilege. They are replaced by stores open to the public, which transform the physiognomy of the cities in a few months.[1] The co-operative feeding of the workers at minimum prices is abolished. The new state stores sell at the "commercial" prices—it is the consecrated term; that is, at the market prices, ten to twenty times higher. But you can find everything there.

I do not have at hand the comparative index numbers. May I be permitted to refer to my personal experience? In Leningrad, in 1926, a family of four persons enjoying a standard of living comparable to that of the skilled worker in France or Belgium spent 2.50 rubles per day for its food. In order to eat in about the same way in 1935 it would have to spend around 40 rubles per day. So far as food is concerned, therefore, the value of the ruble has fallen to about one-sixteenth of what it was ten years ago. By how much have nominal wages risen in this space of time? The social inequalities have increased. The wages of the vast majority of wage earners have not doubled, the rise being about 80 per cent. The stabilization of the ruble thus leads us to record a substantial reduction in real wages in the past ten years.

From 1931 to 1935 the masses of workers and peasants lived on famine rations; properly speaking, there were no

[1] The stores reserved for the personnel of the government, the G.P.U., the party committees, continue to exist half-secretly; to be more exact, illegally. The rule: in the absence of any control by public opinion, the bureaucracy never acts honestly and itself transgresses all the laws and all the regulations which it enacts.

longer wages. You worked in the factory not in order to earn 100 printed rubles that were much easier to procure by speculating a little on matches, but in order not to lose your bread card, your lodgings, your passport, your party card. . . . An inestimable step forward, however little it may be, for wages are henceforth a reality. Emerging from the black years, the workers have few demands. The standard of living of the new workers driven towards industry by the misery of the countryside is very primitive; they are overjoyed at no longer being hungry. Faces are clearing up. Stalin, who did not show his face in public for almost two years, at the beginning of the collectivization, mounts the tribune and declares: "Life has become more joyous." Millions of disks record these precious words. Little girls holding bouquets in their arms march across the screen singing: "Life has become more joyous." Red calico is hung above the streets, proclaiming that "life has become more joyous." Squadrons returning from manœuvres cry out in a manly voice that "life has become more joyous." Tourists stirred by the sights note down in their memorandum books that "life has become more joyous." The newspapers show every day the portrait of the gifted Leader, surrounded by his collaborators who applaud smilingly. They have become more joyous. The newspapers show the Father of his Country drawing to his bosom a little Tartar girl, a little Mongol girl, a little Uzbek, a little Tadjik girl, a little Samoyed girl. . . . It rains decorations.

# 7·

# *The Kirov Affair: A Year of Terror*

A RELAXATION HAD TO TAKE PLACE IN INTERNAL POLICY after this reform. The foreign policy rendered this relaxation eminently desirable. The offers of a united front made to the socialists in the West could not reasonably be accompanied by the continuation of political persecutions in the country. The U.S.S.R. could try to look like an advanced, civilized state, in contrast to Hitlerite Germany, where the heads of communist militants were falling, where books were being burned on the public squares, where Jews, liberal intellectuals, socialists, and communists populated the concentration camps, where Hitler had his own companions-in-arms assassinated on June 30, 1934. . . . But skilful at manœuvring though it is, the bureaucracy is neither perfect master of itself, nor capable of dominating the forces that it evokes against itself. Its realistic, selfish, military, and administrative mentality, devoid of all scruples, causes it to ignore the moral values, which have a certain existence just the same. In the absence of any control, it goes far in its abuses. In the absence of any contact with the rather hostile masses, it remains inclined to panic.

On the eve of the abolition of bread cards, Kirov, the representative of the Political Bureau in Leningrad and confidant of Stalin, falls, brought down by a revolver shot in the head, fired by a communist, Leonid Nikolayev. An unprecedented fact: one of the recognized leaders of the party falls under the fire of a party member. Perhaps it would have been wiser to regard this assault as the act of a desperate person or a madman. (It is quite possible that he was one in reality; everything is shady in this tragedy; darkness, police provocation, lies, massacre.) The government preferred to confer upon it, amid a hideous uproar, the character of a political action. Undoubtedly convinced in its innermost heart that in the eyes of its Bolshevik opponents, the founders of the party, and the October fighters who remained in the party, it deserved death, the bureaucracy inculpated an entire tendency. Here, it thought, is a good opportunity to get rid of it.

Let us follow the events. On December 1st, the day of the *attentat*, there appears a decree of the Central Executive Committee of the Soviets introducing a modification into the penal procedure and providing for the completion of the preliminary examination of all terroristic affairs within ten days and their immediate transmission to military tribunals, judging in camera without admitting defence counsel. The death sentences shall be executed immediately after the pronouncement of the verdict. More expeditious and harsher than many despots, the Executive renounced its right of pardon.

On December 2nd and 3rd, the arrest of all the young communists of Nikolayev's circle. Removal of the head of the Leningrad G.P.U., Medvedyev, Fomin, and others. (Later, they will be sentenced to severe penalties for having failed to prevent an attempt at assassination of whose preparation they were aware. The reasons given for this sentence establish the fact that there was police provocation.) The same day more than 100 persons are discovered in the prisons of Leningrad, Moscow, Minsk, and other centres, charged with terrorism. They had been arrested before the *attentat* of Nikolayev, without having themselves committed any *attentat*; most of them, it appears, for having entered the U.S.S.R. illegally. By retroactive application of yesterday's decree, 114 persons will be condemned and immediately executed on December 5th, 10th, and 11th.[1]

The innocents are shot, but with regard to the guilty one the law that has just been promulgated, limiting the preliminary examination to ten days, is violated. Ten days do not suffice to make Nikolayev and his fellow accused say what it is insisted that they be made to say. The preliminary examination is prolonged to December 20th.

On December 16th the arrest in Moscow of fifteen former leaders of the Leningrad Opposition who were readmitted into the party after several recantations. Among them the oldest member of the Central Committee of Lenin's time, the former chairman of the Leningrad Soviet and the Communist International, Zinoviev; and the literary executor of Lenin's works, former chairman of the Moscow Soviet, Kamenev. Both of them belonged with Stalin to the ruling triumvirate that ousted Trotsky from power. An official communiqué announces that "their complicity in the *attentat* not being established, they will be deported."

On December 30th the secret trial, sentencing, and execution within the hour of fourteen young Leningrad communists. According to the official communiqué, they confessed to having formed an oppositional group of the

---

[1] Here the most bitterly unpleasant reflections force themselves upon you. Let us not recoil from them.—Several Bulgarians were shot and the Sofia press underlines the forebearance of Göring towards Dimitroff, Popoff and Taneff!—If, on the morrow of the Marseilles *attentat* in which Alexander of Yugoslavia lost his life, the Belgrade government had acted like the Stalinist government, how many socialists and communists would have been ordered massacred!—Do they imagine that in the class struggle they can give the enemy such examples and such precedents with impunity?

Zinoviev tendency. Two of them, knowing of Nikolayev's intentions, are supposed to have confessed that they assisted him. They were all former active militants of the Communist Youth.

In December and January, throughout the U.S.S.R., 2,000 to 3,000 members of the party who once belonged to the Zinoviev tendency are arrested.

On January 18th Zinoviev, Kamenev, Yevdokimov, Safarov, Fedorov, Gertik, Bakayev, and many of their comrades are sentenced to terms ranging from five to ten years' imprisonment, for having formed a tendency within the party. A hundred other communists are sent into concentration camps or deported. Those are the published figures; the number of those condemned is actually much higher. According to the unspeakable custom, the accused testified against themselves without restraint or dignity. Nevertheless, whatever may have been their complaisance before the tribunal, they confessed only to the crime of having grumbled a few times.

In December, January, February, in almost all the places of deportation, the most prominent Trotskyists, the majority of whom had recently come out of prison after having spent five years in it (since 1928), are arrested, sent to Moscow, put in confinement. They will soon be subjected, by administrative measure, to new terms of five years' imprisonment. That is the fate of my Orenburg comrades, Pankratov and Pevzner. Yakovin is arrested in Stalinabad, Solntsev in Western Sibera. Solntsev, one of the most talented of the young leaders of the Opposition, will soon die of the consequences of a hunger strike. . . .

At the end of February begins the purging of Leningrad. The T.A.S.S. agency communicates to the press that two hundred former nobles, superior officers, gendarmes, and policemen of the old régime have been expelled from the city for infraction of the law on passports. The T.A.S.S. agency lies, as usual. *Thirty, fifty, perhaps a hundred thousand persons* are not just expelled from Leningrad; they are deported from it to the regions of the Volga, the Urals, Central Asia, Siberia. All of them were previously supplied with regulation passports, which shows that no doubts had been raised about their political loyalty. Citizens who are not the object of a single charge are sent to the concentration camps by the thousands. The decrees of the G.P.U. simply say: ". . . is considered socially dangerous and is interned for three (or five) years." The man to the concentration camp–forced labour; the woman deported. As a rule, they are not former servitors of the old régime, but engineers, scholars, artists, functionaries, workers, in a word, collaborators of the new régime. Whole families leave, with the sick, the invalids, the pregnant women, the dying. The dying die on the railroads, the pregnant women give birth in the stations. A French technician, sympathetic to communism, who lived in Leningrad in this period, writes: "Last March and April [1935], I witnessed the arrests in Leningrad, followed by deportations *en masse;* the total number of the deported, counting their families, must have come close to a hundred thousand. . . . The railroad stations were bottled up for two weeks. The railroad had to refuse to accept baggage. The unfortunates sold their personal property on the railroad platforms and eight days later the state stores could be seen chock-full of second-hand furniture to sell. . . . I knew several of the deported. They were very honest collaborators in soviet technique and science, petty bourgeois in origin, who rallied or who were, in any case, very resigned, guilty at most of imprudences of language reported by stool pigeons. Some of them were former socialists or democrats like those who are called to join the ranks of the People's Front. . . ." I confirm this testimony on every point.[1] Some twelve to fifteen hundred of the Leningrad deportees came to Orenburg. Among them were many women, children, old folk, whom poverty promptly decimated. Whole trains passed by, loaded with poor souls sent into Kazakstan. They were often refused work; they were generally paid less than the others because they were not free to depart. The G.P.U. sent them into godforsaken villages or transferred them to its sheds in the North. Stalin meanwhile delivered a speech in which the press saw a turn towards humanism. . . . He recommended to think of the man, he revealed that "the cadres decide everything." We could see this slogan displayed on every wall in letters a half-metre high. Under these posters I met architects, doctors, jurists, navigators, shipbuilders, high-class engineers, physicists, musicians—deported without knowing why, useless, idle, demoralized, exposed to the vexations of the entirely uncultured local authorities. . . . Persons of German or Polish origin were numerous among these deportees. Others had relatives abroad and thought that a harmless correspondence must have sufficed to render them suspect. . . . The purging of Leningrad seems to have been undertaken on the personal initiative of Stalin.

In May the Societies of the Old Bolsheviks and the

---

[1] Berger, "U.S.S.R. 1935," in *La Révolution Prolétarienne*, September 25, 1935, reproduced as a pamphlet by the Society of the Friends of the Truth About the U.S.S.R.—I was personally acquainted with the deportation of two guardians of the Hermitage Museum, Troynitsky and Philosophov, well known in the scholarly world; of the young architect Tkachenko, soon afterwards pardoned, but whose family was left in deportation; of Mme. Doctor Kerensky, sister of the former head of the provisional government. . . . Leningrad theatre artists were sent to the sands of Kazakstan, to the hamlet of Toorgay, which can be reached only by caravan, on camel-back.

Former Hard-Labour Prisoners are dissolved by administrative measure. Their members kept up a certain frankness in speaking within very restricted circles. Several are arrested (notably the anarchists Novomirsky and Sandomirsky), and both clubs are shut down. Vera Figner, Lydia Akimova, Anna Korba, each of whom devoted half a century of exemplary service to the revolution—half of it in convict prison—will no longer have a tranquil corner where they can say, in all intimacy, what they really think.

The Yenukidze affair breaks out in the summer. Aveli Yenukidze, old Georgian Bolshevik, has fulfilled since 1918 the delicate functions of secretary of the Central Executive of the Soviets. He countersigns all the decisions of the presidency of the U.S.S.R. Respected for his unassailable probity, he is suddenly accused of political demoralization, driven from the party, driven out of public life. He disappears. It is whispered about that he sent packages to his nephew, Lado Yenukidze, young Trotskyist imprisoned for years. That's serious. His friends, his collaborators, their families, their friends, their acquaintances—all are thrown into prison, interned, deported. . . . The real reasons behind this affair remain obscure. Perhaps old Yenukidze knew too well the history of Bolshevism in the Caucasus, the history that a zealous *arriviste*, Lavrenti Beria, whose sudden rise coincides with the elimination of the old man, is in the process of recasting in order to aggrandize the place occupied in it by the Leader. In the big meetings of the party, the orators of the Central Committee, who recoil from no enormity, affirm that the complicity of Yenukidze in the assassination of Kirov has been demonstrated. . . . And this palace drama serves, in the propaganda carried on abroad, to show how the régime struggles against bureaucratic corruption!

The second Kamenev trial probably took place at about the same period. A secret trial in which 36 accused figured, of whom two were executed (one of them a G.P.U. agent). An alleged plot against Stalin was involved. Kamenev countered the accusation with the most clear-cut denials. He was sentenced to ten years in prison. Anybody who knows the moral physiognomy of this writer, one of the most cultured and most moderate men in the Bolshevik party, has no need of his denials. The story of this trial was told by Dr. Anton Ciliga, who met Kamenev in the Verkhne-Uralsk prison.

A police purging of the party takes place in the meantime. All the members who, in 1927–1928, manifested sympathy for the Opposition, even though they have become right-thinkers for the past six years and been assigned to positions of confidence, are expelled, arrested, sent to concentration camps or deported, most of them on the charge of Trotskyism. Trotskyism is rediscovered in mathematics, in music, in chess. . . . Several thousand communists are in this batch.

Then begins the official purging of the party, by verification of the individual files. It will send from 150,000 to 200,000 communists to prison. . . .

My conviction, founded upon a knowledge of the men, of the milieu, of the doctrines, is that the *attentat* of Nikolayev was the gesture of an isolated individual. At the very most, the terrorist gave a few confidences to his two or three closest comrades, among whom the G.P.U. acknowledged that there was an informer. The significance of this *attentat* is none the less profound. Supervening in a heavy atmosphere of unanimity, saturated with official optimism, it reveals an inward-driven crisis, and what a crisis! It also shows the blind alley into which led the tactic of disavowal and apostasy, adopted more out of cynicism than cowardice by the oppositional elements readmitted into the party after Zinoviev and Kamenev. Revolutionary action cannot be suited to such recantations, undoubtedly dictated by a sort of Inquisition but agreed to out of sordid motives foreign to true socialist courage. Woe to those who forget that the proletariat cannot be served by cowardly manœuvres, by abdications of conscience, by mental reservations, by capitulations and impostures. . . . Let us not be astonished that a youth should reach the point, in this suffocating atmosphere, of despairing of everything save his own despair. Let us not be astonished, either, that the bureaucracy should seize upon this occasion to rid itself of its hidden adversaries. The madness and the cruelty which make it lose all sense of moderation are amazing as a confession of tremendous moral weakness; but the political calculations, which result in the measures taken against the Zinoviev tendency, are wretchedly, sordidly correct. Such an opportunity to bury these men will not present itself again.

The point of view of the only opposition whose intransigence has broken with these practices for eight years is expressed by Trotsky in these words: "The unjustifiable atrocities, born of the bureaucratic methods of collectivization, as well as the abominable browbeatings and violences inflicted upon the best elements of the proletarian vanguard, inevitably arouse rancour, hatred, the thirst for vengeance. Terroristic states of mind can be seen emerging among the youth. . . ." But "if the bureaucrats, in their self-adoration, imagine that they are making history, we do not share their illusion. It is not Stalin who has created the bureaucratic apparatus, but the apparatus that has created Stalin in its own image. The replacement of Kirov by Zhdanov has changed nothing. . . . The replacement of Stalin by some Kaganovich would produce no greater change. . . ." The bureaucracy established the authority of its new representative figure by publicity methods by which it submits Stalin to a plebiscite every day—Stalin whose authority, in the long run, is its very own. "That is why individual terrorism is impotent and ridiculous in our eyes. We have not unlearned the first elements of Marxism. The destinies of the bureaucracy and of the Soviet régime depend upon factors of a world historical importance. Only the successes of the international proletariat can restore to the Soviet proletariat its self-confidence." [1]

---

[1] L. Trotsky, "The Terrorism of Bureaucratic Self-Defence," *Bulletin of the Opposition*, in Russian, September, 1935.

# 8.

## *A Democratic Constitution (1936)*

THE NINETEENTH YEAR OF THE REVOLUTION COULD, IN ITS turn, be a year of relaxation. The raising of the material condition of the masses is slightly increased. Measures of tolerance are enacted towards the believers, some churches are going to reopen, they will be permitted to ring their bells. A circular letter moderates the ostracism, with regard to work, against persons who once belonged to the bourgeoisie. The Cossacks, restored to their rights, recover their uniform and are invited to resume their traditions as small proprietors and soldiers. Access to the institutions of higher learning is granted the children of capitalists, tradesmen, priests, officers. The press announces, finally, the early adoption, on the proposal of the Leader, of a new Soviet Constitution which will be "the most democratic in the world." Universal suffrage, secret ballot, liberties. The draft of it is submitted to the masses. A concert of eulogies immediately rises to the Leader. The journals relate that an academician deems "this monument of Stalinist wisdom to be imperfectible" and that a provincial piano teacher compares it with Beethoven's Ninth Symphony. Those are not exceptional notes, they set the general tone. The constitutional text is translated into several languages, is placed on sale abroad under the title: "A Happy People."

The first article of the new fundamental law defines the U.S.S.R. as "a socialist state of workers and peasants." And the functionaries? It turns out that the real holders of power are ignored. Article 10 recognizes the personal property of citizens, protected by the law. Inheritance is guaranteed. So it always was, at least in law. . . .

Article 124 guarantees as in the past—which never prevented anything—religious freedom and the freedom of anti-religious propaganda, which seems to be rather superfluous. Article 125 guarantees the citizens the freedom of speech, of press, of assemblage, and of demonstration. It is copied without alterations from the previous constitutions which were never applied. Article 127 guarantees the inviolability of the person: "no person may be placed under arrest except by decision of court or with the sanction of a State Attorney." Administrative penalties seem to be abolished. But what are the decisions of the court worth and who is it that guarantees the respect of the constitution tomorrow more than today? Article 128 establishes the inviolability of domicile and the secrecy of correspondence, already established by international postal conventions, which never prevented the black cabinet from reading all correspondence sent abroad and from confiscating a notable part of it. The citizens have the right to work, to rest (paid vacations), to education. Here is something new, on the contrary, and more serious:

Article 126 makes clear that "the most active and politically conscious citizens from among the working class and other strata of the toilers unite in the Communist party . . . which represents the leading core of all organizations of the toilers, both social and state." The constitution thus affirms the leading rôle of the Communist party, the only legal party, and implicitly signifies that the non-communist citizens are neither among the most active nor the most conscious. What remains of the freedom of speech, of the press, of assemblage, of demonstration, where only one single party can exercise them? Actually, this is a tremendous retreat in comparison with the previous Soviet Constitutions. What remains of universal suffrage if the elections must take place on the slates of a single party and of branch organizations directed by this party? A plebiscitary comedy on the Italian or German style, which will at most permit the elimination, at the bottom, of the candidates who are most odious to the population because of their venality or their brutality.

The structure of the state is profoundly altered. Having disappeared in actuality a long time ago as organs of power, the soviets now disappear in law, reduced to the rôle of municipalities. The Soviet system gave the workers, considered as forming the revolutionary class, the political hegemony over the peasant masses; the equality of vote will now permit the bureaucracy to foist upon them, in any given case, rural majorities. The new legislative and executive organ, the Supreme Council, formed by two chambers elected for four years (Council of the Union and Council of Nationalities, equal in rights), is not a parliament because it is formed only by a simulacrum of consultation of the electoral body and is no longer a congress of soviets. . . . The question is why the word "soviets" still figures in the name of the state. It can only be for the purpose of abusing the historical tradition.

Instead of the seven federated republics, there will now be eleven, the Transcaucasian Federation being dissolved: Russia, the Ukraine, White Russia, Azerbaizhan, Georgia, Armenia, Turkmenistan, Uzbekistan, Tadjikistan, Kazakstan, Kirghizistan (comprising a large number of lesser republics and autonomous territories). Article 17 allows each republic the right to separate from the Union. . . . Only, the People's Commissariats of Defence, of Foreign Affairs, of Foreign Trade, of Ways and Communications, of Posts and Telegraphs, of Water Transport, of Heavy Industry, of Defence Industry are common to all the republics; the apparatus of the Commissariat of the Interior, a veritable ministry of police, is in fact the most centralized and the most potent, even though there are supposed to be parallel Commissariats of the Interior in all the republics; the machinery of justice is likewise centralized. . . . The federated republics thus have no more possibility of expressing an intention to separate than the elector will have, for example, to vote socialist, for lack of a socialist candidate.

Abroad, this draft of the constitution, called "liberal and democratic," is fairly well received. In the country itself, the party opens up a campaign of discussion, persons allow themselves to express criticisms and the press soon apprises us that "the counter-revolutionary elements" who thus manifested themselves are being treated as they deserve. . . .

The liberal year suddenly changes face in August. On the 12th appears a decree raising the age of military service from 21 years to 19 years. The classes of 1914 and 1915 are to be called to the colours in a few days, which yields an increase of immediately available effectives of 500,000 men. The Finnish and Swedish journals announce the deportation *en masse*, as a strategic measure, no doubt, of the inhabitants of the frontier regions of Karelia towards Vologda in the interior. On August 14th a communiqué of the Supreme Procurator of the U.S.S.R. announces that a trial will be opened on the 19th before the Supreme Military Tribunal, against three of the oldest leaders of the party, Zinoviev, Kamenev, and Ivan Smirnov, and thirteen of their accomplices, accused of having organized terroristic *attentats*. . . . The mere wording of the accusation leaves no room for doubt: probabilities and truth have nothing to do with the current political operation. Lenin's companions are doomed to capital punishment.

. . . At the Extraordinary Congress of the Soviets in November 1936, the new constitution is triumphantly adopted by unanimous vote.

# 9.

# *The Zinoviev-Kamenev-Smirnov Trial*

AS FAR BACK AS JUNE 5TH *Pravda* HAD HURLED A STRANGE threat of annhilation in the direction of the "Trotskyist monsters," accused vaguely of having turned to "espionage, plots, and terrorism." On August 1st, upon a signal from the Political Bureau, the Secret Service launches a campaign. Not another day passes without the press announcing the discovery of centres of Trotskyist counter-revolution in the party organizations and the editorial boards of the official organs. Many arrests are thus made public; but a far greater number of them remain secret. In Minsk the editors of the *Zvezda* (*Star*) reveal themselves as counter-revolutionists, as do the Directors of Education and of the Censorship. In Leningrad, entire party committees are affected. In Stalinabad (Tadjikistan), the governmental milieux are decimated. In Armenia too; there the secretary of the party, Khanjian, blew out his brains rather than lend himself to the proscriptions. In Leningrad, Moscow, Kharkov, Dniepropetrovsk, Kiev, Baku, Gorky (Nizhni-Novgorod), there are nothing but arrests. Plots are discovered in all the republics of Transcaucasia and Central Asia: arrests of leaders. A vast case of treason is mentioned in the Ukraine where, among the guilty, are named one of the founders of the first soviets in that country (together with Eugenie

Bosh and Piatakov), who returned by miracle from the shambles of the civil war, Yuri Kotsiubinsky, later secretary of the Legation at Vienna and Warsaw. The former Commissar of War of the Petrograd Commune, Kliavs-Klavin, is arrested; a cousin of Stalin, Dimitri Djugashvili, is arrested. The language of the journals changes suddenly: it is no longer a question of counter-revolutionary actions, but of treason, of separatism, of terrorism, of espionage, of sabotage. . . . And it becomes plain that the great political operation in progress differs profoundly from all the preceding ones by the fact that the victims are chosen this time from within the Stalinist party, from among its most faithful and most important functionaries, all of whom, however, belong to the old Bolshevik generation, the one that accepted all the responsibilities from 1917 to 1923. Even before opening, the Zinoviev-Kamenev-Smirnov trial appears like an attack directed basically at this generation. Perhaps it is also a case of being unable to prepare the death of the former leaders of the party without subduing the entire old party in advance, by means of terror. The innumerable persons accused of Trotskyism are in reality docile functionaries of the Stalinist party who made their career in the struggle against all the Oppositions. . . .

The indictment is published only on the very day when the proceedings are started: not without reason. A hundred times over it involves Trotsky, the indomitable outcast, exiled at the moment in Norway. It is important to make it impossible for Trotsky to reply in the press or to put to those who accuse him any precise questions that may blow up the indictment before the executions. It is the Kirov affair, already exhausted by two trials and several waves of repression, that rebounds again. Part of those accused in the 1935 trial for moral complicity have disappeared. Why?

In exchange, new culprits have been found, several of whom—men with great names in the history of the revolution—had been arrested twenty-three months before Nikolayev's *attentat*. They include Ivan Nikitich Smirnov, former precision-machinist, one of the founders of the party, veteran of the illegal work under the old régime, October fighter, later the inspirer of the Fifth Red Army which challenged Kolchak, president of the Revolutionary Committee that sovietized Siberia, People's Commissar of Posts and Telegraphs, oppositionist of 1923 who rallied to Stalin in 1928, appointed director of the automobile plants of Nizhni-Novgorod; Sergei Mrachkovsky, one of Trotsky's collaborators during the civil war in which his name became illustrious; Ter-Vaganyan, younger by ten years (born in 1893), militant and Marxian theoretician; an old Bolshevik administrator, Holtzman. . . . Zinoviev, Kamenev, Yevdokimov, the latter a former worker, one of the defenders of Petrograd in 1919, subsequently secretary of the Central Committee; Bakayev who was head of the Cheka in Petrograd in the gravest hours of the civil war—these men were already judged, as we know, in January 1935 for being politically responsible for the assassination of Kirov—a thoroughgoing investigation had not made it possible to establish against them any evidence of actual complicity—and sentenced to long terms of imprisonment. Reingold, former Under-Secretary of State for Finances; Dreitser, one of the victors over Kolchak in 1919, and one of the heroes of the Polish campaign in 1920; Pikel, man of letters, former secretary of Zinoviev, completes the list of the Bolshevik group of the accused. All ex-oppositionists, they have been capitulators since 1928–1929. Smirnov and Holtzman retained hidden sympathies for the Trotskyist Opposition. Zinoviev and his friends broke with it, we already know, back in 1928. Five other accused are unknowns. They are young people of German origin or formation, *whom their fellow accused see for the first time* (except for a single one, Moissei Lurye, known to Zinoviev). The thesis of the indictment, *propped exclusively by the confessions of all the accused*, is this:

At the end of 1932 the ex-Trotskyists readmitted into the party, Smirnov, Mrachkovsky and Ter-Vaganyan, came together with Zinoviev and Kamenev in order to constitute with them a clandestine Central Committee (they say a "Centre" in order not to profane the respected words "Central Committee") of the Opposition and to prepare terroristic *attentats* against the party leaders. An instruction from Trotsky bade them do it. At the end of 1934 Kirov was actually killed: this was supposed to be on the order of Zinoviev, who is himself supposed to have received it from Trotsky. Trotsky and his son, Leon Sedov, send to Russia several terrorists from abroad, who obtain the necessary passports and visas with the co-operation of agents of the Gestapo, or Secret Police, of the Reich. These are Olberg, Berman-Yurin, Fritz David, Moissei and Nathan Lurye, who admit having prepared *attentats* against Stalin, Kaganovich, Voroshilov, Zhdanov, Kossior, Postyshev, Ordjonikidze *and others* (*sic*).[1]

The trial opens on August 19, at 12:10 P.M. in the large Hall of the Columns of the Moscow House of the Trade-Unions, in the presence of a numerous audience, handpicked by the Secret Service, and of some foreign journalists. Three military judges, a secretary, an assistant judge. Ulrich, "army jurist," one of the oldest judges of the revo-

[1] There is no mention of an *attentat* against the president of the Council of People's Commissars, Molotov. . . . (An omission remedied in the Novosibirsk trial of November 1936.—*Trans.*)

lutionary tribunals, renowned for his harshness, presides. Vyshinsky indicts. Procurator-General of the U.S.S.R., he is a former Menshevik social democrat who turned at the end of the civil war and who, in the struggle against Bolshevism in 1918, took part in the sabotage of the provisioning of the Ukraine. He has the experience of all the big trials since 1930. The accused begin by renouncing the aid of counsel. Many of them, however, could have made good use of it. But they have their reasons, too, for not defending themselves, since they will accuse themselves unremittingly. Attorneys, without even contesting the confessions of their clients, would not have failed to ask the tribunal if the intention to commit a crime, which was not committed, indeed constitutes in the eyes of Soviet law a crime liable to capital punishment. If complicity by virtue of adherence to an unexecuted plan, by virtue of outlining such a plan or promising co-operation in it, can be punished just as severely as a crime really accomplished. If, finally, the failure to execute a projected crime is not a strongly attenuating circumstance. . . . Nine of the accused,[1] acknowledged strangers to the Kirov affair, will in fact be sentenced only for *attentats* which did not take place and the mention of which would have provoked smiles if the slightest smile were admissible in all this. Berman-Yurin was supposed to shoot Stalin at the XIII Plenum of the Executive of the Communist International; but he did not succeed in obtaining an admission card. . . . David, however, did succeed in penetrating the Congress of the Communist International, but he found himself too far away and he lacked resoluteness. . . . Nathan Lurye saw Voroshilov's automobile in the street but judged that it was moving too fast to be shot at.

---

[1] Dreitser, Pikel, Olberg, Berman-Yurin, Holtzman, Fritz David, Reingold, the two Luryes.

Elsewhere, in Cheliabinsk, *he thought* of going to a factory where Kaganovich and Ordjonikidze were to speak, in order to shoot them. . . . In Gorky, Olberg was only able to "draw up the plan" of an *attentat* which his arrest prevented him from accomplishing. . . . These things are seriously related in a country where terrorism has had its virtuosi and its practised technicians.

The accused who accuse themselves—without producing the slightest material proof of their allegations—of these crimes of intention were always arrested before being able to make an actual gesture. How did they enter the U.S.S.R.? It is known how difficult it is for the ordinary mortal to obtain a Soviet visa. Olberg, Lett by birth, speaking Russian and German, was nevertheless able to sojourn in the U.S.S.R. with the passport of a citizen of Honduras, which he declared he had bought with the co-operation of a Hitlerite agent. They are disquieting figures, who reek of intrigue and provocation. Agents provocateurs or the playthings of agents provocateurs—no doubt may be entertained on that score. Three of them once belonged to the German Communist party and, within this party, to the coterie of Heinz Neumann [1]—not to the Opposition.

The only official report of the proceedings published, far from being stenographic, is obviously edited for the purposes of agitation. Each time that a defendant discusses a point of detail—the only thing he permits himself—the report states: "The accused tries in vain to dispute that . . ." How does he try it? Is it really in vain? On the other hand, the fragments of dialogues in which the accusation has the advantage are given almost in full. Almost, for the initiated

[1] Neumann was Stalin's man of confidence for a long time. Played a rôle in the Canton insurrection of 1927. Fallen into disgrace, his group was liquidated by the G.P.U. Reported imprisoned in the U.S.S.R. (?)

reader discovers at every point gaps, passages without context, badly fitted patching, contradictions that are slid over. . . . The manner in which the proceedings are conducted is unqualifiable. We are witness to an atrocious comedy. Everything is reduced to a sort of dialogued lecture repeating the texts of the indictment. Confessions that vie with one another, petty amplifications of remarks made or heard. Not a piece of evidence. Not a single witness apart from selected defendants. Monstrous gaps through which you shudderingly see that all is false. . . . All the speeches can be summed up in a few lines:

"Yes, we did form a clandestine terroristic organization in 1932. Yes, we did receive and approve the instructions from Trotsky to wipe out Stalin and his principal collaborators. Yes, we did prepare the assassination of Kirov, and other *attentats*, which failed. Yes, we do repent, we are aware of the magnificent work of Stalin and our complete defeat as oppositionists. Yes, we did not even have a political platform, because the triumph of the general line left us bankrupts, we did not even have any principles left to defend. . . . Yes, we are the basest of wretches, the accomplices of the Gestapo, the instruments of fascism, we do merit the supreme punishment. Yes, we do now admire the gifted Leader; we would like to live for him, we do consent to die for him. Only one man in this world is worse than we, more criminal, more fascistic, more vile and more perverse: Trotsky."

There is the tone and it endures: it endures for whole sessions. A howl of death rises from this hall towards the exile of Norway, rises and rages with such hatred, such perseverance that the very reality of it is exceeded and you hear nothing more than a horrible raving. . . .

But what is the meaning of these revelations made in open

court by Kamenev, Zinoviev, and their confidant, Reingold, a new personage who emerged to take up the rôle of an attentive listener around the old leaders, for years, and to tell everything today? A pretence is made at being surprised by them, as if everything had not been rehearsed during the preliminary examination. It is suddenly learned that Sokolnikov who, in 1917, collaborated with Lenin in drawing up the program of the party, who signed the Brest-Litovsk Treaty in 1918, who represented more recently the U.S.S.R. at London, is in the plot, together with Serebriakov, a former secretary of the Central Committee; Karl Radek, whose inculpation is announced by the journals at the very time they are publishing his envenomed diatribes against the accused and Trotsky; Bukharin, the most renowned of the former theoreticians of the party, now director of *Izvestia*, who demanded under his own signature an investigation against himself; Rykov who succeeded Lenin in the presidency of the Council of People's Commissars, today People's Commissar of Posts, Telephones, and Telegraphs; Tomsky, founder and for many years leader of the Soviet trade-union organization; Smilga who played such a great rôle during the October Revolution and the civil war; Piatakov, Under-Secretary of State for Heavy Industry, member of the Central Committee; Uglanov, former secretary of the Central Committee. . . . It is learned that the Old Bolsheviks Gertik, Grinstein, Radyn, Faivilovich, Hertzberg, Arkus (one of the State Bank directors), Sharov, Shliapnikov, Medvediev, Eismont; the heroes of the civil war Schmidt, Gayevsky, Putna (military attaché at London); the historians and publicists Sliepkov, Anyshev, Seidel, Friedland, Yakovlev, the former head of the Communist International of Youth, Shatskin; Stykhold, who is one of the first group of the organizers of the Red Army—it is learned that all these men and many others are terrorists or the accomplices of terrorists! Most of them are in prison; many of them, like Eismont, Riutin, Smilga, since 1932–1933. . . .

A veil falls, the truth bursts out in full. All the surviving members of the Central Committee that made the October, Stalin excepted, are indicted. The whole Bolshevik Old Guard is compromised. It is the trial of a generation and of an epoch. A journal of émigrés will be able to publish this sarcastic cartoon: two citizens standing under a monument of Lenin ask: "What is he saying?—He is repenting for having collaborated with Trotsky. . . ." Another veil falls at a stroke, the police machination appears in all its hideousness. Why *sixteen* accused on these benches? Who has chosen them? How? The prosecutor Vyshinsky declares that twelve men accused of the same plot are the object of a separate investigation. Why? Thirty-eight other accomplices are mentioned in the course of the hearings. The very numbering of the dossiers cited shows that the preliminary hearing was directed at thirty-eight inculpated persons, at least. But only the sixteen present consented to lend themselves to this stage-play. The others are bargaining or resisting, they are not yet ready. The conditions under which the secret examination must have been held may be guessed by observing that the depositions of the most disquieting young figures, like Olberg, run to as high as 262 pages (and it is on the last page, at his last interrogation, that he suddenly remembers his relations with the Gestapo!). Whereas those of the Old Bolshevik leaders run between 10 and 32 pages. The examination of the former began at the beginning of the year. Ter-Vaganyan, on the contrary, made his confessions only on August 14th, that is, the very day when the prosecutor signed the indictment, less than a week before the trial. He was skewered with the others to be shot only at the very last moment. . . .

The scenario is so sloppy that it does not bear the slightest examination. Did the terrorist Central Committee (the "*Centre*") exist? According to the indictment, it is supposed to have been formed at the *end of 1932:* from certain depositions it is seen that it nevertheless ceased its activity in the *fall of 1932*. Before it was formed? Smirnov says that it never met. . . . Zinoviev says that it existed "actually up to 1936," when all its alleged members were in prison, some since the last days of 1932, others since the end of 1934. The prosecutor, in his indictment, corrects it and affirms "up to 1934." . . . Zinoviev exaggerates! But another accused exaggerates still more in his confessions. Holtzman, an Old Bolshevik who looks like a paunchy businessman, who bears himself with dignity, who, after the verdict, will refuse to solicit a pardon, confesses to having made an appointment with Trotsky's son, Sedov, for the *Hotel Bristol* in Copenhagen; to having gone with Sedov, still in Copenhagen, to see Trotsky and there receiving instructions on the necessary terrorism. We shall soon learn that there is no *Hotel Bristol* in Copenhagen; and that Sedov never went to this city, where Trotsky spent only eight days in 1932 amid a well-known circle which can provide not a few witnesses. We will learn that it can easily be proved that Sedov was in Berlin at the time, from which he had daily telephonic conversations with his father, a list of which can be found on the communications registry kept at both ends of the wire. The thought comes to mind that Holtzman gave these details in order to facilitate the refutation of the lie that was forced on him.

These are the only verifiable precise details in this affair, for great care is exercised not to ask for any. If everything had not been kept secret until the last moment, if the trial and the execution had not been hurried through in a few days, Trotsky, in the foreign press, would have been able to put simple questions like the following to the agents provocateurs: "You affirm that you saw me on this date and at that place. Did I wear a beard or not? Describe the hotel, the room, the surroundings. . . ." But when he was first enabled to read the "confessions" that dealt with him, the accusers-accused were already dead.

One of the most dubious of the accused, Olberg, citizen of Honduras and charged with teaching in Stalinabad, finally brings proof that the terrorist instruction of Trotsky exists. Sedov had him read it in Berlin: "In the message that he wrote when he was deprived of his Soviet nationality, Trotsky affirmed the necessity of killing Stalin." At last we have proof! This message of Trotsky to the Executive of the Soviets, dated Prinkipo, March 1, 1932, was published in various languages. Some of the lines have a prophetic ring today: "Oh, to be sure [wrote the outcast], Stalin has not yet said his final word. We know his arsenal: Lenin weighed him and appraised him. But all that he has left is personal vengeance. . . ."—"You know Stalin as well as I do. Many of you, in your conversations with me or those close to me, have judged him many times without illusions. The strength of Stalin has always lain not in himself but in the bureaux: in himself, at most, to the extent that he is the most consummate incarnation of the automatism of the bureaux. . . . Stalin has led you into a blind alley. You cannot emerge from it without liquidating Stalinism. You must trust to the working class, give the vanguard of the proletariat the possibility of revising the whole Soviet system, from top to bottom, by free criticism. The last urgent advice of Lenin must finally be put into effect: remove Stalin!" The terrorist instruction is therefore Lenin's. The prosecutor, Vyshinsky, insists upon making two of the accused admit that the word of Lenin: *remove*, means *kill* when it is pronounced by Trotsky. Ter-Vaganyan confesses to having received from Trotsky the advice to "fight the leadership of the party violently." He is made to admit that *violently* meant "by assassination." And there you are.

These reports are edited with such dishonesty that it is impossible for us to know definitely if Smirnov [1] did confess or not, and what it is that he did confess. Because of his high moral authority, the man who could be called the Lenin of Siberia, the former head of the Fifth Red Army that beat Kolchak, the man who, together with Trotsky, saved the young republic in the battle of Sviazhsk, is indispensable here. A former oppositionist who went over in 1928, his sympathies for the Opposition are genuine; he once saw Sedov in Berlin, he collaborated secretly in the *Bulletin* published abroad. The indictment declares that he acknowledged having belonged to the clandestine "Centre," having remained in touch with Trotsky up to 1933, having received from Trotsky, through his son Sedov, the instruction to resort to terrorism. At the session of August 20th, according to the official report, he replies in the affirmative to the question: "Did you receive from Trotsky the instruction to resort to terrorism?" This seems to be categorical, but exactly fifteen lines before we see that "Smirnov tries to deny everything"; and forty lines farther on that he "tries to deny having transmitted the instruction" which, moreover, is no longer an instruction of

---

[1] The Old Bolshevik party counted three Smirnovs, all three enjoying a great authority. Ivan Nikitich suffered the fate that is known; the other two, one of whom belongs to the extreme left (Vladimir) and the other to the right, are in prison.

Trotsky, but a personal opinion expressed by Trotsky's son. These are strange scenes, we are on the brink of a revelation or of a rupture of something. The prosecutor reads a fragment of Smirnov's deposition (confession) at the preliminary examination of August 13th (the eve of the publication of the indictment! and from this date alone it follows that Smirnov's resistance was broken only at the last moment, probably under the pressure of an affair already entirely concocted in the name of state reasons). "Well?" asks the prosecutor. Smirnov is silent. The prosecutor bids him reread himself, aloud, several lines of the deposition. Smirnov obeys, in a mechanical voice, and they pass on. How can you fail to have the impression before this scene that the accused was on the point of breaking the pact that bound him to the accuser? From now on, Smirnov is lost; even though he was arrested twenty-three months before the Kirov affair itself: this troublesome witness must not live. It is not finished: "For three hours," say the newspapers of August 21st, "Smirnov does all he can to duck responsibility. . . ." The report becomes an inextricable tissue of contradictions and patchwork. The prosecutor having committed the imprudence of asking the accused: "When did you leave the Centre?"–Smirnov replies: "I didn't think of leaving it because there was nothing to leave. . . ."

*Vyshinsky:* Didn't the Centre exist?

*Smirnov:* What are you talking about?

This is said contemptuously–the Russian words are much more significant–everything collapses. . . . The prosecutor appeals to his assistants, the other accused. Did the Centre exist? They reply in chorus: yes, yes, yes, yes. And the report resumes: "Smirnov again tries to deny that. . . ." And so on throughout. When he is asked if his fellow accused are lying, he is silent. He has the air of saying: "I am playing the part agreed upon, but don't expect me to put my heart into it. . . ." And he lets fall, in Zinoviev's direction, this phrase full of contempt: "Zinoviev speaks like this because he is Zinoviev"—and that means: a man who never stands up.

On the other hand, what zeal the other accused display! So much so that they get into a jam at every turn. Lucky that there are no defence attorneys! They are talking about a fantastic letter of Trotsky's on terrorism and defeatism, received from abroad and written in sympathetic ink on a page of a magazine. Dreitser received it, he said, with the writing brought out, and sent it 4,000 kilometres farther to Mrachkovsky, in Kazakstan. Both of them recognized the writing. Good; but the second recipient also declares that he received this letter written in sympathetic ink *not brought out!* Nobody pursues the point. I pass over many secondary episodes in order to keep to the essentials. Never does the complaisance of the victims stand out clearer than when they are asked for the reasons that made them act: "The feeling of our defeat and the triumph of Stalin," they reply. Kamenev, old white-haired intellectual, the most refined politician among them, perhaps the most authentic statesman there has yet been in Russia, replies subserviently as it was so obviously agreed in advance that he would reply:

"—The thirst for personal power."

And the only word that ought to be on every lip, which, by itself, implies a capital accusation, a fighting platform, a sufficient explanation of the trial—the word *bureaucracy*—is not once pronounced! All the open or covert oppositions see in the bureaucratization of the régime the ruin of the proletarian revolution. The old leaders of the party who are here have written and said it more than once. But, faithful to the commitments made, these politicians do not put a single political question. And you understand why not one oppositionist, not one authentic Trotskyist, figures in the trial! Yet there are no less than half a thousand of them, in captivity for eight years. Not at all complaisant. There are some inculpated in affairs linked with this one, for the aim is to get rid of them; but they will be strangled in the dark. They will not be permitted to explain themselves before the foreign journalists, have no doubt on that score.

Hours are taken up in speaking of the Kirov affair. Bakayev, Zinoviev, Kamenev admit that they prepared this *attentat* down to its minutest detail. In the course of the two investigations of 1934–1935 they succeeded in deceiving the Inquisition even while confessing what it asked them to confess at that time. . . . But why isn't there brought forward in court the letter written by the murderer of Kirov to explain his action, a letter that has never been published? Why isn't there once mentioned the attempt that was made so maladroitly at that time to implicate Trotsky in the affair by resorting to the services of a Lettish consul? Why are there not once mentioned the facts, which have remained secret, about the trial of the heads of the Leningrad G.P.U., sentenced at that time for not having prevented the act of Nikolayev, the preparations for which they were acquainted with? Finally, why is there such a complete silence on the second trial of Kamenev, a rigorous secret to this day, which ended on July 27, 1935, with a sentence of ten years' imprisonment, but which is referred to in the indictment without the slightest comment? [1] So it was three times that they tried to break the resistance of old Kamenev: first trial in January 1935, second trial in July 1935, third trial in August 1936. . . .

---

[1] See above, Chap. VII.

Zinoviev, Kamenev, and Reingold accuse the former groups of the Workers' Opposition, of the right wing of the party, of the left-wing Stalinists, one after another, of having been in solidarity with them. Let us quote Kamenev: "Tomsky told me: Rykov thinks as I do . . . and Bukharin too, but Bukharin, for tactical reasons, wants to gain the confidence of the party. . . ." After three days of violent discussions in his party cell, old Tomsky, hounded by his denouncers who insult him in the customary meeting-room phrases, returns home and puts an end to his days. A hopeless situation. Throw light on it? Impossible. Defend oneself? What for? Undergo this horrible cat-and-mouse game, confess what they demand you confess, humiliate and debase yourself, begin all over again, go to prison? Everything is finished, the reaction is indeed the stronger, farewell revolution. Tomsky killed himself on August 23rd, the very day of the opening of a hearing against him, Rykov, and Bukharin (the latter two will benefit by a no-cause!). It is a dignified end.[1]

The examination takes hour after hour to go over the same material without adding anything to it except a luckless excursion into the political domain. In order the better to prove that Trotsky advocated defeatism in case of war, Vyshinsky exclaims that . . . But I had better translate it, it is too brilliant:

"But perhaps all this is an invention, imagination, empty chatter of the accused who are trying to say as much as they can against the others in order to mitigate their own fate? No! This is not an invention, not fantasy! It is the

---

[1] Along the road followed by Stalin this is the third famous suicide. Skrypnik, Old Bolshevik, People's Commissar in the Ukraine, Stalinist from the beginning, blew out his brains in 1933. Lominadse, once the leader of the young Stalinist left wing, in 1935.

truth! Who does not know that Trotsky, together with the accused Zinoviev and Kamenev, several years ago formulated his Clemenceau thesis, that they said that in case of war they would wait until the enemy was within eighty kilometres of the capital in order to take up arms against the government of the soviets, to overthrow it? This is an historical fact. It cannot be denied. *And that is why* it must be admitted that the depositions of Berman-Yurin and Fritz David in this connection correspond to the truth. . . ." (*Izvestia*, August 23rd, p. 2, col. 8.) The *that is why* which I underlined is really rather good. But what is this Clemenceau thesis, "defeatist and insurrectionary"? Was Clemenceau a defeatist and did he take up arms against the government of France?

Asked in 1927 about the attitude that the Opposition would observe towards the ruling bureaucracy in case of war, Trotsky replied, in substance: "We would do what Clemenceau did against Poincaré in France. The Germans were at Noyon, the war was being lost, but the criticism of Clemenceau did not disarm the country; quite the contrary. We would criticize mercilessly a government which could only sabotage the defence of the revolution, we would end by putting the bureaucrats in their place and carry on the war as revolutionists." At that time the Opposition excluded all resorting to violence or to mass action; it took up its position inside the party and sought to be the instrument of a reform of the régime. It had to be muzzled before the "Clemenceau thesis" could be converted with impunity into a defeatist and insurrectionary thesis. This gives us a good idea of the value of the political arguments of the prosecutor.

We certainly do not know just what Smirnov did confess. The summation says textually: "Smirnov denies with the greatest obstinacy. He has only admitted having been one of the leaders of the illegal Trotskyist centre. . . . Even then, he confessed it in a humorous form. . . ."—"Yet I have every reason to contend," continues the prosecutor, "that he confessed to the following . . .", and that is, to having transmitted a terroristic instruction which he denies having transmitted. . . . You can perceive the procedure of logical analysis—in which the logic, by the way, is very peculiar—which is used to elaborate such confessions. "You confess to being a Trotskyist, and Trotskyist means defeatist and terrorist; hence, you confess to being a defeatist and terrorist. . . ." Smirnov is embarrassing. Imprisoned for almost two years prior to the Kirov affair, how is he to be inculpated? The prosecutor devotes more than an hour to him. And all of a sudden, from a few words in his peroration, we learn that the accused said in the hearing a mass of things that are not to be found in the published trial reports, that they made allusions to the terrorism of the great party of the People's Will which executed Alexander II in 1881. Didn't they recall that Lenin's brother, Alexander Ulianov, was hanged in 1887 for having participated in a plot against Alexander III? Here, Vyshinsky raises his voice. "These comparisons do not bear criticism. As Bolsheviks, we have always been the opponents of individual terrorism, but we pay homage to the sincerity and the heroism of the terrorists of the People's Will. . . . But you, you are a band of arrant counter-revolutionists, you represent the vanguard of the international counter-revolution. You aligned yourselves against the freedom and the happiness of the people! . . . I demand, Comrade Judges, that these mad dogs be shot, one and all!"

The journals clamour on that day: *Shoot the mad dogs!*

The accused now rise, one after another, to pronounce

their last words. They are new indictments of themselves, of Trotsky, new acts of impassioned contrition before the party and its Leader. They proclaim that they deserve death, that they merit no indulgence, that they ought to be shot, that it would be doing a good deed to shoot them! Yevdokimov exclaims: "We were bandits, assassins, Fascists, agents of the Gestapo. I thank the prosecutor for having demanded for us the only penalty that we deserve." Dreitser, Reingold, Bakayev speak the same language. Bakayev, convulsed, leans in the direction of Zinoviev, aged, wasted, his mane like a woman's, and upbraids him for having brought them all to this. . . . Pikel expatiates on the ideological errors of Zinoviev, recalls that he himself was once a prosecutor and, in that capacity, a collaborator of Ulrich, who is judging him this evening, and suddenly launches into an exalted eulogy of the Stalinist draft of the constitution, which has revealed to him the "true soul of Bolshevism." . . . Kamenev and Zinoviev once more denounce Trotskyism—in which they are probably sincere, having spent a large part of their lives in combating it—proclaim their indefectible attachment to the party, renew their confessions, express their shame at being there by the side of dubious figures who come from police offices, like the Olbergs, Berman-Yurins, Davids, and Luryes. And there, too, they must be fully sincere. "I adjure my sons," says Kamenev, "to employ their lives in defending our great Stalin!" He grows indignant, in passing, at the fact that the foreign press will exploit this trial. . . . "I am fifty-four years old and I am not afraid of death. Not having known how to live to serve the revolution, I am ready to serve it by dying." And these words, for me, ring true; they are true. Zinoviev takes upon himself all the responsibility for the plots. Holtzman speaks contemptuously of the fascist scamps, his fellow accused, and adds that he asks for no clemency. Since all the reports are abridged and adulterated, it is hard to extract the true meaning of the words. Holtzman behaved with dignity, he seems to have been a genuine oppositionist. His last words are perhaps a slap in the face of the agents provocateurs and they say clearly that he expects nothing from the judges. The reports of the last words of Smirnov are also peculiar. According to the Soviet journals, he reproaches himself for having resumed the struggle against the party in 1931, denies all responsibility for what might have been done after his arrest (and nothing was done before it), bids his comrades break with Trotskyism, "for our country has no other road but the one it is following, has not and cannot have any other leaders than those whom history has given it. . . ." A reserved resignation to accomplished facts. . . . "I accept in advance the verdict of my party."

The Olbergs, Davids, and others implore the clemency of the judges.

* * *

Even before the trial a campaign began in the factories, where the party secretaries had resolutions voted for with enthusiasm, demanding the death penalty for the enemies of the people. All the journals are inundated with reports of this kind, which they publish:

"At the Stalin Automobile Plant in Moscow, the non-party worker Semenova says: The Trotskyist-Zinovievist monsters sought to darken our happy life . . . We demand that they be annihilated, they must no longer crawl on our land!" The writer Count Alexis Tolstoy, White émigré at the beginning of the revolution, uses the same language at the assembly of men of letters of Leningrad. Little Eva Nerubina, schoolgirl in Stalino, writes a poem that ends with these words: "Let us shoot them like dogs!" Transmitted by telephone the same day to *Izvestia*, it is printed in more than a million copies. From the depths of the Far East, by telegraph, it is reported that the old Chinese workers, Shi Gang-li and Chiang Lian-siay, declare: "Trotsky is a dog!" A woman worker of Cheliabinsk exclaims: "We love our great Stalin like a first-born son, like a beloved father. . . . I ask for only one thing: wipe out these monsters!" The miners of the Stalin pit write to the "Great Leader of the great people, to the friend and beloved teacher, to the hope of toiling humanity, Joseph Vissarionovich Stalin" that he must, "with tenfold vigilance, track down and annihilate these wretches." The *Izvestia* editorial of August 23rd, probably written by Bukharin, asserts that "They have nothing in their souls unless it be a bestial hatred, matured in ten years, against *Our sun Stalin* and his genius, victorious over counter-revolutionary impurity. . . ." —"There will be no pity shown!" (The verdict has not yet been pronounced, let us note, at the moment when the official organ of the government affirms it so categorically.) . . . "The entire people demands that . . . these mad dogs be shot, one and all!" These words recur everywhere. No doubt the Leader himself had pronounced them and approved them for propaganda. In these days he has become at once "*Our Sun*" and "*Our Well-Beloved*," as he is called by the active members of the party who assemble in Moscow and by peasants who send him a message. The journals unleash a similar campaign for an investigation to probe to the bottom, relentlessly, the complicity of the other surviving companions of Lenin, Bukharin, Rykov, Uglanov, Radek, Piatakov. There is no longer a question of Tomsky, as if the investigation into his case has become superfluous. The Professors Speransky, Lavrentiev, Oberhardt, Razenkov—and others—supplicate Stalin not to forget that "science regards HIM as a leader, a well-beloved father, a banner . . ."—"They are beasts with human faces," says a worker of Lipetzik, "they must be treated like bandits. . . ." The academician Komarov is also of this opinion. Friedrich Adler, de Brouckère, Citrine, Schevenels, having sent a brief telegram to the Soviet government in the names of the Labour and Socialist International and the International Federation of Trade-Unions, asking that the accused be given the guarantees of justice considered normal in civilized countries, are treated as accomplices of the terrorists and of the Gestapo by *Pravda* and *Izvestia*. "The only ones who can take up the defence of these blackguards—the accused—are rascals who have lost all conscience and who voluntarily accept the shameful rôle of supplicants of the head of the Gestapo, Himmler." In Russia, Adler and de Brouckère would not be able to escape ten years of imprisonment as "accomplices of the bloody dogs." Eight academicians and fifteen professors demand the death penalty for the accused and praise the "great beloved sage, our Leader. . . ." The artist emeritus of the Republic, Klimov, writes, enchanted at having read the verses of the schoolgirl Eva Nerubina: "Yes, let us shoot them like dogs . . ." The worker Stepanov declares: "I am seventy years old and I have been working for fifty-two years in this factory. . . ." From the heights of his half-century of servitude, he demands that these rascals be annihilated so thoroughly that not a trace of them is left. Former ambassador of the soviets, one of the men of October, one of the good fighters of the civil war, an old friend of Trotsky, one of the oppositionists of 1923–1927, the same Antonov-

Ovseyenko who was the first to enter the Winter Palace at the head of the sailors, writes that "since 1928, when he had recognized his mistake, he declared himself ready to shoot his former political friends." Piatakov, himself also a former oppositionist, Rakovsky, linked to Trotsky by twenty years of friendship, deported for seven years, and rallied to Stalin only yesterday—both kneel to worship the Leader and demand, in terms that you blush to quote, the death of their former comrades. . . .

A death resolution, voted in the factories, proclaims that "the life of our leader Stalin is the most precious life for humanity." The editor of *Izvestia* writes in his editorial of August 24th that "the true humanism, the only humanism, lies in the defence of the régime which, under the leadership of the great Stalin, assures the new life, the free life, to millions of men." And he concludes by quoting an opportune phrase of the great proletarian humanist, Maxim Gorky: "If the enemy does not surrender, you knock him down."

Who would dare, under the fire of this totalitarian artillery, to abstain from voting for a resolution—only to disappear the same night, as an accomplice of Friedrich Adler, of de Brouckère, of the Gestapo, of the terrorists? In Rostov-on-Don, the professor of sociology Khalilov says before his students that he has found this trial "peculiar." This seems to be suspicious, the phrase is promptly reported, a newspaper of September 1st announces, in relating the incident, the arrest of this "terrorist-Trotskyist." . . .

* * *

The verdict is rendered on August 24th, at two in the morning, as was to be expected: death for all. According to the law of December 1, 1934, verdicts of death pronounced in affairs of terrorism are not subject to appeal or recourse and must be executed forthwith. The Sixteen listen, impassive; several of them—dubious supernumeraries—have "a flippant manner," according to the journalists. "I shall never forget," writes the correspondent of the *Daily Telegraph*, "the expression of Zinoviev, his head bowed, his hands joined as if in prayer, as Ulrich read the sentence in a dry voice, in short pithy sentences. . . ." With the reading terminated, are they going to conduct the victims directly to the place of execution? No, a stay of seventy-two hours is granted them, an exceptional and illegal act, so that they may address an appeal for clemency to the Executive of the Soviets. Holtzman and Ivan Smirnov refuse to do so. The Executive is old Kalinin, their comrade of yesterday, who takes his orders from Stalin. No doubt the Leader deems it wise not to give any, but since he does not give the order for clemency, the death sentence becomes mandatory. Besides, all this has already been deliberated by the Political Bureau. Nadyezhda Constantinova Krupskaya, according to certain accounts, writes to Stalin to ask him for a pardon for men whom she has known for so many years; he has her answered that he cannot put any pressure upon the highest magistracy of the state. Really, he cannot. . . . This timid intervention will soon be expiated by Lenin's widow when she signs a hideous statement on the execution of the terrorists. "You've got to, Nadyezhda Constantinova, because the socialist press is exploiting your name. . . ." Poor woman.

The Executive having rejected the appeals, the execution takes place at the dawn of the 25th, even before the expiration of the legal stay. The reason for this precipitateness seems to lie in the fear of foreign intercession.

As a rule, the condemned is called upon at night to quit

his cell. He does not know where he is going, the turnkey does not know where he is conducting him. The elevator brings him down to the main floor. There, when he is made to take a cement staircase, powerfully illuminated, he begins to understand. . . . He follows a cement corridor bordered by gutters. He knows nothing; as a rule he does not even know that he has been condemned to die, if the G.P.U. has invoked the death penalty administratively. A man—who himself knows only one thing and that is that he must kill the one who is being brought to him—emerges behind him on padded feet and sends a bullet through his head. The water spouts are opened, the body rolls into a trap or is pushed into a recess. Next! It may be that it was not even deemed necessary to apprise the Sixteen of the rejection of their appeal. Called by surprise, before the expiration of the legal stays, they understood only at the last minute. But in this last minute they perceived many things; and few men have died with such frightful bitterness—betrayed and tricked. . . . No witnesses; the cellar smothers all sounds; a few reliable executioners act without knowing anything exactly. Silence, secrecy. I was confined in the Lubianka when the thirty-five functionaries of the Commissariat of Agriculture were executed there for a bizarre affair of sabotage and intelligence with Poland (March 1935). No sound disturbed the silence of the perfect prison.

* * *

The newspapers of the 25th print on the first page the smiling portraits of the Leaders at the Tushino airfield, where an aerial celebration took place. In small type, in the bottom corner of the fourth page, under the miscellaneous section, a notice records the fact that justice has taken its course.

"Since it is over," writes *Pravda,* "we breathe better, the air is purer. Our muscles acquire a new vigour, our machines turn faster, our hands are nimbler. . . . We shall see new industrial records. . . ." It was never before known that blood lubricated machinery so well. . . .

*Izvestia* says that a "storm of approval is passing over the country; the workers are thanking the Supreme Tribunal by the millions." Their will is done! Had not Mme. Doctor Sophie Bortman, children's doctor, written: "No mercy for the enemies of the people!" The government listened to the doctor. The workers of the dramatic theatre named after Gorky approve. Peasants of Voronezh approve. "Long live the great friend, the father and the teacher of all the workers. . . ."

The *Pioneers' Pravda* expresses the joy of the children. Colony No. 5, formed of abandoned orphans, thanks the "beloved Chekists" for having shot the bandits and declares: "This verdict is ours." Little ones, boys and girls eight and ten years old, exclaim with joy: "Let these dogs perish. . . ."—"Oh, how we should have liked to shoot them ourselves!" And they send a message of affection to the well-beloved Leader.

Alexis Stakhanov exults. Mary Soban, member of the Communist Youth, the daughter of an American worker, relates before an audience of Rostov workers, that when her mother and she heard the loud-speaker announce the verdict, they could no longer contain themselves and they clapped their hands. "So great was the satisfaction of this honest proletarian family." The writers are content. The artists applaud. The woman worker Yevdokimova of the "Commune de Paris" plant in Moscow, exclaims, happily: "These dogs died like dogs!" (A Yevdokimov has just been shot.) Stakhanovists deplore the fact that Trotsky is alive.

The academician Williams considers that the verdict was "dictated by the noble sentiments of proletarian humanism in the interest of the happiness and the freedom of millions of workers."

Why did a social democrat have to come along to darken the bright memories of this day? Professor Tandler, Viennese physician, refugee in Moscow, died suddenly upon learning of the execution. You can clearly recognize there the feebleness of a petty bourgeois nature. . . . He must have been, at bottom, a "masked enemy." . . .

# 10.

## *Explanation and Sequel of a Crime*

THE CORRESPONDENT OF THE HAVAS NEWS AGENCY, HAVING attended the trial, gives his opinion in circumspect terms. He thinks that the accusations and the confessions are not entirely devoid of foundation; but that it cannot be said up to what point the accusations are founded; and that, in any case, the element of truth they do contain has been widely exploited for definite purposes. . . .

Bowdlerized though the official accounts of the trial are, they reveal to the reader who knows the men, their ideas, and their struggles, the modicum of truth that there is in this whole affair. The Old Bolsheviks dedicated a black hatred—and still do—to Stalin, whom they dread even more than they honour him by command—a hatred based on resentment, fear, and political hostility. They had capitulated to him in vain, they could not meet together intimately without grumbling, without asking themselves how it would all end, what to do—what to do, despairingly, in order to get out of the blind alley.

The whole spurious plot so laboriously erected by the inquisitors becomes clear when one reopens an authentic enough document dated July 11, 1928. It consists of notes written down by Kamenev on his conversations with Bukharin, meant to be sent to Zinoviev, then in exile in Voronezh. (The Trotskyist Opposition got hold of it and published it in a tract.) Bukharin arrived, agitated, "shivering, his lips trembling"; he seemed to be "at his wits' end." "The G.P.U. is trailing me and watching you. Let nobody know that we have seen each other!" What does he say? "Stalin's policy is fatal for the revolution. He is leading us to the abyss. . . . He is an intriguer who subordinates everything to his thirst for power. He changes his theory in order to get rid of somebody at the proper moment." On these intensely tragic pages, certain lines are stained with blood today, ten years later. The besetting refrain: "He will strangle us all."—"What is to be done? The subjective conditions are maturing in the Central Committee for removing Stalin, but they are not yet ripe. . . . Stalin knows only vengeance . . . the dagger in the back. Remember his theory of *sweet revenge. . . .*" ("One summer's eve, talking frankly with Dzerzhinsky and Kamenev, Stalin is supposed to have said: To choose the victim, to prepare every detail of the blow, to gratify an implacable revenge and then to go to bed. . . . There is nothing sweeter in the world.")

Bukharin compares him with Genghis Khan, speaks of the police régime, enumerates all those among the leading figures of the party who dream of removing Stalin but do not yet dare, who flinch at the last moment, who take fright as soon as it is spoken of. Bukharin, Rykov, Tomsky, Uglanov, still in power, already feel themselves lost. . . . Aren't we finally going to combine against him, dare to defend ourselves? "He will strangle us. . . ."

No, there is no plot, there is no terrorism. A plot was impossible in this atmosphere of proscription, of police surveillance, of informing, of doctrinal divisions. No plot—but hatred, fear, and hopeful waiting, behind the appearances—which deceived nobody—of fidelity to the well-beloved Leader.

* * *

Let us try not to reason here as readers of detective stories and let us bear in mind that we are dealing with political people par excellence. All those who knew a Zinoviev in the international congresses and a Trotsky in exile, know that, for these men, the personal life is not separable from political action and that the latter takes precedence over everything; know that men of this training are incapable of thinking otherwise than as Marxian politicians and that, on the other hand, they are capable of breaking instantly with anyone who departs to any serious extent from Marxian methods. But so long as we remain faithful to these methods, *remove Stalin* means to break with the bureaucratic policy of the Leader, to drive him from power. It is a matter of a political action and not of an assassination which would very likely have an opposite result, since it would not affect the bureaucratic machine and would only decapitate a clique which is really provided with many heads. On the other hand, assassination would discredit politically its authors. The General-Secretary suddenly placed in a minority, resigning in an instant, locked up for greater security—that is what was dreamed of in so many of the secret meetings. It would actually have been a political event and it did seem possible, since all the old men of the early days feared him and wished for his elimination. An assassination, on the other hand, would have transferred the power to a Kaganovich (or a Voroshilov), propped up by the High Commissar of the Secret Service, and would have permitted precisely the Stalinist coterie to rid itself, by means of repressions, of its political opponents.

At the moment of the Kirov affair, imprisoned Trotskyists—whom I know—asked themselves if it was not a Stalinist second edition of the "Röhm stroke." Finally, one can follow Trotsky's reactions, day by day, in the numerous articles he published. Quoting an old article which he gave in 1911 to the *Kampf*, a Viennese socialist magazine, he writes:

" 'Whether or not the terrorist act, even if "successful," throws the ruling circles into turmoil, depends upon the concrete political circumstances. In any case, such turmoil can only be of short duration; the capitalist state is not founded upon ministers and cannot be destroyed with them. The classes it serves will always find new men, the mechanism remains whole and continues its work.

" 'But the turmoil which the terrorist act introduces into the ranks of the toiling masses themselves is far more profound. If it is enough to arm oneself with a revolver to reach the goal, what need is there for the strivings of the class struggle? If people in high positions can be intimidated by the noise of an explosion, what need is there then for a party?'

"To this article which counterposed to terrorist adventurism the method of preparing the proletariat for the socialist revolution, I can add nothing today, twenty-three years later."

On the act that cost Kirov his life, Trotsky delivered the following judgment:

"The subjective motivations of Nikolayev and his partisans are a matter of indifference to us. Hell itself is paved with the best of intentions. So long as the Soviet bureaucracy has not been removed by the proletariat, a task which will eventually be accomplished, it fulfils a necessary function in the defence of the workers' state. Should terrorism of the Nikolayev type spread, it could, aided by new, unfavourable conditions, render service only to the fascist counter-revolution." [1]

---

[1] Trotsky, *The Kirov Assassination*, pp. 16*f*. (New York, 1935.)

Since Plekhanov's break with the future terrorists of the People's Will (*Narodnaya Volya*) around 1879, this has always been the inflexible doctrinal attitude of the Russian Marxists, even in the epochs when terrorism, pursued by the Social Revolutionary party, proved effective in the struggle against the autocracy. Trotsky represents in this case a half-century of tradition. Let us take note that he grants the Stalinist bureaucracy a function, useful in spite of everything, in the defence of the proletarian state. We know that he has not hesitated to break, in the course of recent years, with all those among the militants of the international Opposition who expressed doubts on the proletarian nature of the Soviet state or who advocated, with regard to this state, any other attitude but that of unconditional defence in the event of war.

The policy of Zinoviev and Kamenev consisted in getting back into the good graces of the party in order to be present on the day of the regroupment. However baffling may be their lying confessions—that extraordinary political and moral suicide that made their execution possible—the explanation is clear to anybody who knows these men and it is contained in a few words: devotion to the party, usefulness.[1]

Founders of the Old Bolshevik party, unable to conceive of living outside its ranks, they professed that it was necessary to stay inside at all costs, even at the cost of forswearing thoughts, of abdicating all dignity (is one's dignity put on the scales when the interests of the revolution are in-

---

[1] I translated as "usefulness" a Russian word which would be more accurately rendered by "conformity with the aim pursued"—that dreadful little phrase that I heard pronounced there so often.—*Trans.*

volved?), of feigning to bow to the officially worshipped Leader, regarded in their innermost heart as the worst grave-digger of the revolution. Hence, their reiterated capitulations, their double game of being and yet not being oppositionists, their infernel position as perpetual suspects. In order the better to discredit them—for these men, the only surviving companions of Lenin, remained formidable rivals because of their basic attachment to Bolshevism and of their past—the most humiliating apostasies were periodically demanded of them. They came out of prison or they returned from the hamlets of Central Asia in order to ascend the tribune of the congresses and make their apologies—once more—before the Leader. Then they returned to the shadows, and everybody knew that they existed, retaining their judgments at bottom. They existed in spite of the humiliations inflicted and accepted. They would continue to exist so long as they were alive. The ordered disavowals did not diminish them any more because the profound reason for the statements was known—their attachment to the party. . . . Besides, in a country without law, everybody knows that the only defence left lies in evasion, the only salvation in cowardice. You adapt yourself, you "play 'possum," you wait. And the power, which knows it, is infuriated at these passive men. . . .

That is why the following language, approximately, is used to them in the private conversations in the cells situated several stories above the execution cellar:

"You are, whatever you may say or do, our unalterable opponents. But you are devoted to the party—we know that too. The party demands a new sacrifice of you, more complete than the preceding ones. A political suicide. The sacrifice of your consciences. You will confirm it by yourselves providing for capital punishment. Only then will it be possible to believe that you are really disarming before the Leader. We demand this sacrifice from you because the republic is in danger. The shadow of war hovers above us, fascism is rising all around us. We must strike at Trotsky in his exile, at all costs, discredit his nascent Fourth International, make a holy alliance around the Leader whom you execrate but whom you acknowledge, because he is the strongest. If you consent, you have a chance to live. If you refuse, you will disappear, in one way or another."

When you know, as does anyone who has lived there for a long time, the psychosis of war that the leaders spread throughout the U.S.S.R., you understand the power of this appeal addressed, after all, infinitely more to the spirit of devotion than to the spirit of cowardice. And it is all the more effective because most of the accused were old opponents of Trotsky, long ago disposed to discredit him by any means. (Smirnov and Holtzman were exceptions and their attitude was very peculiar; but the same general reasons also held good for them. Smirnov, bowing before reasons of state, seems to have consented only to *confessing one thing*.)

To refuse would perhaps mean to give oneself more chance to live, but it would surely mean to break with the party. They could not refuse. . . .

Others, in all probability, did refuse. Shall we ever know?

A half-certainty guaranteed them life, in addition to the promises that were probably made to them. First, Soviet law was explicit in the days when there was a Soviet law. *The law does not punish or avenge*, it confines itself to defending society. The criminal who has disarmed, who, by his confessions and his attitude, has rendered himself powerless to do harm, may not be punished for what he has done; he must not be subjected to vindictiveness; he may only be isolated from society for a certain time, as a measure of precaution and towards the end of re-education. They flatter themselves on applying this principle to the—at first glance—most incorrigible old offenders. Tourists are readily made to visit the G.P.U. colony at Bolshevo, not far from Moscow, where a number of bandits with more than one life on their consciences, work in guarded freedom, go to the club, study Stalin, take part in the Stakhanovist brigades. Panait Istrati, amazed, exclaimed upon leaving it: "What a pity that one must have assassinated several persons in order to enjoy such welfare!" They had neglected to tell him that, in addition, one must have given away his accomplices.

Two precedents were no less explicit. The principal defendants in the two large similar trials, likewise prepared with the shrewdest admixture of lies, fear, and devotion, in accordance with the case, were not executed. The engineer Ramzin who accused himself in 1930 of having formed a clandestine Industrial party, sabotaged the industrialization, prepared a foreign intervention in contact with the General Staff of a power which is today very friendly, never ceased working for the Commissariat of Heavy Industry and was recently rehabilitated along with his principal accomplices. He is rich and esteemed. (I should very much like to know what happened, on the other hand, to the two Leningrad teachers who were driven out of the trade-union for having refused to vote for the death penalty against this traitor? The fault surely still weighs heavily upon their destiny.) . . .

The old socialists who accused themselves shortly afterward of the same crime, although it flew in the face of all probability, in a trial which was a bewildering imposture from beginning to end (they admitted having prepared a foreign intervention under instructions from the Socialist International), are alive; in various prisons, to be sure. To prepare a foreign intervention against the country is, after all, a greater crime than that which Zinoviev, Kamenev, and their fellow accused were bidden to charge themselves with; and the founders of the party, the heroes of the civil war (Mrachkovsky, Smirnov, Dreitser) could not, in all good logic, be treated with greater severity than the traitors. . . . Only, good logic amounted to nothing in all this.

There was, therefore, a sort of bargain concluded between the accused and the Leader, accepted out of devotion to the party and with a remnant of human and political hope. "He won't dare, he won't go that far; after all he, too, is one of the old ones of the party"—that is what they must have said to themselves in their horrible moments of doubt.

And they understood their mistake only at the very last moment, when their hands were tied to make them go downstairs. . . .

What impulses did Stalin obey in dispatching the old members of the Political Bureau? The clearest is the consecration of personal power. If he has himself called "Leader of Leaders, the most gifted genius of all times, sun, our father," it is not only in order to breathe the low-grade incense which escapes from his own press services. His power is absolute, unchecked, perpetual. Who would think of voicing an objection if it pleased him to designate his successor? It will be asked of him, someday, like a favour that he will confer upon his good people. . . . The consecration of a personal power, which is in such contradiction to socialist principles and the Bolshevik tradition, cannot be effected without the elimination of the Old Guard of October. However passive the remnants of it may be, it is impossible for them not to think, and by that alone they constitute a threat for the future.

In spite of the persecutions, Zinoviev, Kamenev, Smirnov benefited by a somewhat privileged political position. The party, the entire country knew that those old ones, after having built up the party with Lenin and made the revolution, no longer shared, for the last twelve years, the responsibility of the power. The millions of victims of the forced collectivization, of the years of famine, of the years of terror against the workers, did not permit any reproach to be made against these men. Hence, one could dishonour them officially, continue to debase them or, silently, as with Smirnov, to immure them. Yet, through it all they retained a certain grandeur and could make up a replacement crew.

There is no more replacement crew.

The consecration of the personal power is only one of the aspects of the consecration of a policy. It may be said that the Soviet Thermidor, which lasted for years, is consummated. *Il Messagero*, the Italian fascist organ, was not mistaken in declaring that the *Enragés* of the Russian Revolution had been put to death. The bureaucracy fears above all else the explosive power of the ideas which it pretends, out of necessity, to adhere to in order to retain the old banners. It must put an end to the generation that incarnates these ideas. The Old Bolsheviks—and I understand by them the men who stood firm until the death of Lenin—are today in the anachronistic position of the former Jacobins under the Thermidorian reaction.

Now the socialist revolution, frustrated by the *parvenus*, differs from the bourgeois revolution (1789–1793–1800) in this sense, that it does not lead to a stable order in harmony with itself. Until it will have discharged the agreement, signed by the victorious insurgents of October 1917, which will be presented to it inevitably, tomorrow or the day after, by millions of workers, it will live under the menace of internal convulsions. The bureaucracy does not exercise a legitimate authority; it cannot invoke either the divine right of the old régime or the natural laws of bourgeois positivism; it is reduced to disavowing itself by asserting that it is "fighting the bureaucracy"—really!—that it only represents the workers, that it is working for the welfare of the workers. . . . A false situation that cannot be perpetuated and that can last only thanks to a constant intervention in the ranks by the ministry of police of the totalitarian state. But it is wise in foreseeing the coming turns. They are undoubtedly being prepared. It may be that we are on the eve of great changes at home or of grave events abroad. In either case, the revolutionary potential of the masses must come into play. The problem is to reduce it by anticipation.[1] A clean-up in the rear, in case of war. A warning to the Russian proletariat that the events in Spain, supervening after the great June strikes in France and Belgium, are stirring up the depths, dangerously. . . .

The Opposition nevertheless exists under a multitude of forms. Invisible, it is silent, sometimes betraying itself by a joke. So much the worse for the joker. The Opposition also exists under a form the very heroism of which may appear to be absurd: several thousand intransigents of all the shadings of working-class thought—and some without shadings, having formed themselves as best they could,

[1] The crime is that, in reducing it, the revolution is disarmed before the future. If there are no socialist or communist replacement crews at the next turn of history, *who* will take over the directing of events? Do not think that the relentless bureaucratic reaction is not stirring up currents of anti-socialist reaction, also still latent.

without knowing exactly what they are—represent it in the prisons, the concentration camps, the places of deportation. The most dangerous and, moreover, the most numerous are those who adhere to the October Revolution, primarily the Trotskyists. They have a leader, eminently intransigent, a figure that has become legendary as the equal of Lenin, the organizer of the insurrection and the organizer of the victory, the only oppositionist who never capitulates, the deportee of Alma-Ata, the banished of the Island of Prinkipo, the banished of Norway, the banished of Mexico. . . . He is out of reach, he is missing from the batch of the shot and so long as he remains alive the replacement crew will be able to come together again, since a head subsists and it is precisely the grandest head. Terrorism had to be invented because only this charge permitted the execution of the one while indirectly striking the other, Trotsky. How?

By making life as hard for him as possible. It must be said that, in this respect, the Stalinist government has permitted itself a good deal, with a curious success. It is foreboding. Never did the ministers of the Tsar, who did often fall under the fire of authentic terrorists, dare to demand in such terms the expulsion of a socialist leader from a country of Europe. Since the U.S.S.R. must speak to all the countries where Trotsky may find exile in the same language it used towards Norway, it follows that it means to have him refused asylum everywhere, that is, to impose his internment upon the foreign governments. The stupefying thing is that it has succeeded for the time being. A precedent is thus created which the totalitarian régimes will know how to profit by, let there be no doubt about it. The Stalinist reaction has just dealt a direct blow at the right of asylum—one of the last frail guarantees of the freedom of opinion in the world.

By disqualifying the idea of the Fourth International, which has become disturbing to the leaders of the Third, since they feel that they have left a vast empty space in the labour movement by abandoning all revolutionary activity and perspective. Dimitroff writes: "We see today why Trotsky needs to create a Fourth International and who is served by this dirty collection of infuriated petty bourgeois individualists, self-infatuated upstarts, agents of the Gestapo and other police." [1]

By making Trotsky indefensible for the imprisoned Trotskyists who will be called up to de-solidarize themselves from an "agent of the Gestapo." No doubt they will be able to reply: "Oh, we know that! It's exactly what was

---

[1] This article by Dimitroff, which at the same time heaps insults upon the leaders of the Socialist International, would be worth quoting in full if it were not really so futile. The Hottentots are sometimes calumniated by having attributed to them morals that are supposed to be expressed in this saying: "If I steal the cow of my Kaffir neighbour, that's all right; if he tries to steal mine, that's a crime." Dimitroff knows better than anyone else how a high treason trial is staged in a totalitarian régime: and having come back safe and sound from the Leipzig trial he is in a position to make some not uninteresting comparisons between the greater or lesser propensities for legal assassination in the Hitlerite and Stalinist régimes. I note in passing that he has the effrontery to write: "The documents presented at the trial have proved . . ." etc.; and "everything required of a public trial in order to prove the terroristic culpability of the Trotskyist-Zinovievists was there in abundance." Now, there was not a single piece of material evidence to prop up the accusation; not a single proof figured in the trial! To finish with Hottentot morals: A dispatch published by the Soviet agency, T.A.S.S., protested at the same time against the scandalous procedure followed by the Japanese in Manchukuo. Desirous of seizing the lands of certain White Russians, the Japanese arrested them, made them confess, in the course of a secret preliminary investigation, that they had engaged in espionage for the Reds, tried them scandalously without guarantees of justice and put them before a firing squad. . . .

said about Lenin and all the rest of us in 1917. Just remember Alexinsky's documents, and the sealed train, and the millions of the German General Staff that we were supposed to have received when we didn't have a spare shirt. . . ." But the custom is not to allow any reply. Up to now Trotskyism was outlawed as a form of opposition; beginning with the Zinoviev trial, it is outlawed as a form of high treason, which justifies recourse to the harshest measures against the intransigents. . . .

By making discussion impossible between oppositional and Stalinist communists. Many of the latter, ignorant of the history of the first ten years of the revolution, imagine in all good faith that they are serving the cause of the proletariat by giving their adhesion to the bureaucratic régime.

They live on counterfeited ideas. At the moment when the official Communist parties, obeying the gifted Leader, are passing from internationalism to nationalism, from the class struggle to class collaboration, from anti-militarism to militarism, from the proud thoughts of Lenin to a suspiciously combinatory neo-socialism, it must be seen to that no conversations are conducted between Stalinist workers and oppositional communists. Between the two there is now blood.

The struggle between the Oppositions and the bureaucracy is no longer one of two different tendencies of the labour movement, but has become a class struggle.

No more correct general judgment of this crime has been delivered than that of Otto Bauer: "The execution of the Sixteen is a tremendous misfortune for the international working class." We cannot yet measure its consequences. In the Russian Revolution, this trial marks a date comparable to that of the 9th of Thermidor, without aiming to draw the analogy too closely. Supervening at the moment when the working class needs moral unity and active solidarity—rising above the divergence of doctrines and tactics—in order to live and triumph, at the moment when non-party workers, socialists, anarchists, syndicalists, Stalin-communists and Trotskyists are lying down to sleep in Spain in the same trenches, and dying from the same bullets, this legal massacre of great militants of the Russian Revolution is surrounded by such odious circumstances that it signifies not only a cruel schismatic leaven, but a new decline in human values which we all need in order to breathe. . . . Socialism will not vanquish fascism unless it brings men entirely different morals than those. From all this bloodshed, from this irruption of lies, from all these police intrigues, from this debasement of the vanquished, from this ferocity of the victor, from this Borgian justice instituted in the first state of the workers and peasants, from this devotion to the party that leads to a nameless demoralization—shame, sordidness, horror, discreditment and anguish rebound upon idea-forces of a vital importance. Years will be needed, after these infamies, to rebuild in the mind of the masses the idea of the proletarian party, that puissant cohort of free men associated by common thought and discipline of action. Years will be needed to resuscitate the emancipating conception of the dictatorship of the proletariat of Engels and of Lenin.

And how much further the human dignity of our time has been humiliated!

On the morrow of the trial, the arrests continue, accompanied by alterations in the governmental personnel. Karl Radek is arrested. He is not only a companion of Lenin; he was with Karl Liebknecht, Rosa Luxemburg, and Leo Tyschko in Berlin, in the tragic days of 1919. Chance alone enabled Radek to escape their fate, in that same Moabit prison where his friend Tyschko had just been brought down. For years he heaped up vileness in the service of the Leader; the worst was, perhaps, the vileness of yesterday, the unspeakable article he was made to write to demand the death penalty against his comrades of thirty years of struggles. Semi-official spokesman of Stalin in foreign policy, he suddenly disappears and, when the European press is stirred up about it, *Pravda* finally denounces him as a suspicious counter-revolutionary intriguer. Will he be tried with Sokolnikov, Putna, Serebriakov, as is anticipated? After the outcome of the trial of the Sixteen, are similar agitational spectacles, founded upon the complaisance of the accused, still possible? Yes, if the accused are unaware of the fate of the Sixteen. . . . The head of the Secret Service, Yagoda, is abruptly dismissed; he is transferred to Posts, Telephones, and Telegraphs, with his associate Prokofiev, one of the oldest Chekists. Did he concoct yesterday's affair too maladroitly? At all events, he knows too many things; besides, he, too, is an old one from 1917. Moreover, in 1927–1928 he sympathized with the Oppositions which wished in the dark for the elimination of Stalin. Rykov and Bukharin benefit by a "not enough evidence." Then the ones who were shot did tell the truth in accusing themselves, in accusing Trotsky, in accusing Radek, but lied in accusing Rykov and Bukharin? Believe it who can. The strictly political and perhaps provisional no-cause leaves them at the mercy of the Leader. Pardoned, they no longer really have any influence; sooner or later it will be perceived that their mere presence is disconcerting and they will have to be put out of the way. Piatakov disappears, undoubtedly inculpated. Arrests everywhere. The proscriptions have their logic. The whole October generation must be outlawed. Whatever its last representatives may be made to do, to say, and to write, words no longer count. Stalin knows that these men may someday take hold of themselves again and that, in their heart of hearts, they are his implacable judges.

The very precipitateness with which the trial was announced, conducted, and terminated shows premeditation. Now we understand the bizarre Yenukidze affair of 1935 and the dissolution, at the same time, of the Society of the Old Bolsheviks. The secretary of the Bureau of the Executive of the Soviets, devoted though he was to Stalin, might have hesitated to reject the appeal for pardon of the Sixteen. The Old Bolsheviks might have muttered against the decapitation of the old party.

Yagoda makes way, at the head of the Secret Service, for a petty functionary drawn from nowhere by the Leader: Yezhov. A new generation formed out of yesterday's unknowns and who represent nothing more than the good pleasure of the General-Secretary thus occupy the leading posts, little by little: Zhdanov in Leningrad, Khrustchev in Moscow, Lavrenti Beria in Tiflis, Yezhov in the ministry of police. . . .

# 11.

# *Stalin's First Foreign Policy (1927-1934)*

IN THE BEGINNING THE FOREIGN POLICY OF THE PROLETARIAN revolution is essentially a rupture with the past. It consists in appealing, in the midst of the World War, from the imperialist governments to the assassinated peoples, in publishing and tearing up the treaties, in abolishing secret diplomacy, in proclaiming the will to peace of the workers. Later on, the ups and downs of the revolutionary movement in Europe force Soviet policy through several different phases, but there is a great continuity of spirit in all of them. When the hard-pressed Republic is desperately resisting the Germans, the diplomatic notes of Chicherin are S.O.S. calls incessantly addressed to the proletarians of the world. Towards 1920, the Republic being saved, the Communist International consolidates its power of radiation, and its policy, paralleling the policy of the Council of People's Commissars, is one of revolutionary expansion, that is, of active support to the revolutionary attempts in Europe and in Asia. Lenin deems necessary the risky offensive against Warsaw, for its success would signify the sovietization of Poland, would bring closer the victory of the proletariat in Germany and would deal a decisive blow to the Versailles system. At the same epoch, a Congress of the Peoples of the Orient meets in Baku, showing the interest that the Communist International has in the revolutionary possibilities of Asia. Lenin writes his theses on the national and colonial question. A short time previously, Russian troops commanded by Blumkin, in the shadow of Kuchuk-Khan, had attempted to arouse the North of Persia. Finally, in 1923, the Comintern and the Soviet government are ready to give thoroughgoing support to a German Revolution whose failure—let us remember—inaugurates the political crisis in Russia.

Towards 1927–1928, at the moment when the bureaucracy arrives brutally in power, the Chinese Revolution is in its ascendant phase. The forecasts of Lenin are being realized—shouldn't this be the time to recall his theoretical advice? But another social stratum holds the levers of command and it must proceed from a different ideology. The Chinese Communist party is ordered into enslavement to the Kuomintang, which first paralyses it, then compromises and strangles it. The admirable trade-unions of Shanghai are surrendered, after their victory, and despite the admonitions of a handful of militants, to the headsmen of Chiang Kai-shek, who is in partnership with Stalin and whose arms have been assured success by heads of the Red Army, like Blücher and Olgin. The International forbids the Chinese revolutionists to form soviets at a time when only councils of workers could have put themselves at the head of the mass movement. You see communist ministers, directed by agents of Stalin, participating in the Wuhan coalition government, which represses strikes and agrarian uprisings. Day after day the toiling masses are led into ambush. Victories which would have been easy, according to all indications, escape them at the last moment. The departments and the emissaries of the International collaborate with the heads of the reaction. There isn't a trace of the doctrine and the strategy of Lenin in all this. For the class struggle

Stalin substitutes the conception of the "bloc of four classes," formulated in the bureaux by an old Menshevik who came over belatedly. Stalin considers that the important thing is not to frighten either the Chinese bourgeoisie or the powers. . . . Where Lenin sought to exhaust the revolutionary possibilities, he seeks, by extending his sway as widely as possible, to exercise a moderating influence in order to guarantee the security of the bureaucratic state. The interests of the *parvenus* prove to be opposed to an extension of the revolution and are aimed much more at extending the national sphere of influence of the Russian power.

Protests arise by the thousands. Stalin, unmasked by the Opposition and unable to overcome it save by vying with it, executes an abrupt turn-about-face. The insurrection of Canton is unleashed on the occasion of a party congress, assembled in Moscow (the Fifteenth Congress), and the Comintern launches the slogan of soviets right in the midst of the débâcle of the Chinese Revolution. . . .[1] Defeat after defeat, blood upon blood, incoherence, the infamy of mean tricks—are all added to the most revolting errors: a Chen Du-hsiu, great communist militant, is drenched with abuse—while a Kuomintang headsman decapitates his son—because he passes over to the Opposition. At the end of March 1927 twenty Chinese communists who had taken refuge at Karakhan's, in the Soviet legation at Peking, and been arrested there in defiance of international law, are executed by slow strangulation. Among them the scholar and poet, Li Ta-chao.

During the collectivization, the foreign policy of the U.S.S.R.—from which the activity of the Comintern cannot be separated—presents two aspects: the U.S.S.R. is ac-

[1] Stalin's representative in Canton, Lominadse, committed suicide in 1935 in Magnitogorsk, at the moment of being arrested.

tually disinterested in what is happening in the world, but maintains, for propaganda uses in the interior, an extremist ideology that dominates, in turn, the tactic of the sections of the International. Before this, communist circles in Moscow ascribed to Stalin the intention of liquidating the Red International of Labour Unions—to begin with—and of relegating to second place the Communist International, whose impotence and corruption he bitterly derided; but surnamed "the grave-digger of the revolution" by the oppositionists, he is compelled to try playing a different rôle on the world scene.

He is unable to admit the defeat of the Chinese Revolution, in which his responsibilities are terrific; and the official thesis, supported every day by the press, is that the Chinese Revolution is marching from victory to victory. . . . Are there not Soviet territories in Hunan, peopled, it is affirmed, by 40,000,000 inhabitants, and "as large as France"? The revolution is also rising in Germany, as proved by the electoral successes of the German Communist party. . . . The International prescribes to the Western parties the tactic of "class against class," an absurd tactic of isolation destined primarily to fight the socialists, who are labelled Social Fascists. The slogan is: destroy the social democracy first in order to vanquish fascism. During the Red plebiscite in Prussia, you see the communists unite with the Nazis against the social democratic government of Otto Braun. An insane strategy, and it would be interesting to know what Thälmann, who applied it so zealously, thinks of it today.[1] Right in the midst of the depression of the

[1] It will be remembered that in 1925 the German Communist party had made it possible for Field Marshal von Hindenburg to be elected to the presidency of the Reich by maintaining the candidacy of Thälmann against the social democrat Müller. The united votes of the two labour parties would have carried the socialist candidate.

French labour movement, Molotov, speaking of the "radicalization of the masses," explains that the question of power stands before the French proletariat. . . . The report of Stalin to the Sixteenth Congress of the Communist Party of the Soviet Union (1930) would be of a stupefying ignorance were it not a masterpiece of demagogy destined to deceive the masses in the country itself. Souvarine sums it up very exactly in eight lines: "The globe is mined with antagonisms, the most acute of which opposes the United States to England; the League of Nations is rotting on its feet; socialism is losing all its influence and the Communist parties are marching from victory to victory; the stabilization of capitalism is coming to an end and the revolution is rumbling everywhere; the bourgeoisie is looking for a way out in the war against the U.S.S.R., above all in France, 'the most aggressive and the most militaristic in the world,' etc. . . ."[1] At this moment the economic crisis coincides with a deep crisis in the labour movement, the counter-revolution is threatening everywhere, it can be seen rising in Germany with sure tread—and it can even be unfailingly predicted that the anti-socialist tactic of the Comintern will give it an easy victory. For having proposed, while there was still time, the united front of the labour parties against Nazism, Trotsky—clamorous voice in the desert—will be treated as a Hitlerite by *Pravda.* This criminal tactic will result in the crushing of the German proletariat without a struggle: for, divided at this point, it is no longer capable of any effective resistance. The last-minute attempts at a united front will be nothing more than poor gestures of distraction.

The explanation of this policy by the agitational needs

---

[1] B. Souvarine, *Staline*, p. 478.

in the interior of the U.S.S.R. is inadequate. A very complex psychological phenomenon must also be taken into account. The bureaucracy appeals for the industrialization and the collectivization to the revolutionary energies; its own ideological evolution has not yet been completed. It has not yet matured, in 1932, for the complete abandonment of the Bolshevik doctrine. This abandonment will become psychologically possible only a few years later, after the economic victory at home.

From another angle, the responsibilities of the Stalinist reaction for the disaster in Central Europe go far beyond mere questions of tactics. The Marxists explain the victory of the October Revolution in Russia by the fact that at the decisive moment the bulk of the middle classes (the peasants) supported the proletariat. At the moment when the German crisis opens up, the desolating experience of the forced collectivization is under way in the U.S.S.R., followed all the more closely in Germany because the famine and the terror affect the old German colonies of Russia and give birth there to a mass movement of emigration. Can the middle classes of Germany be expected to pronounce themselves in favour of communism under such conditions? In this sense the Stalinist reaction supplements the work of the Versailles Treaty, which it will soon be reduced to defending.

# 12.

## *Stalin's Second Foreign Policy (1934-1936)*

THE COLLAPSE OF WORKING-CLASS GERMANY SUDDENLY creates a new situation in 1933. The "Comintern line" traced by the Leader, has always been right: anybody, in Russia or elsewhere, who permits himself to doubt this is a traitor. . . . But what is Hitler going to do? If he perseveres in the path of the Rapallo Treaty, the Stalinist reaction remains ready to come to terms with him as it did with Mussolini, the only foreign chief of state who has never been attacked personally in the Soviet press. Waiting expectantly, *Pravda* still writes at the end of 1933 that the working class should not distinguish between the fascist states and the pseudo-democratic states. The resolute hostility of the Third Reich is needed, its armaments, its negotiations with Poland and Japan, before the bureaucracy returns to a more correct evaluation of the importance of democracy —even bourgeois—for the working class of the West. On this point, too, the ideas of Marx, Engels, and Lenin no longer have any standing with the bureaucracy. And how could it show itself sincerely attached to workers' liberties in other countries when it itself refuses these liberties to the workers? But the U.S.S.R. has lost its natural ally, the German proletariat. What is to be done?

To the successes and the excesses of the reaction in the

interior there corresponds, as was to be expected, beginning with 1934, a foreign policy which strives primarily towards a rapprochement with certain great capitalist powers. By lavishing assurances that have not been published, the U.S.S.R. obtains *de jure* recognition from the United States. Diplomatic relations are resumed with Bulgaria and Rumania. Under what conditions? Communists are demonstratively hanged in Bulgaria while the first plenipotentiary minister of Tsar Boris is received in the Kremlin. About three thousand Rumanian communists and socialists are arrested on the eve of the arrival in Bucharest of the first plenipotentiary minister of the U.S.S.R. "We will not surrender an inch of our territory," proclaims Stalin; but he renounces Bessarabia, still depicted on all Soviet maps as a territory forcibly torn from the Republic. The U.S.S.R. enters the League of Nations in September 1934. The Geneva organism ceases to be a league of imperialist pirates for the defence of the Versailles treaty of brigandage (all these are expressions of Lenin, and Stalin himself repeated them more than once), and it becomes the safeguard of peace in the world. The generation of Lenin and Trotsky refused to weigh minutely the intentions of the diplomats between July 25 and August 4, 1914, in the question of the origins of the war. In its eyes the two imperialist coalitions, equally interested in a new division of the world, were equally culpable. But by the Versailles Treaty, the victorious coalition created a situation pregnant with the worst dangers for civilization. You can see today how correct was the revolutionary criticism of this treaty. No matter, a purging of the libraries will suffice.

The totalitarian state sets in motion its machine for manufacturing ideas. The Radeks will multiply their allusions to German war guilt. A signal to the press—and articles, fillers, chronicles, couplets dedicated to the fatherland—plain fatherland and no longer proletarian—will follow in droves, creating a whole new vocabulary. Escadrilles of Soviet aeroplanes land in Prague and in Le Bourget. Czechoslovakian and French escadrilles arrive in Moscow. Banquets. On May 2, 1935, MM. Laval and Potemkin sign in Paris the Franco-Soviet agreement of "mutual assistance in case of non-provoked aggression on the part of a European state." (France refuses flatly to intervene in case of Japanese aggression in the Far East.) A similar pact is signed between the U.S.S.R. and Czechoslovakia. In May, M. Pierre Laval proceeds to Moscow, is received by Stalin. At the end of their interview, an official communiqué attests that "M. Stalin understands and fully approves the policy of national defence pursued by France in order to maintain its armed forces at the level of its security." M. Stalin therefore formally disapproves of socialist and communist anti-militarism. For the two fundamental theses of Lenin: "No national defence in a capitalist régime" and "transformation of the imperialist war into a civil war," M. Stalin substitutes his understanding and his unreserved approval. . . .[1] If the French bourgeoisie is led to fight to defend its colonies (and, at bottom, that is the most real danger of war), it will be able to count on the Red Armies. . . . For his part, M. Pierre Laval, who at least has the incontestable merit of not claim-

[1] ". . . The president of the Council, M. Laval, recorded the fact that it was on the initiative of M. Stalin himself that the paragraph concerning the policy of national defence of the French government had been included." (*Le Petit Parisien*, June 20, 1935.) "Addressing himself directly to M. Péri, who represents the communist group in the commission [of Foreign Affairs, in the Chamber of Deputies], M. Laval declared: "Why did I go to Soviet Russia to conclude an act of peace, if I am to be perpetually attacked in France and discommoded in my activity by those who call themselves here the translators of Soviet thought and doctrine? There is a hypocrisy in that that has lasted long enough." (*Le Petit Journal*, same day.)

ing to be either a socialist, a Leninist, or the leader of the world proletariat, and who is only making a good business deal in all this, understands and undoubtedly approves the progress of Soviet armaments proclaimed from the top of various tribunes by Marshal Tukhachevsky. Effectives in 1930: 600,000 men; in 1934: 940,000 men; in 1936, 1,500,-000 men.[1]

On September 22nd, a decree re-establishes ranks in the Soviet Army. Another decree creates five marshals of the U.S.S.R. Edicts provide for the creation of new insignia of command, gold and silver stripes. The marshals will wear gold stars half a decimetre in size on their collars and sleeves. The Commissars of the Secret Service will be no less bedizened than the new generals. . . . There remains to ask oneself what titles, what stripes are to be thought up for the one who dispenses all of them and whom his panegyrists call "the Grand Marshal of socialism"? Let us wait. The Turkmen poets compare him with the sun, and he smiles.

---

[1] According to Tukhachevsky's report to the Soviet Congress in 1935, the growth of the forces of the U.S.S.R. in the course of the first Five-Year period was 300% for the aerial army; 2,475% for speed tanks; 760% for light tanks; 792% for medium tanks; 535% for submarines; 1,100% for coastal guards; 470% for torpedo boats; for machine guns it varies between 250% and 700%.

Other figures, no less imposing, were given at the Extraordinary Congress of the Soviets in November 1936. Admiral Orlov made known that, in comparison with the forces existing on January 1, 1935, the increase of the submarine fleet is 715% at the end of 1936. . . . The under-chief of the aerial forces has just announced from the tribune that the U.S.S.R. has 7,000 aeroplanes, 2,000 of them of the first class, at its disposal. . . . "Germany and Japan," he says, "are trying to bring into play 18,000 aeroplanes all told. If it were necessary, we would be able to supply 100,000 aviators. . . . In a few months, we shall dispose of several hundred aeroplanes capable of 600 kilometres an hour. . . . In the whole World War, 17,500 tons of explosives were thrown by enemy aircraft upon the territories of France, England, and Russia. Five flights of the Soviet bombardment fleet would suffice today to transport the same quantity of explosives." (Session of November 29th.)

Only autocrats can decide upon peace and war at their pleasure, without consulting assemblies. . . . Without the constitutional organs of power having deliberated thereon, M. Stalin declares one morning that if Japan makes an attempt upon the territorial integrity of the Mongolian Republic, the U.S.S.R. will intervene. M. Stalin says it to Mr. Roy Howard, a bourgeois journalist from America, and the Soviet workers thus learn, incidentally, that their blood has been disposed of. In other respects, too, the conversation of M. Stalin with Mr. Roy Howard deserves to be dwelt upon. Here is the principal passage:

*Mr. Howard:* Does this, your statement, mean that the Soviet Union has to any degree abandoned its plans and intentions to bringing about a world revolution?

*M. Stalin:* We never had such plans and intentions.

*Mr. Howard:* You appreciate, no doubt, Mr. Stalin, that much of the world has long entertained a different impression?

*M. Stalin:* This is the product of a misunderstanding.

*Mr. Howard:* A tragic misunderstanding?

*M. Stalin:* No, a comical one. Or, perhaps, tragi-comic.

Is the tragedy of the world revolution, therefore, to end for M. Stalin as a farce? Is the Bolshevism of the bureaucrats drowned in combinations to go to the point of forswearing the past of the Bolshevism of the revolutionists? The habit of lying with impunity and the necessity of lying enormously here brings the Leader of the Communist Party of the Soviet Union and of the Third International into a blind alley. Nothing is more tragi-comic than his remarks. What! wasn't the Third International, the party of the world revolution, founded in Moscow? Did not M. Stalin himself take the floor in its congresses and its commissions? Did he not intervene, alas! in order to guide the activities of the various Communist parties? Wasn't all this printed throughout his book, *The Problems of Leninism*, translated into all the European languages? The Finnish Revolution, supported by Russian troops in 1918; the Soviet Revolutions in Bavaria and Hungary; the Communist insurrections in Germany; the march of the Red Army on Warsaw in 1920 and the formation at the rear of this army of a Revolutionary Committee of Poland with Markhlevsky and Dzerzhinsky; the aid given by the Russians "in money, artillery, arms, and counsel" to Kemal Pasha; the rôle of the Red Army in the sovietization of Georgia; the mobilization of the Russian party in 1923 to support the German Revolution which was considered ready; the rôle of the Comintern in the revolutionary attempts in Bulgaria (1923–1924); the magnificent rôle of the Russian communists in the Chinese Revolution of 1927; the rôle of a Blücher, today marshal of the U.S.S.R., in the victorious march of the Kuomintang army from Canton to Shanghai; the rôle of the Russians in the organization of the Soviet territories of China from 1928 to 1935 [1]; the rôle of the Russians in the foundation of the republics of Tana-Tuva and of Mongolia, which are in reality Soviet protectorates—are all these tragic-comic misunderstandings?

Would it not have been much more honest and much less stupid on the part of M. Stalin to say simply: "We did once follow a policy of solidarity and of revolutionary expansion, but we are now abandoning it"?

At this moment, and undoubtedly for this reason, the epopee of the last rear-guard battles of the Chinese Revolu-

[1] This rôle, like that of the Stalinist bureaucrats throughout the Chinese Revolution, was not always a glorious one. It has been made public in the U.S.S.R. that the G.P.U. of the Chinese soviets liquidated several Trotskyist conspiracies. Revolutionists have therefore massacred other revolutionists—by order—in the mountains of Hunan.

tion is coming to an end. A new manœuvre is executed in China in 1934–1935—the abandonment of Eastern China, populous and relatively industrial, by the small Soviet armies under the command of a revolutionist of rare temper and value, Mao Tse-tung. From Hunan they withdraw painfully towards Chendu and farther north, in the purely agricultural regions of the centre. They seek to draw closer to the frontiers of Mongolia. . . . They abandon the populations who relied upon them and, giving up the re-kindling of a real hearth of the revolution in artisan and industrial China, they gain the steppes of Central Asia. They cut the communications between Nanking and Chinese Turkestan, where Soviet influence is filtering in. The spectre of Bolshevism departs the fertile valleys of old China, leaving the field free to imperialist competition. There can be no question of maintaining soviets in China while seeking the friendship of the big colonizing powers.

The policy of the Third International undergoes a parallel evolution. And how could it be otherwise? Just like the government of the U.S.S.R., the Executive Committee of the International gets its instructions from the Political Bureau of the Russian Communist party, that is, from the General-Secretary of this bureau. . . . The International has not met in congress for seven years; and now a World Congress is suddenly convoked in Moscow in 1935. There Dimitroff, invested by Stalin, makes solemn proposals for a united front to all the socialists of all countries. It is no longer a matter of "arousing the socialist workers against their traitorous leaders" and of denouncing social fascism. The Comintern sheds its skin and extends a fraternal hand to those it insulted yesterday. To fight war and fascism—for it is no longer a problem of fighting capitalism, generator of wars, and of preparing the proletarian revolution—the

Comintern shows itself ready to make any concession, provided that the question of the Russian socialists is not raised, provided that it is not asked finally to open up the prison gates for them. Cynicism and a vast contempt for human nature are needed in order to make these offers of collaboration to international socialism, while at the same time meaning to keep in Soviet prisons *all* Russian socialists. But the bureaucracy cannot yet make any concession at home, not even the smallest real one, to workers' democracy. The seriousness of Dimitroff's offers is attested in France by the change of attitude of the Stalinist leaders of the C.G.T.U.[1] who, after having resisted unity for years, abruptly accept all the conditions of Jouhaux. The fusion of the two French C.G.T.'s results in reducing to nothing the Red International of Labour Unions, in which the C.G.T.U. was the only existing organization outside of the state-ified Soviet unions. The Stalinists commence, by means of that boring-from-within which has already yielded them astonishing results among the intellectuals, the systematic conquest of the united C.G.T.

The French Communist party changes face, tactic, program, language, ideology, without any apparent effort, without a change in personnel, like an astonishingly well-trained party in which those who pull the strings can obtain anything with ease. It rallies to national defence, becomes a good French party, allies itself amicably with the socialists and the radicals against whom it employed the tactic of "class against class" not so long ago, situates itself at the right wing of the socialists, no longer mentions the dic-

[1] Unitary General Confederation of Labour, the Red trade-unions controlled by the Communist party. The C.G.T., the General Confederation of Labour, is the former parent body, a minority of which separated from the radical-controlled Lille Congress in 1921 and remained under the control of the moderates until the recent re-unification.—*Trans.*

tatorship of the proletariat, expresses its admiration for Joan of Arc, seeks to bring to power the same M. Daladier whom it treated as an assassin on February 6, 1934, defends the Versailles Treaty, worships today everything that it burned yesterday. And faced with the menace of the fascist leagues, the socialists accept an alliance with the Communist party without seriously raising the question of the fate of their brothers in Russia. You have the impression that with the Franco-Russian alliance once more ratified, the Third International, foreseeing the war, is endeavouring to cement in advance the sacred union. Dimitroff and Thorez assiduously play their rôle in the "policy of peace" of Stalin.[1]

Where does this policy of peace lead to and is it proper to call it that? The Stalinist bureaucracy sincerely wants peace to the exact extent that it is afraid of war. It knows that it will not be possible for it to fight for a long time to come, for several serious reasons:

1. The precarious state of transportation (worn railroads, no highways, a road network that is beneath any criticism, too few automobiles, in spite of the immense effort spent—successfully—in the creation of an automobile industry).

2. The indigence of the masses and the latent conflict between these masses, especially the peasants, and the power.

3. The discontentment of the nationalities among whom it is constantly necessary to repress nationalist tendencies,

---

[1] The same tactic produces elsewhere simply clownish results. In the August 1936 number of *Lo Stato Operaio*, official organ of the Italian Communist party, we find an appeal for the reconciliation of all Italians, from which we quote the following remarkable lines:

"Italian people! Fascists of the Old Guard! Young Fascists! We communists adopt as our own the fascist program of 1919 which is a program of peace, of freedom, of defence of the interests of the workers, and we say to you: Let us fight unitedly to realize this program!"

which are quite capable of moving speedily to the point of separatism.

Should I underline again the fact that the reaction itself has created these perils? The wearing out of transports results from the anarchic execution of the Five-Year Plans; the régime's conflict with the masses, we already know. If the problem of nationalities is more complex in itself, the forced collectivization and the dictatorship of the Secretariats gave it its present gravity.

The Red Army leaves every observer with an impression of youth, of solidity, of virility. Completely re-equipped in the last six or seven years by a government which was not hampered by any control of expenditures, still profiting by the moral achievements of October, object of a constant selection of men and of a labour of totalitarian education pushed further than anywhere else, it would certainly perform marvels in the vastest battles and in the most scientifically conducted ones. . . . The young men who comprise it did not go through the war. From childhood on, they have been prepared for it, not without fortifying them against "demoralizing pacifism," "petty bourgeois sentimentality," "debilitating intellectualism," and other evils of the same order. The exploits of this generation would undoubtedly give the world something to think about and would cost the enemy dearly. Could they be decisive? With these million men consumed in a few months, the outcome of the events would depend, for the U.S.S.R., on the economic situation at home, on the state of mind of the masses and of the international proletariat. Knowing this, the régime exerts itself to postponing the conflicts which it considers likely. Will it be able, tomorrow or after tomorrow, to master the circumstances which it is nevertheless contributing to create? Will it want to, when it feels itself strong enough? [1] What psychosis of encirclement will its policy create in Germany? What an impulsion it gives to the armaments of the capitalist countries by making the country look like an entrenched camp filled with aeroplanes, tanks, motorized artillery, new inventions!

The régime's policy of security is strictly that of the ruling bureaucracy. The security of the first republic of the workers would demand other measures and would rest on other associates. In times gone by the Red Army—of which Sokolnikov once said before me to French comrades, during a parade under the Kremlin walls: "Look at the army of the Third International!"—was able to conquer without marshals, led by worker-commissars, roughly dressed in black leather, to whom the offer of stripes would have appeared even more laughable than insulting. It conquered, thanks to the profoundly revolutionary character of a policy whose honesty in breaking with all diplomatic intrigue really corresponded to the aspirations, conscious or not, of the masses of the entire universe. A government of the workers would perhaps have an excellent opportunity today to apply the old socialist program of the armed nation, in order to put an end to militarism and the psychological reactions which it determines from country to country. But in order to arm the nation it would be necessary to be its emanation, to have nothing to fear from it. Having gone

[1] In perspective, another problem may be visualized in a certain number of years. Knowing the mentality of the rulers of the present régime, it is permissible to ask if they will be able to resist the temptation to make war when they feel themselves ready. A caste of empirical and tough *parvenus* seems to have all the requisite qualities for joining the imperialist game. But before that time other factors will intervene, such as can, if not annul, then at least counterbalance its influence: the awakening of the proletariat of the West is today an achieved fact; the awakening of the Russian proletariat is only a matter of time. When the day comes, it will be the working class of the U.S.S.R. upon which it will depend to impose peace or to conduct the revolutionary war.

over from militant internationalism to national socialism, refused all freedom to the workers and maintaining itself against them by police and terror methods, the bureaucratic régime is aware that it can no longer count upon the unreserved support of the advanced elements of the international proletariat and consequently the toiling masses influenced by these elements. It finds it safer to come to terms with the bourgeoisie of certain countries. Everything is connected. In foreign policy as in domestic policy, the incompatibility of the two conceptions is absolute. All proletarian socialism must be abandoned in order to maintain the dictatorship of the *parvenus*.

* * *

False and dangerous situations often result from that. When in July 1936 the civil war breaks out in Spain, the Stalin government rallies first of all to the non-intervention agreement and observes it scrupulously, quite the contrary from Germany and Italy which send the Rebels aeroplanes and munitions. The U.S.S.R. does not want a Spanish Revolution, for she dreads the complications in Europe and, at home, the consequences of the awakening of the revolutionary spirit in the world. The latter is perhaps the reason for the Zinoviev-Kamenev-Smirnov trial and for the vast police operations undertaken against the Old Bolsheviks most faithful to the bureaucracy itself. But the technical intervention of the fascist powers threatens to guarantee the victory of General Franco; that would mean the disruption of the Mediterranean equilibrium and the encirclement of France, the only actual ally of the U.S.S.R. The policy of non-intervention which is translated into conference at Plymouth while the Italians occupy the Balearics and Caproni trimotors and Junkers take off to give Madrid to the mutinous generals, proves to be a pretty sorry deception. The Soviet ambassador to Great Britain, Maisky, simply declares to the Non-Intervention Committee that the U.S.S.R. will henceforward behave exactly like certain other powers signatory to the pact. Thus, the Capronis will meet the Soviet trimotors in the Castilian air; the Italian fighting tanks will collide with the tanks from the Sormovo plants. At the beginning of November, the straightening out of the situation beneath Madrid is achieved, Republican Spain seems to be saved. As a consequence, Stalin, who has just had his former comrades of Lenin's Political Bureau shot, acquires a new popularity in Russia and in the labour circles of the world. He will be pardoned many executions if he takes on the appearance of saviour of the Spanish working class. It goes without saying that his inaction in this situation would have doomed him to the most profound discreditment.

But to him it is not a matter of supporting a workers' revolution; it is a matter of maintaining a certain equilibrium of the powers and of manœuvring with the masses to whom whopping lies must be told. And the Communist party of Spain declares, obedient to the instructions it receives, that its only aim is "the defence of republican order in the respect of property." Its spokesman in Madrid, M. Hernandez, adds that if the anarchists are not of this opinion, it will not be hard to bring them to heel (August). Whether you want it or not, a revolution is taking place on the peninsula as an inevitable defensive reaction. The property of the mutineers should have been confiscated, and the exploitation of the expropriated industries should have been confided to the trade-unions. Tomorrow the need of reconstructing on the ruins will impose a managed economy and rationing, while the sacrifices and the exploits, the armament and the actual situation will give the political preponderance to the workers' organizations. The Stalin-communists are the only ones, in the Generality of Catalonia, to wish for the return, pure and simple, to the social state prior to the civil war, whereas the radicals even of the Catalan Left (*Esquerra*) declare themselves disposed to tread the path of social reform "as far as necessary." You see the bureaucracy seeking to guarantee its grip on the labour movement of Spain and doing it very openly. A party of oppositional communists, basically hostile to the bureaucratic system, exists in Spain, more influential in many localities than the Stalinist party. It is the P.O.U.M., the Workers' Party of Marxian Unification, founded by an old oppositionist of the Third International, Maurin,[1] and by a former friend of Trotsky, Andrés Nin, who for ten years filled the office of secretary of the Red International of Labour Unions in Moscow. In October-November, the Soviet ambassador to Madrid and the Communist party, acting jointly, obtain the eviction of the P.O.U.M. from the Defence Junta of Madrid, the prohibition of the newspaper of this party—it is the first assault upon freedom of opinion within the anti-fascist front—while a gang sacks the headquarters of the P.O.U.M. Youth with impunity. In Barcelona the consulate of the U.S.S.R. goes so far as to denounce the oppositional communists, in a note to the press, as "paid agents of international fascism." The Stalinist sheet, *Treball*, makes it exact: "Agents of Franco-Hitler-Mussolini" and draws its proofs from the Moscow trial. . . . You see the Stalinist bureaucracy intervene in Spain in order to prepare there the repression of the revolutionary tendencies that combat it and to profit by the aid it lends the republic in order to assure its own political hegemony within it.

[1] Maurin was shot by the Rebels.

# *Conclusion*

*No problem has been resolved.*

DOES THIS RÉGIME OFFER ANY GUARANTEES OF STABILTY? THE importance that repression has there demonstrates the opposite, in spite of the solidity of the apparatus. The agrarian problem is not resolved. In the *colkhozes* themselves you can see taking shape a whole category of farmers in the process of enrichment, who, sooner or later, will emerge as *kulaks* on a new basis and among whom the spirit of property will inevitably manifest itself. In order to be lifeworthy, the collectivization would have to be accepted because it conforms to the interests and the mentality of the agrarians. The labour problem is not resolved. In one way or another, before many years have elapsed, the new working class in the process of formation will launch the struggle. The problem of nationalities is not resolved. So long as the nationalities have not obtained a freer statute within the Union, which only a Soviet democracy could offer them, they will breed separatist aspirations. The economic problem is not resolved. You cannot live indefinitely on a paper ruble, which is used essentially to defraud the workers of a part of their real wage and which, as a consequence, only provides the bookkeeping of the state with a thoroughly defective instrument. The difficulty of exchange between town and country, the scarcity of commodities, the low per capita consumption, the housing crisis, the transportation crisis, the lack of roads, the enormous disproportion between the war industries and the others, demand solutions that will not be found without crises. The spiritual problem is not resolved by the totalitarian management of all intellectual and moral activity; in the long run the sterility and suffocation will make themselves felt by debilitating the whole social organism. The political problem, far from being resolved, can only arise in increasingly disturbing terms. The selection of new leaders is taking place by methods that lead inevitably to the power of servile and unscrupulous *arrivistes*. The institutions are lacking in flexibility. They are incapable of development. Up to now, the political spirit of some old bureaucrats, Marxists, after all, by virtue of their previous training, permitted them to make up for the defects of the mechanism. We have seen that all this resulted in imposing upon the country enormous overhead expenses and immeasurable suffering. But there is no longer a replacement crew that offers the socialist guarantees of the Old Bolshevik generation. Who will be the masters of this despotic apparatus tomorrow?

The problem of the Oppositions is not resolved. That they are all in prison and that the men who represent them die behind bars settles nothing. Soviet society, far from becoming more homogeneous, becomes increasingly differentiated from year to year. It therefore has many ideologies confronting each other. A Soviet democracy could count upon the masses to make its socialist tendencies prevail. The repression, by creating a vacuum in people's minds and by preventing the development of innovating revolutionary thought, threatens to leave the masses disarmed some day in face of reactionary currents.

*A new régime of exploitation has installed itself.*

The dictatorship of the proletariat has given way to the dictatorship of the bureaucracy over the proletariat and society. The exploitation of labour is restored to the profit of the newly privileged. Through the medium of the totalitarian state, the Soviet worker is sometimes exploited by foreign capitalism. When, in 1931–1932, at the peak of the world crisis, the U.S.S.R. exported its wood, petrol, fruits, and foodstuffs below net cost, while hunger installed itself permanently in the homes of the builders of the Five-Year Plan, isn't it plain that by the juggling of prices on the international market capitalism made the Russian workers pay the costs of the crisis? It would be in place to investigate what part of the surplus value is taken off the wages of the Soviet workers and consumed by the bureaucracy and what other part is contributed in various forms to foreign capital. The economic explanation for the disarmament of the old animosities between Stalinism and the bourgeoisie of various great powers need not be sought elsewhere. "We are moving towards the disappearance of the state by the re-enforcement of the state," declared Stalin and his theses-maker, Stetsky, in 1934. This impudent formula, diametrically opposed to the program of the October Revolution, well corresponds to the needs of a class of new exploiters. However, the usurpation of power by this class "was possible and has endured only because the social content of the bureaucratic dictatorship is determined by the relations of production established by the proletarian revolution" (L. Trotsky). The bureaucracy cannot yet find its salvation outside of the preservation of collective property and managed economy. In this sense it continues, in a certain measure, the socialist work by methods which, it is true, are flatly anti-socialist. Borrowed now from the arsenal of capitalism, now from the pre-capitalist routine of old Russia, these methods fall with all their weight—if not in a rain of blood—upon the heads of the workers. From the usurpation an inexorable logic generates the terror against the masses and the most serious economic mistakes which, in turn, by creating panic and stirring up dangers, bring in their wake disastrous psychoses among the leaders. The industrialization was a colossal exploit, due less to the totalitarian state than to the functioning of the potential of the revolution. If the bureaucracy was able, almost with impunity, to treat the workers as it did, it is because it swore to them every day to employ their sweat and their blood in the construction of socialism. To what extent did it work for socialism? To what extent did it work to the discreditment and the ruin of socialism by piling up errors and crimes? The future will tell, and the future does not depend exclusively upon the bureaucracy. If it seems to us just to acknowledge certain merits in the work of the Russian bureaucrats, it is in the manner in which Marx, in the *Communist Manifesto*, acknowledges the revolutionary and creative rôle of the bourgeoisie.

*A Soviet democracy would have done better.*

But right here, on a theoretical point, we are forced to a severe judgment. All that was done in the U.S.S.R. under the dictatorship of the *parvenus*, would have been done much better by a Soviet democracy (standing behind a dictatorship against the fomenters of capitalist restoration).

The authentically workers' and peasants' state would have been able to save the costs of maintaining the privileged class. Equalitarian in its aspirations, concerned with assuring all the workers at least a minimum of welfare, it would not have been obliged to foist upon them overwork, the famine, and now the terror. Its policy would easily have been firmer, more clear-sighted, and more human, the special interests of the ruling camarillas being unable either to distort or divert it. From 1924–1925 it was possible to curb the formation of a rural bourgeoisie without leaving the framework of the N.E.P., without achieving it as a result of that civil war against the peasantry that was the forced collectivization. Begun at the right time, the industrialization would have improved the relations between town and country; Russia would not have known the famine of 1932–1934 and the perils which that famine gave birth to. Hence, it would not have been obliged to devote the best of its last forces to armaments, which, in turn, have become a source of danger, because of the anxiety they create among eventual adversaries. Useful admonitions to the rulers were not wanting. Since 1922 Trotsky has advocated an industrialization plan to ward off the conflict between the socialist state and the countryside. Sokolnikov, Piatakov, Preobrazhensky took up these ideas again on numerous occasions, even before they became the program of an opposition.

The bureaucracy itself could, it seems, have a less disastrous policy without difficulty, if it had displayed more general culture and socialist spirit. Its infatuation with administrative and military methods, joined to a penchant for panic in critical moments, reduced its real means. In despotic régimes too many things depend upon the tyrant.

The industrialization, pursued in a republic of free workers enjoying—even if poor—a genuine well-being, would have changed the face of the world to a very appreciable degree. What would the radiating force have been of a U.S.S.R. that was genuinely sovietic, truly socialistic, in which human dignity would be revealed as superior to what it is in the old countries, richer and better equipped? Would the rise of fascism in several countries of Europe, drawing behind it a part of the middle classes, have been possible in face of this example?

*The past of Russia weighs heavily upon the present of the U.S.S.R.*

A great rôle in this failure of the socialist revolution is played by the influence of old Russia. The factors engendered by its historic formation continue to operate with an amazing power. In political morals especially, the continuity is terrible. Malicious or ignorant critics sometimes ascribe to the socialism they seek to combat, what harks back in reality to the past, to the Russia of the Tsars Alexis Mikhailovich the Silent, Ivan Vassilievich the Dreadful, Peter the Great, who was also in reality the Madman, the Cruel, the Knave, the Barbaric, Nikolai I the Policeman. . . . The historian Kliuchevsky devoted a study to the testimony of foreigners on the Muscovy of the sixteenth century. There on every page you find again the present-day reality. The absence of juridical notions, the miserable condition of the people, the wiles of the great, their distrust of foreigners, their desire for an enclosed empire, their tendency to isolation due to the inferiority complex of Russia with respect to her Western neighbours. You find it all again, even down to the economic endeavours: in the sixteenth century the tsars establish model farms with the assistance of foreign specialists; they import equipment, suffer defeat after defeat in their innovations, not without torturing and executing the subordinates whom they make responsible for them. They establish a monopoly of the fur trade, of Volga fish, of rich stuffs. Fishermen and hunters owe all they get to the stores of the monarch. The local authorities live by extortion. Obscure intrigues cause the power to shift from one category of nobles to another, the ousted ones being exiled, with their families, to the same regions as today. Assemblies of notables sanction these changes as a formality; iniquitous trials, concocted against the vanquished in the dark of secret chancelleries and torture chambers, terminate in horrible executions. On the plane of repression, the historical continuity leads to the most monstrous resurrections. The arbitrary and mysterious proceedings that a denunciation sufficed to set in motion are revived in our days. The same prisons fulfil the same functions. Monasteries like those of Suzdal and Solovietsky, where heretics were sent, have become "solitaries" for socialist heretics. Villages lost in the northern snows, where for centuries the tsars sent their disgraced servitors, are still peopled with political exiles. As in the olden days, the whole family of the outlaw is punished with him, for nothing in Russian society ever dictated the respect of the individual: it does not count. As in the past, the power, when it turns to ferocious injunctions, imposes upon all its voluntary and involuntary supporters the bond of a shrill complicity. Peter I demands that his *boyards* participate—with their own hands—in the executions over which he presides in the Red Square. Stalin makes all citizens demand the death penalty for those whom he wants to be rid of. Woe to him who refuses to bow, in either case! Guarantees of justice do not exist and never did exist for anybody. As under Alexis Mikhailovich (1645–1676) and under Nikolai I, it is a crime to want to make a trip abroad and you are suspect for a correspondence with London or Paris. Nikolai I made all of Russia adopt models of churches. From the make-up of the periodicals, through the construction of prisons, to the construction of workers' clubs, everything is done today on the standard models of the central government. The more dreaded a tsar was for his police, his gallows, his implacable fiscal laws, his crafty spirit, the more the eulogies of the courtiers surrounded him with a servile concert: "Our Father, the well-beloved, the emancipator, the great, the anointed of God." . . . It was necessary for Stalin to have the oldest companions of Lenin shot, for the official press to call him: "Our Sun." What atrociously edifying details there are in these unparalleled annals! Around 1860 the most remarkable of the Russian thinkers, the uncontested spiritual guide of the young generation, Chernychevsky, was mysteriously thrown into the Petropavlovsk Fortress, judged by a secret commission on forged evidence, condemned to hard labour, defamed and sent to prison. He remained in Siberia for twenty years, reduced to burning what he wrote. . . . Kamenev, also deported, wrote a biography of Chernychevsky, before disappearing in his turn in a jail, seeing all his manuscripts confiscated, being tried three times before secret and complaisant tribunals, on the basis of falsehoods that will be studied later on, and being finally shot. Chernychevsky was accused of complicity with the exiled Alexander Herzen. Kamenev was accused of complicity with the exiled Leon Trotsky. Sixty-six years apart, the fate of the biographer surpasses in tragedy the fate of his subject. Both perished for socialist thought.

*New overturns are inevitable.*

In order better to transform Russian society, bent under the heavy heritage of history, more and better workers would have been needed; a more enlightened and numerically stronger working class. The Russian Marxists, while accepting all the responsibilities in order the better to exhaust the revolutionary possibilities, saw that clearly. At the moment of quitting Zurich for Russia, in March 1917, Lenin wrote:

"The great honour of beginning the series of revolutions caused with objective inevitability by the war has fallen to the Russian proletariat . . . [which] is less organized, less prepared, and less class conscious than the proletariat of other countries. . . . Russia is a peasant country, it is one of the most backward of the European countries . . . [but it can] give tremendous sweep to the bourgeois democratic revolution in Russia, and may make our revolution a prologue to the world socialist revolution, a step forward in that direction. . . . In Russia socialism cannot triumph directly and immediately. But the peasant mass may bring the inevitable and ripe agrarian upheaval to the point of confiscating all the immense holdings of the landowners. . . . Such an overturn would, in itself, not be socialistic as yet. But it would give a great impetus to the world labour movement. . . ."[1]

The titanic work accomplished between 1917 and 1923–1927—between the collapse of the old régime and the consolidation of the Thermidorian reaction—powerfully attests the revolutionary capacity of the workers and the vitality of socialism. Compromised today, the continuation of this work will depend upon new, inevitable, and even imminent struggles. Tomorrow history will bring face to face: (1) The privileged class assembled around the bureaucracy; (2) the peasants; (3) a new working class in the process of formation. Millions of peasants have entered into industry in the course of the last ten years, still further weakening the class consciousness of a proletariat exhausted by the preceding struggles. The large factories are transforming them into workers. A young generation has arisen to fill the gaps. Tomorrow this working class will necessarily engage in a struggle for better conditions of material and moral existence. It will undoubtedly begin with the most elementary

---

[1] Lenin, *Collected* Works, Vol. XX, Bk. I, pp. 85*f*. (New York, 1929.)

demands. In any case, it will engender a painful evolution while waiting to accomplish again, very probably, a revolution.

Already one can discern the direction in which it will have to orient itself. Trotsky emphasizes in *The Revolution Betrayed* that it will only have to make—in the present state of things—a political revolution: to reconquer power. It will not need to affect the property régime. It will demand a more socialistic distribution of the national income: increase in wages and restrictions on the privileged, first step towards their abolition; the freedom of opinion and, now, the legalization of Soviet parties, the separation of the parties from the state, the freedom of speech, of press,[1] of assemblage, of association, of demonstration; guarantees of individual liberty at least equal to those that capitalist society accords its members in the most civilized countries; and the immediate suppression of the unspeakable régime of interior passports, the destruction of the police apparatus (G.P.U., Secret Service provided with discretionary powers, administrative punishment); the passing over from the permanent army to the armed nation and, immediately, the democratization of the army by the suppression of ranks and decorations; the establishment of the legality and impartiality of the courts, the restoration of the right to defence counsel. It will be necessary for the revolution to renew the tradition of socialism, to affirm the value of human life by abolishing the death penalty. All this presupposes the restoration of the régime of the soviets, that is, of a genuine democracy in which, whatever its representative and

---

[1] What form, for example, might the freedom of a nationalized press assume? Lenin proposed in 1917 to grant every group representing a certain number of workers (10,000) the right to publish a paper.

legislative institutions may be, the assemblies of workers will have their word to say on all things.

The Stalinist bureaucracy seems to be neither susceptible of developing in this direction nor capable of abdicating. On the contrary, it is very conscious of the working-class threat and resolved to defend itself without worrying about the means. Everything points to the fact that the Russian working class will be obliged to sustain a stubborn and bloody struggle, which has, after all, already begun in the boundless resistance of the political prisoners. Bloody it already is. . . . Wherever evolution is not possible, the violence of the masses must sooner or later impose its solutions.

The awakening of the Russian working class is conceivable only in relation with the awakening of the working class of the West. And just as for the other belligerent countries of 1914–1918, one can set approximately the years 1938–1940 as the time when, the lean years passed by, the masses of the U.S.S.R. will have more or less finished the recuperation of their physical strength. They will reach maturity somewhat later than the Western proletariat, for the civil war prolonged their ordeals until 1920.

If the power of the bureaucracy appears to be formidable, it is certain that someday it will collide with an incalculable workers' power which will have on its side economic necessity, the aspiration of the masses, the constantly invoked tradition of October. A spontaneous general strike was on the point of crushing the autocracy in 1905. It seems to us that the working class of the U.S.S.R. will have no more effective weapon, at least at the beginning of tomorrow's struggles, than the general strike. And if the totalitarian state concentrates all power within its hands, it will perhaps discover that in aligning the unanimity of the toilers against the privileged, it is working its own doom. . . .

*A capitalist restoration is hardly likely.*

The essential thing today is that the war should not interrupt the reconstitution of the Soviet proletariat and the recuperation of the strength of the Western proletariat. The bureaucracy may, it is true, hurl the U.S.S.R. into some disastrous adventure at the end of which (and it knows it, which is a guarantee of peace for us) it would inevitably meet its doom, but in such a chaos that a counter-revolution, of the peasants at first—which would re-establish the rights of small rural property—would become highly possible.

The socialization of the means of production corresponds so well to the needs of the community that a capitalist restoration still does not seem predictable. The Soviet Thermidor was accomplished on the plane of collective property. Trotsky judges that the bureaucracy would be led to alter the property régime to its own advantage if its domination were prolonged without encountering any resistance. Another hypothesis, just as disturbing, seems to me more plausible: the rulers of the régime, seeking support in the foreign bourgeoisie, will come to terms with it for some sort of joint exploitation of labour. The bureaucracy, thus paying tribute to international capitalism, would assure itself of valuable alliances, of peace, or of chances of victory in the war; the collective ownership of the means of production would be maintained, and capitalist exploitation—indirect—restored in addition to state-ified exploitation.

*Socialized economy, the plan, and the psychological achievements remain.*

What then remains of the conquests of the proletarian revolution?

Socialized economy, directed by a single plan, whose

power proved extraordinary during the period when capitalism floundered in the crisis. A stage is crossed in economics. The accession of the backward nationalities of the old empire to civilization. The vigorous rough draft of a transformation of man. It is no longer deniable that the masses can triumph, impose a new property system, organize collectivist production; that man can live without the direct power of exploitation over his fellow man, without need or profound desire to enrich himself; that new incentives to work, more efficacious than the old, can be found in the collective interest; that the equality of races and of sexes, the priority of labour, socialist ethics and thought have powerfully begun the renovation of society; that we have acquired an historical experience of incalculable scope.

Nineteen years after having conquered power, the workers of Russia must still prepare themselves to reconquer all at the cost of new battles. But their point of departure is no longer the centuries of oppression and of defeat. They have behind them imposing victories. It has proved possible to rob them of the fruits of these victories, to be sure. They know, they feel, however, that no curse weighs down upon them. The exploits of yesterday guarantee them the future. Nothing is ended, everything begins.

# *Postscript*

---

*The Crisis of the Stalinist Régime.*

I PUT THE FINISHING TOUCHES TO THIS BOOK IN JANUARY 1937. Many of my best friends hesitated to approve its publication. Their attachment to the revolution impelled them to ask if I was not drawing too black a picture of the Soviet Union of today; if the involuntary or even unconscious resentment of an outlaw was not playing some part in the book. May I be permitted to dwell for a moment on the latter point? Individual destinies scarcely count in the dramas in which the future of the world is at stake. Like nature itself, history in the making is neither just nor unjust: it is necessary. Sometimes it grinds down those who fervently seek to make themselves its instruments. That's not very important, provided the right road is found, the end reached and that marching men clear the bar. The revolutionist imbued with this conviction is no longer subject to rancor, bitterness, resentment, to the puny little considerations of his insignificant personal adventure. Little would we mind being iniquitously, absurdly swept aside if the new society were really born. But that is precisely what is such a long way off.

The past year shows that all the oppositions which, in the last fourteen years, stood up against the bureaucratic régime, underrated its profoundly counter-revolutionary power and, still more, its inhumanity. The judgments formulated hitherto by the Left Opposition to which I belonged, sinned only in indulgence and optimism, because the Opposition stuck to preserving at all costs the last chances, however feeble, of a political redressment, of a great reform which would have brought the Soviet Union back to the road of socialism. Let us therefore cast up the balance of the twentieth year. . . . A pitiless year, marked by numerous trails of blood.

I wrote above, in connection with the Zinoviev-Kamenev-Ivan Smirnov trial: "the trial of a generation and an epoch." An estimate of higher than 10,000 is made of the Old Bolsheviks, fighters of the October and the Civil War, who have been driven out of public life, arrested, and who disappeared in the months to follow. Suspicion grows apace and, since the accusations hurled at the heads of Lenin's companions who have been massacred are incredible, the whole of the old party must be wiped out, because it understands their enormity.

Karl Radek, Rakovsky, Piatakov—upon command—had just asked in abominable terms for the death of their comrades of a lifetime, when they were arrested in turn, with numerous others, as accomplices of the Sixteen who were shot. The "Trotskyist" conspiracy, in short, embraced all the founders of the Soviet Union. A second trial, that of the Seventeen, opened on January 23rd, before the Supreme Military Tribunal, presided over by the same Ulrich, with the same prosecutor Vyshinsky. It was an enlarged repetition of the trial of August 1936. The Seventeen confessed, confessed that they had been Trotskyists, that they had planned the dismemberment of the Soviet Union, that they had had intelligence with Japan and Germany, that they had organized 3,500 railroad wrecks (a sub-Commissar of the People for transportation, by the name of Lifschitz, took upon himself this preposterous charge), that they had organized a mass of *attentats* which did not take place. Now they were repenting and, doomed to the death penalty, they worshipped the Gifted Leader. There is no more mystery in these command-confessions of men wedged in between their devotion, their demoralization and death, than in those of the Zinoviev trial. With some two or three exceptions, the Seventeen did not know of the execution of the Sixteen, so that they too had reason to count upon the clemency incontestably due their obliging behaviour. The hastily patched-up imposture ended by refuting itself when a witness (Romm, the Washington correspondent of the Moscow *Izvestia*) related an interview that he allegedly had with Trotsky in Paris, in the Bois de Boulogne, at the end of July 1933. Trotsky was soon to prove without difficulty that after his arrival in France toward the end of July, he had confined himself to Royan, in the Lower Charente district, some 503 kilometres from Paris. . . . Piatakov related, amid general stupefaction, that in December 1935, he had proceeded from Berlin to Oslo by aeroplane in order to receive instructions from Trotsky. The Norwegian authorities promptly established the fact that not a single foreign aeroplane had arrived in Oslo in that period. Instead of proceeding to other easy verifications, there was a hurried shooting of Piatakov, whose obviously false confession blew up the trial. Falsehood upon falsehood, imposture upon imposture, blood upon blood. The trials of the Inquisition were cleaner. At least the sorcerors had the excuse of hysteria and the inquisitors that of faith.

The trick played, badly played, thirteen men are executed in the night between the 1st and 2nd of February 1937. Which men? Three friends and collaborators of Lenin:

Yuri Piatakov, who sovietized the Ukraine in 1918, considered by Vladimir Ilyich, in his Testament, as one of the most competent administrators in the party, who went back to Stalinism in 1928, one of the directors of Soviet finances and of the industrialization, sub-Commissar of the People of Heavy Industry up to the day when he was arrested. (And the People's Commissar of Heavy Industry, Sergo Ordjonikidze, member of the Political Bureau, will die, following this execution, of a quite comprehensible embolism.)

Leonid Serebriakov, former railwayman, former secretary of the Central Committee, who once carried out confidential missions in the United States, an oppositionist deported in 1927 who went back to Stalin in 1928.

Nicholas Muralov, old Bolshevik, one of the heroes of the three Moscow insurrections (1905, February 1917, October 1917), military governor of Moscow after the seizure of power, an old Trotskyist oppositionist who was broken by eight years of persecution.

Two great combatants of the Civil War, Drobnis and Boguslavsky, a director of the chemical industry, a director of transportation, some victims of minor stature, spies, agents-provocateurs. Gregory Sokolnikov, of the Central Committee of October 1917, later People's Commissar of Finance, then ambassador to London, is spared: ten years of prison. Karl Radek, the journalist ready to say or do anything, the closest man to Stalin among all the former oppositionists who came over to him, saved the trial by his statements, knavish but more intelligent than those of his fellow-accused. There is no doubt that he made his conditions in advance. Ten years' imprisonment. Let us bear in mind that he said two extremely interesting things: That he is not confessing out of concern for the truth but "out of concern for utility" (*Izvestia,* January 30, 1937, p. 2, col. 3) and that "the Trotskyists of France, of Spain and of other countries will pay for it with their heads if our example teaches them nothing." The threat is direct.[1]

Those shot are either buried or cremated. Their families are deported—poor families! Official communiqués make known that the successor of Lenin as chairman of the Council of People's Commissars, Alexis Rykov, and the ideologist of the early days of the revolution and of Stalinism, Nicholas Bukharin, both arrested, have "refused to confess their crimes." Obviously: they know what confessions lead to. They disappear without a trial, like all the unobliging accused, who number hundreds.

We are now in March 1937. The old Bolshevik generation is liquidated. Its last few survivors, the Krestinskys, Rudzutaks, Bubnovs, Antonov-Ovseyenkos, Litvinovs, compromised and deprived of influence, must disappear sooner or later. It becomes plain that the two trials of imposture have marked the phases of a vast police blow against the men of 1917. At the beginning of April, the heavy machine for grinding down revolutionists makes a sudden lurch in another direction. Stalin undertakes to rid himself of those who were the docile instruments of his recent stroke; he is afraid of his too well-informed accomplices. After having perfidiously removed him and shifted him from the Commissariat of the Interior to that of Posts and Telegraphs, he causes the arrest of his minister of police, the Fouché of the Russian Revolution, the organizer of

[1] How can we fail to recall it after the Communist Party of Spain has provoked the fall of the Caballero cabinet on the question of outlawing the P.O.U.M. (Workers' Party of Marxian Unification) and obtained this measure from the Negrin cabinet, followed by the apprehension of all the leaders of the P.O.U.M. and the arrest of a thousand of its active workers? This at the risk of killing the Spanish revolution and of weakening irremediably the republic.

all the repressions for more than ten years, the creator of the most populated concentration camps in the world, the stage-manager of the first trial—Henrick Grigorievich Yagoda, a 1917 Bolshevik. In his fall, Yagoda brings with him almost the whole leading personnel of the G.P.U. I can no longer have any doubt about it: the examining magistrates who, in the secrecy of the prison cells, dictated the false confessions of the Zinovievs and the Piatakovs, were promptly shot. "Yagoda can be reproached for everything," I wrote. "All the crimes desired of him, he committed on command, and he could not commit a worse and more unpardonable crime than to defend himself, for that he could only do by accusing. . . . Lost beyond redemption." At the present moment, it is not known what has become of him.

The inexorable logic that necessitates the disappearance of those who hold the worst State secrets, places the Gifted Leader in a blind alley. Nobody in his entourage is henceforth sure of the morrow; and in face of everyone's hypocritical fear, masked by adoration, he himself feels sure of nobody. No genuine collaboration is any longer possible with him, no sharing of power. The members of the Political Bureau come together in meeting, they hesitate to look each other in the face, and everyone weighs his lightest word. The party destroyed, the governmental circles decimated, the political police decimated, only the army subsists, a still intact force, having at its head great soldiers of the Civil War. At the top of the military hierarchy stands Voroshilov, whose prestige in the country is less compromised than that of Stalin. The head of the morale of the army, a vast organization of education and of police surveillance, Yan Gamarnik, sub-People's Commissar of Defence, collaborated for a long time with Yagoda: he understands everything, he knows everything, he must therefore disappear. He commits suicide forty-eight hours after having been elected a member of the Moscow Party Committee; according to an unofficial version, he is supposed to have been killed while resisting those who came to arrest him. Dead, he is suddenly denounced, early in June, as an "enemy of the people, Trotskyist traitor, agent of the enemy." This signifies that the services which he directed are going to be pitilessly purged; and they are of essential importance in the army. The blow struck at Gamarnik reaches Voroshilov, who was unable to defend his principal collaborator; it reaches the whole High Command, until now spared by the proscriptions, although made alert for many months now by the arrests of such noted generals as Vitovt Putna, Dimitri Schmidt and Primakov, men with the finest service records behind them. What is taking place at that moment? The obscurity of the communiqués published on the Tukhachevsky affair makes you think of smoke screens. Undoubtedly, the High Command did murmur; nothing, nothing more than this was or is possible. Men of war, knowing each other for twenty years, asked themselves in the intimacy of their confusion, to what disasters the suspicious madness of the Leader is leading the country—and what to do. Timid objections on their part to the purges being planned or carried out, anxious words exchanged among intimates—these sufficed for them to be shot without trial after being arrested by surprise. Two successive and contradictory communiqués are thereupon published: one speaks of a trial behind closed doors, of high treason in the interest of Germany, of confessions; the other, issued several days later and signed by Voroshilov (without doubt for the purpose of thoroughly involving his responsibility and of ruining his credit), mentions Trotskyism and denounces a plot against Stalin in vague terms. Whatever the case may be, eight of the most remarkable chiefs of the Red Army were shot on June 2nd or before. At one stroke, Stalin decapitated the extraordinary staff of the generals of the revolution. Tukhachevsky, army commander at the age of twenty-five, conqueror of Kolchak in 1918–1919, gloriously vanquished beneath Warsaw in 1920, victor over Antonov's peasant mutiny in 1921; Marshal of the U.S.S.R.; Kork, Yakir, Eidemann, Primakov, Feldman, whose biographies are epic, yesterday the commanders of the most important military regions–shot, shot. Muklevich and Levandovsky, disappeared. The names of all who disappeared are not yet known. Voroshilov, discredited. Whether his closest collaborators had been traitors, or he allowed them to be massacred as such without it having been true, what credit does he deserve? There remain the Marshals Blücher and Yegorov who, in order to compromise them, were made to figure among the judges of a secret trial which most likely never took place. . . .

No reaction follows in the prostrated country. The dark blows come in raging succession, ravaging all circles. Proletarian writers and dramatists, those who dictated yesterday the official theses and patterns, are denounced in their turn as Trotskyists, enemies of the people, because they were once grouped around a distant relative of Yagoda, an agitator and an infinitely servile bureaucrat, Leopold Auerbach, former general secretary of the Association of Proletarian Writers; with him go to the prison the Polish émigré Bruno Jascinski, the dramatist Kirshon, the novelist Libedinsky and a host of others. Purging of the Academy of Sciences. Arrests of the jurists Chlenov and Pashukanis. Purgings everywhere. Proscription upon proscription.

What other régime could afford the senseless luxury of thus decimating its cadres?

The death of Yan Gamarnik has other repercussions in the country of his birth, White Russia, where the principal members of the government are accused of treason. The president of this republic, Cherviakov, puts an end to his days (in June) and they have the effrontery to write that it is the result of "family trouble." In July comes the brusque removal of the president of the most important republic of Central Asia, Feisula Khodjaev, noted personality of the Soviet Mussulmanic world; his brother is alleged to have committed suicide. The persecutions grow apace: no sooner does a man fall than all his collaborators and friends follow him.

The same repressions, inexplicable to an uninitiated mind, in the sphere of production. All you have are "Trotskyist nests" successively discovered in the chemical, electrical, military and automobile industries, in metallurgy, in the gold mines, in the Central Planning Commission. . . . What is the general resultant disorganization, what are the effects of this panic and this savagery on the productivity of the enterprises? It is impossible to learn. Sober official communiqués announce executions by the dozen in the Far East. "Agents of the enemy, Trotskyist traitors, enemies of the people. . . ." Who is thus being shot? What is becoming in this frightful nightmare of the genuine oppositionists, imprisoned, interned, deported for years now—the ones who refuse to submit? It is impossible to learn.

Let us endeavour to conclude. Is there, then, a scattered opposition throughout the country, among all the functionaries, the military men, the administrators, the intellectuals? No. Whoever knows how the present directors were selected, on the basis of servility and passive obedience, cannot have the slightest doubt on this score. But there is disorder, panic, terror, mute reproval, passive resistance—atomic, as it were. Not being sure of the morrow, nobody dares to assume a responsibility. All the statistics, all the balances, all the figures are false because nobody ever dares tell the truth, because everybody takes refuge in lies, in irresponsibility, in what is expedient. Every text is falsified. The problem is to repeat the words of yesterday while killing yesterday's ideas. That's the result of despotic methods of administration and the suppression of all freedom. The totalitarian machine has worn the social texture down to the thread.

After Thermidor, that is—without wishing to force the analogy—after the liquidation of the revolutionary generation, comes Brumaire, that is, the liquidation of the Thermidorian generation. The new privileged caste or class seeks in this way to guarantee its reign. The present crisis is that of its cadres and its methods. The men of the revolution had to be eliminated so that the newly privileged might install themselves solidly. In this respect, the Thermidorians themselves, Stalinists from the first hour, were not sufficiently sure. But in its struggle for power against the Oppositions, the toiling masses, the traditions of October, Marxian thought, the bureaucracy, led to resort unceasingly to violence, finished by isolating itself from the country and by having at its disposal nothing except simple and barbarous methods of government, extremely costly from the economic standpoint and disastrous from the standpoint of the selection of the cadres. Stalinism, which incarnates the bureaucracy, is beginning to suffocate it; it is not lifeworthy, for it allows nothing to live. It is defined by fear, by knavery, by terror, by a frenetic determination to endure. It can stay on top only by paralyzing to a very large degree the economic life itself of the country: it has now become an obstacle to the very development of the productive forces. If, on the other hand, it is swept away —for the directing coterie is henceforward at the mercy of its own blunders—the bureaucratic reaction, appealing to new men without socialist training of any sort, will most likely seek its salvation, at home, in concessions to small peasant property, in seemingly democratic reforms, in a reconciliation with the non-party people, rendered indispensable by the liquidation of the Bolshevik party; and abroad, in a more intimate co-operation with the capitalist states. In either case, the socialist idea remains momentarily vanquished, the workers having no interest at the board; in either case the bureaucratic régime stabilizes itself without resolving anything and continues to repress harshly any allusion to the real aims of the October Revolution; in either case, given the nationalization of the means of production, a proletariat of more than twenty million young men continues to mature, amidst poverty and oppression, for those inevitable struggles that are calculated before long to change the face of this sixth part of the world.

Paris, July, 1937.

# Thirty Years After the Russian Revolution

WHAT A TERRIBLE ROAD WE HAVE TRAVELED THESE LAST THIRTY years! The greatest event of our times, the event most charged with hope, seems to have turned upon us. What now remains of the unforgettable enthusiasms of 1917? Many men of my generation, who were among the first ranks of communist activists, now have nothing left but bitterness toward the Russian Revolution. Of the participants and witnesses, almost none have survived. The party of Lenin and of Trotsky have all been shot. Documents have been destroyed, hidden, or falsified. The only survivors in any numbers are the émigrés, who were always opposed to the revolution. They write books, they teach, they have the support of the still powerful forces of conservatism; forces which, in this period of global upheaval, would never relent or display any true objectivity. What a poor excuse for logic, which—pointing accusingly at the dark spectacle of Stalinist Russia—attempts to prove the failure of Bolshevism and therefore of Marxism and even socialism. A piece of sleight-of-hand that succeeds easily in the face of all the problems gripping the world and that won't loosen its grip in the foreseeable future. Are you forgetting the other failures? Where was Christianity during periods of social catastrophe? What has happened to liberalism? What has conservatism produced, in either its enlightened or reactionary form? Did it not give us Mussolini, Hitler,

Salazar, and Franco? If it was a question of honestly weighing the many failures of different ideologies, we would have our work cut out for us for a long time. And it's far from over.

Any event is both definitive and transitory. Its development in time is often unforeseeable. Before forming an opinion on the Russian Revolution, let us recall the many changes of outlook and perspective about the French revolution. The enthusiasm of Kant, when he heard that the Bastille was taken, the Terror, Thermidor, the Directorate, Napoleon. Between 1789 and 1802 the republic of liberty, fraternity, and equality appeared to make a complete turnaround and deny its own origins. The Napoleonic conquests, creators of a new order in all but the title, are striking—if one examines the map—by their similarity to those of Hitler. The Emperor became the Ogre, the civilized world united against him, and the Holy Alliance fought for the reestablishment of the old regime in all of Europe. Nevertheless we see now that the French revolution, by ushering in the power of the bourgeoisie, the spirit of industry, and scientific inquiry, actually fertilized the nineteenth century. And yet, thirty years after the event, in 1819, during the time of Louis XVIIIth and Tsar Alexander, did it not seem the costliest mistake in history? How many to the guillotine, how many wars and struggles, just to arrive at a wretched restoration of the monarchy.

*II.*

It is entirely natural that the falsification of history should now be the order of the day. Among the inexact sciences, history is the one that threatens the most interests, both material and psychological. Myths, errors, tendentious interpretations swarm about the Russian revolution, although the facts are easily available. Obviously it is simpler and more attractive to talk and write without informing oneself first.

It is often said that "a violent coup by the Bolsheviks in October/November of 1917 overturned a nascent democracy." Nothing could be further from the truth. No republic had been proclaimed in Russia and not a single democratic institution existed, outside of the Soviets and the Councils of workers, peasants, and soldiers. The Provisional Government headed by Kerensky had refused to carry out agrarian reform, refused to open peace negotiations clearly demanded by popular opinion, and refused to take effective measures against the forces of reaction. It existed in a transitory, ephemeral state between two vast, ongoing conspiracies: that of the generals and that of the revolutionary masses. Nothing pointed to the development of a democracy with socialist tendencies—the only theoretically viable outcome under the circumstances. By September 1917 the only alternatives were either a dictatorship of the reactionary generals or else a dictatorship of the Soviets. Two historians on opposite sides of the issue clearly agree on this question: Trotsky and the right-liberal statesman Milyukov. The Soviet, or Bolshevik, revolution was the result of the failure of the unstable and ineffectual moderate democratic revolution led by the liberal bourgeoisie and temporizing socialist parties after the fall of the autocracy.

It is also claimed that the insurrection of 7 November (25 October, according to the old calendar) was the work of a small minority of conspirators, the Bolshevik party. Again nothing could be more contrary to the proven facts. 1917 was a year of mass action, amazing in its variety, multiplicity, strength, and in the perseverance of a popular initiative whose thrust was clearly toward Bolshevism. Agrarian unrest spread throughout all of Russia. The old discipline within the ranks of the army crumbled under the weight of widespread insubordination. Kronstadt and the Baltic fleet categorically refused to obey the Provisional Government, and it was only the intervention of Trotsky, who met with the Soviet at the naval base, that averted armed conflict. In Turkestan the Tashkent Soviet took power in its own name. Kerensky was threatening the Kaluga Soviet with his artillery, and on the Volga an army of forty thousand men refused his authority. In the suburbs of Petrograd and Moscow, red-guards of workers were forming. The Petrograd garrison placed itself under the authority of the Soviet. Among the Soviets themselves, the majority passed peacefully and legitimately out of the hands of the moderate socialists and to the Bolsheviks, who were among the most surprised at this development. The moderate socialists were turning their backs on Kerensky, who could count on no one, except for the military, which by this time had lost all credibility. It is for this reason that the insurrection in Petrograd succeeded almost bloodlessly, in a great wave of enthusiasm. Reread the words of John Reed and Jacques Sadoul on this question; both of whom were eyewitnesses! The Bolshevik "conspiracy" was literally carried into power by a colossal and rising wave of public sentiment.

It is worth remembering that the Empire crumbled in February-March 1917 under the pressure of the unarmed population of the Petrograd suburbs. The spontaneous fraternization between the troops of the garrison and the demonstrating workers sealed the fate of the autocracy. Later on there was an attempt to identify the unknown individuals who instigated this fraternization; some were identified, the majority remained anonymous. The leaders and the most capable militants of all the revolutionary parties were at that moment all either in prison or outside the borders. The small groups still active in Petrograd were so surprised at the turn of events that the Bolsheviks even planned to publish an appeal to the workers to return to the factories! Four months later, the experience of a coalition government under the liberal bourgeoisie and the moderate socialists had produced such profound anger that by the beginning of July the garrison and the population of the suburbs themselves organized a vast demonstration whose slogan was the demand for power to the Soviets. The Bolsheviks disapproved of this measure taken by unknown elements, and only joined it unwillingly, guiding it to a painful and dangerous conclusion. They felt, and probably with reason, that the rest of the country would never follow the example of the capital. Naturally they became the scapegoats. Calumny ("German agents") and persecution fell upon them. From that moment on, they understood that if they did not take in hand this mass movement, the generals would succeed in taking power by force.

In September 1917 General Kornilov entered the fray with the open complicity of elements in the Kerensky government. Lenin and Zinoviev went into hiding, Trotsky was in prison, and the Bolsheviks were run to ground. The troops of Kornilov, however, fell apart of their own accord, as a result of their contacts with the railway workers and other militant workers.

The civil servants of the autocracy clearly saw the revolution coming; they simply had no means to prevent it. The revolutionary parties awaited it; but they would not have been able, they could not have provoked it. Once events had taken their course and the uprising was upon them, all that was left for anyone was to participate with either more or less will and vision.

## *III.*

The Bolsheviks took power because, in the process of natural selection that took place among the revolutionary parties, they showed themselves the most adept at expressing in a coherent, far-sighted, and determined manner the aspirations of the mobilized masses. They held on to power and won the civil war because, in the last analysis, and despite many hesitations and conflicts, the masses supported them from the Baltic to the Pacific. This great historic fact has been recognized even by the majority of the Russian enemies of Bolshevism. The liberal émigré publicist, Helena Kuskova, has written just recently that it is "undeniable that the people supported neither the Whites. . . . nor the struggle for the Constituent Assembly." The Whites represented the monarchist counter-revolution, the Constituents, democratic anti-Bolshevism. Thus until the end of the civil war, in 1920–21, the Russian Revolution took on the aspect of an immense popular movement, to which the Bolsheviks provided a brain and nervous system in the form of leaders and cadres.

It is said that the immediate goal of the Bolsheviks was to establish a monopoly on state power. Another myth! In fact they were concerned about the danger of being isolated in power. Many of them were early partisans of a coalition socialist government. Lenin and Trotsky rejected on principle a coalition with the moderate socialist parties—who had led the March revolution to failure and who refused to recognize the Soviets. But the Bolshevik party sought and obtained the collaboration of the Left Social-Revolutionary Party, a peasant-based party led by idealist/intellectuals generally hostile to Marxism. From November 1917 to July 6, 1918, the Left SRs participated in the government. They, like a good third of the known Bolsheviks, refused to recognize the treaty of Brest-Litovsk, and on July 6, 1918 began an insurrectional revolt in Moscow, proclaiming their intention to "govern alone" and to "reopen the war against German imperialism." Their proclamation, which was broadcast over the airwaves that day, was the first declaration by any party of an intention to rule alone! However they were defeated, and it was left to the Bolsheviks to rule alone. From that moment on, their responsibility increased, and their mentality changed.

And before that, following the split of the Russian Social Democratic Workers' Party into majority (Bolshevik) and minority (Menshevik) factions, were they fundamentally different from the other Russian revolutionary parties? It is common to impute to them an authoritarian character, intolerant and immoral in the choice of means; a centralized and highly disciplined organization containing the germs of bureaucratic statism; a character at once dictatorial and inhumane. Knowledgeable and ignorant writers alike are fond of citing in this regard the "amoralism" of Lenin—his "proletarian jacobinism" and "professional revolutionism." One reference to Dostoyevsky's satirical novel *The Possessed*, and the writer thinks he has clarified the topic. In fact he has only obscured it.

All the Russian revolutionary parties, from 1870–80

on, were in fact authoritarian, highly centralized, and disciplined within and for their illegal activities. All were trained "professional revolutionaries," that is to say, men whose lives were dedicated to the struggle. All were capable at times of a type of "practical" amorality, although fairness would oblige us to credit them with an ardent and selfless idealism, as well. Almost all, proletarian or not, were imbued with a jacobin mentality. All produced both heroes and fanatics. All, with the exception of the Mensheviks, aspired to dictatorship, and the Georgian Mensheviks made frequent use of dictatorial methods. All the larger parties were "statist" by the nature of their structures and by the goals they assigned to themselves. In reality under the important doctrinal divergences, there was a single revolutionary mentality.

Have we forgotten the authoritarian temperament of the anarchist Bakunin and the methods of clandestine organization he used in the First International? In his *Confessions* Bakunin advocates an enlightened dictatorship, but one without mercy—exercised on behalf of the people. The Social Revolutionary Party, which was imbued with republican ideals and was more radical than socialist, developed a rigorously centralized, disciplined, and authoritarian "apparatus" aimed at fighting the terrorist autocracy, which became a fertile ground for police provocation. The Russian social-democratic forces as a whole aimed at the conquest of state power. No one spoke of the coming revolution in more "jacobin" terms than their leader, Plekhanov. The Kerensky government, in which the socialist revolutionaries and the Mensheviks were the dominant force, assumed a dictatorial—though ineffectual, it is true—tone. Even the anarchists themselves, in the areas occupied by Nestor Makhno's Black

Army, exercised a true dictatorship, complete with confiscations, requisitions, arrests, and executions. And Makhno was its "batko," its "godfather" or "don."

The social democrat Mensheviks on the right, like Dan and Tsereteli, hoped for authoritarian rule. Tsereteli advocated the repression of Bolshevism before it was too late. The left Mensheviks, like Martov, were perhaps the only group sincerely attached to the ideal of democratic revolution. For this reason they really constitute, from a philosophical point of view, a happy exception to the rule.

Certain characteristics of Bolshevism gave it an innate superiority over its rival parties, with whom it shared a common outlook. These were: a) its Marxist conviction, b) the doctrine of the hegemony of the proletariat in the revolutionary process, c) its intransigent internationalism, and d) the unity between thought and action. In many individuals this kind of unity of thought and action can come together in a powerful faith in their own point of view.

Marxist realism of 1917 seems somewhat simplistic to us today. The world has changed, and social struggles have become much more complex than they were back then. During the Russian revolution, however, this realism, centered upon a strong awareness of historic and economic realities, was equal to the moment and to the circumstances. It contained antedotes to the contemporary liberal phraseology, the double-dealing, the self-aggrandizing procrastination, and abdication of responsibility, whether honorable or hypocritical. The moderate socialists believed that the country was undergoing a "bourgeois revolution" destined to open it to an era of capitalist development; this, in turn, would necessarily lead to the development of a bourgeois democratic political structure. The Bolsheviks believed that only the proletariat could carry out this "bourgeois" revolution—carry it out and of necessity bypass it entirely. They believed that socialism was impossible in such a backward setting but that a Russia on the path of socialist development would eventually become the example for the European working class. In 1917 Lenin did not envision the blanket nationalization of the means of production, but instead worker control over them. Later on he came around to the idea of a mixed regime of capitalism and state control; only in July of 1918, did the outbreak of civil war force complete nationalization as a defense imperative. The uncompromising internationalism of the Bolsheviks rested on their belief in the coming European revolution, which was to be more developed and more fertile than the revolution in Russia. This vision of the future was not theirs alone; it was a part of the shared foundation of European socialism, even though in actuality the large parties had already given up on this idea of general revolution. The German successor to Marx, Karl Kautsky, was until 1908 one of the prime theoreticians of this revolution. Rosa Luxemburg, Franz Mehring, and Karl Liebknecht all held the same conviction. The essential difference between the Bolsheviks and the other socialists seems to have been a psychological one, due to the particular circumstances under which the revolutionary intelligentsia and the Russian proletariat developed. There was no place in the Czarist Empire for parliamentary opportunism and daily compromise; a brutal and simple social reality engendered a faith at once active and total. In this sense the Bolsheviks were more Russian, and more at one with the temper of the Russian masses, than the revolutionary socialists or the Mensheviks, whose cadres were permeated with a western, evolutionist mentality, democratic in the sense of the developed capitalist countries.

*IV.*

Let us now open the difficult chapter of mistakes and errors. Not without regret for the fact that, in such a brief study, it is impossible to consider equally the faults, errors, and crimes of the powers and the parties who fought against the Bolshevik-socialist revolution. In the absence of such a decisively important context, we will have to content ourselves with an admittedly unilateral point of view.

In 1939 I wrote in my *Portrait de Staline*, published in Paris (Grasset): ". . . the most incomprehensible error—because deliberate—committed by the socialists (Bolsheviks), precisely because of their awareness of history, was the creation of the Extraordinary Commission for the Repression of Counter-Revolution, Speculation, Espionage, and Desertion—later abbreviated to 'CHEKA'—which judged the accused, and mere suspects, without hearing or seeing them; that is, without their having the least possibility of defense. It pronounced verdicts secretly, and carried out executions in the same way. What was this, if not an Inquisition? Certainly, a state of siege is not without severe problems, and a bitter civil-war must impose extraordinary measures. Nevertheless, did the socialists forget that public trials are the only guarantee against arbitrary and corrupt actions. How would it be possible to justify sinking thus even lower than the makeshift methods of Fouquier-Tinville?" The error and the blame are patent; the consequences were horrifying:

the GPU, the even more powerful successor to the Cheka, finished by exterminating the entire revolutionary generation of Bolsheviks. It only remains to mention a few extenuating circumstances in fairness to Lenin's Central Committee; circumstances that, to the eyes of the sociologist, take on a real importance. The young republic lived in mortal peril. Its indulgence toward generals like Krasnov and Kornilov were to cost it rivers of blood. The old regime had resorted time and again to the use of terror. The initiative in the use of terror in the civil war was taken by the Whites in November 1917, in the massacre of the Kremlin arsenal workers. It was taken up by the Finnish reactionaries in the first months of 1918, on the widest possible scale, well before the "Red terror" had ever been proclaimed in Russia. The social wars of the nineteenth century, beginning with the June days of 1848, in Paris, and the Paris Commune of 1871, were all characterized by the mass extermination of the vanquished proletarians. The Russian revolutionaries knew what was waiting for them if they lost. Nevertheless, the Cheka was relatively benign at the beginning—until the summer of 1918. And once the Cheka—after counter-revolutionary uprisings, after the assassinations of the Bolsheviks Volodarski and Uritski, and after two attempted assassinations of Lenin—opened the "Red Terror" and began shooting hostages, suspects, and enemies, it still continued to look for ways to control and channel the popular fury. Dzerzhinski worried about the excesses of the local Chekas; the statistics of Chekists themselves shot for this offense would be very edifying. Recently I reopened a small book (deplorably translated into French) on this subject: *Memoirs of a People's Commissar*, by the Left Social-Revolutionary

Steinberg, in which I found two significant episodes recounted. At the end of 1917, two shots were fired at Lenin in an assassination attempt. Following this, a worker's delegation came to Lenin and said that, if a single drop of his blood was shed by the counter-revolutionaries, the proletariat of Petrograd would exact a hundredfold revenge. Steinberg, who was collaborating with Lenin at the time, notes in his recounting of the incident how upset Lenin was at this idea. The affair was hushed up specifically to avoid tragic consequences. I know through other sources that the two socialist-revolutionaries who fired the shots were arrested and their lives were spared. Later on they became Bolshevik supporters. Two liberal ex-ministers, Shingarev and Kokoshkin, became ill while in prison; it was ordered that they be transferred to hospital. Once there they were assassinated in their beds. When Lenin heard of the crime, he was greatly shocked. A government investigation was ordered, which discovered that the perpetrators were revolutionary sailors, supported and protected by the mass of their comrades. Disapproving of the leniency of the men in power, the sailors took matters into their own hands with an act of terrorism. In fact the crews of the fleet even refused to turn over the assassins, and the People's Commissars were forced to "forget" the entire episode. At a moment when the support of the sailors was a question of daily life-or-death for the revolution, could they have raised a conflict over a spontaneous act of terrorism?

In 1920 capital punishment was abolished in Russia. It was thought that the civil war was almost over. I had the feeling that everyone in the party expected a normalization of the regime, the ending of the state of siege, a return to Soviet democracy, and the limitation of the powers of the Cheka, if not its abolition. All this was possible, which is to say that the revolution itself could have been saved. The exhausted country wanted only to begin its reconstruction. It still had great reserves of faith and enthusiasm. The summer of 1920 marks a fatal moment in the history of the revolution; one that only pure bad faith on the part of historians can explain their failure to see. At a moment when all Russians hoped for a pacification of the situation, Pilsudski threw Polish arms into battle against the Ukraine. This aggression, which was clearly inspired by desire for conquest, coincided with the recognition by Britain and France of the General Baron Wrangel, who was occupying the Crimea. The hardening effect on the revolution was instantaneous. Poland having been beaten, the Central Committee believed it might be able to provoke a Soviet revolution there. This scheme of Lenin's failed with the defeat of the Red Army before the gates of Warsaw. Much worse was the fact that, with a painful and bloody war finished, and the country drained and exhausted, there was no longer any question of abolishing capital punishment or of beginning the reconstruction of the nation upon the bases of Soviet democracy. Misery and danger paralyzed the party-state in an economic regime intolerable to the population and doomed from within, which has been called "war communism."

The uprising of the Kronstadt sailors in early 1921 was precisely a protest against this economic regime and the dictatorship of the party. Whatever its real intentions and its probity, no party would be able to govern a starving nation and maintain its popularity. The spontaneous enthusiasm of the masses had died out. Sacrifices and privations were wearing out the still-active minority within the revolution. Ferocious winters, insufficient rations, epidemics, constant requisitions in the countryside all spread bitterness everywhere, a kind of despair, and an ideologic confusion between bread and counter-revolution. If, in this situation, the Bolsheviks had let go the reins of power, who would have taken their place? Wasn't it their duty to hold on? In fact they were right to hold on. Their mistake was to panic at the Kronstadt revolt, which they could have handled in any number of ways, as we who were there, in Petrograd, knew well.

The errors and mistakes of power are all tied in with Kronstadt 1921. The sailors only revolted because of the brutality with which Kalinin refused to listen to them. Where persuasion and understanding were needed, the president of the Executive Committee of the Soviets used only threats and insults. Instead of being fraternally received, the Kronstadt delegation to the Petrograd Soviet was arrested by the Cheka. The truth about the conflict was hidden from the party and from the country as a whole by the press, which—for the first time—lied shamelessly, saying that a White general, Kozlovski, was in charge in Kronstadt. The mediation effort proposed by the influential and well-intentioned American anarchists, Emma Goldman and Alexander Berkman, was refused. Instead the cannons opened up in a fratricidal battle, and the Cheka later shot its prisoners. If, as Trotsky says, the sailors had changed since 1918, and now expressed nothing but the aspirations of a backward peasantry, it must also be said that the ruling circles had changed as well.

In proclaiming the end of "war communism" and the

start of the "NEP," Lenin satisfied the economic demands of the Kronstadt revolt, after both the battle and the massacre were over. He thereby admitted that the regime, and he, himself, had become bound into an untenable position; one that Trotsky had denounced as dangerous and about which he had demanded changes a year earlier. The NEP abolished requisitions in the countryside, replacing them with an in-kind form of taxation. It reestablished the freedom of commerce and small-scale business—in a word, it loosened the mortal grip on the country of the complete state control over production and exchange. At the same time, it would have been normal to liberalize government policies toward those other socialist and libertarian elements who had opted to accept the authority of the Soviet constitution, through a policy of tolerance and reconciliation. Raphael Abramovitch correctly reproaches the Bolsheviks for not having taken this road in 1921. Instead the Central Committee outlawed the Mensheviks and the anarchists. Unquestionably if a coalition government had been formed at this time, it would have internalized certain dangers, but, and this is well-proven, they would have been less than the danger of this monopoly of power. In fact discontent within the party and the working class forced the Central Committee to declare a state of siege from that moment on. It is true that this state of siege was a mild one within the party itself. The working class opposition, however, was condemned, and purges and exclusions followed.

## *V.*

What were the deeper reasons that motivated the Central Committee to maintain and strengthen its monopoly on power? First of all during critical moments, the Bolsheviks trusted no one but themselves. Carrying a heavy responsibility only aggravated by the Kronstadt affair, they were afraid to open the political arena to competition from the Menshevik social-democrats and the leftist social-revolutionary "peasant" party. Finally and most importantly, they believed in world revolution, in the imminent revolution in Europe, and particularly in Central Europe. A coalition government in Russia would have weakened the Communist International, whose destiny it was to guide and direct the coming revolutions.

Perhaps here we touch upon the greatest and gravest error of the party of Lenin and Trotsky. Here, as always in creative thought, truth, error, wishful thinking, and subjective intuition are all intertwined. Nothing is ever undertaken without a belief in the enterprise, without trying to gauge the tangible givens, without hoping for success, without entering into problematic and uncertain areas. All action is a projection from the real/present moment into an unknown future. From the point of view of the intellect, the justified action is that which does not project itself forward blindly. Seen from that angle, was the doctrine of the European revolution justified? I do not think that we are in a position to respond satisfactorily to that question. My only intention is to delimit it.

There is no longer any doubt that the era of stable, growing, relatively pacific capitalism came to an end with the First World War. The Marxist revolutionaries who announced the opening of a global revolutionary era—and said that if socialism did not establish itself in at least the great European powers, another period of barbarism and a "cycle of wars of war and revolution" (as Lenin put it, quoting Engels) would follow—were right.

The conservatives, the evolutionists, and the reformists who chose to believe in the future bourgeois Europe—carefully cut into pieces at Versailles, then replastered at Locarno, and fed with phrases dug up at the League of Nations—are today remembered as statesmen of blind policies. What is it we are seeing today, if not global transformation of social relations, of relations of production? Of international relations, of power relations, of ideas and customs; in short a world revolution as vital and acute in Indonesia as it is timid and uncertain in Europe. In all this, America, with its prodigious technological strides, its crushing international responsibilities, its contradictory social movements, holds a special place—as befits the richest and best organized industrial power in the world. On the other hand, nothing going on in Japan or Greece, nothing being built in the absolute secrecy of the Siberian wastes of the USSR, nothing happening or brewing in Trieste or in Madrid, is outside of this revolution. The Marxist revolutionaries of the Bolshevik school awaited and worked toward the social transformation of Europe and the world by an awakening of the working masses and by the rational and equitable reorganization of a new society. They expected to continue working toward the time when men would take control over their own destinies. There they made a mistake—they were beaten. Instead the transformation of the world is taking place amidst a terrible confusion of institutions, movements and beliefs without the hoped-for clarity of vision, without a sense of renewed humanism, and in a way that now imperils all the values and hopes of men. Nevertheless the general trends are still those defined by the socialists of 1917–20 toward the collectivization and the planification of economies, the internationalization of the world, the emancipation of oppressed and colonized peoples, and the formation of mass-based democracies of a new kind. The alternative was also foreseen by the socialists: barbarism and war, war and barbarism—a monster with two heads.

The Bolsheviks saw in the expected German revolution the salvation of the Russian revolution. In this it appears they were not mistaken. Under socialist regimes, agricultural Russia and industrial Germany would have had an assuredly peaceful and fertile development. Under this thesis, Russia would have avoided strangulation by its developing internal bureaucracy. Germany would have escaped the dark night of Nazism and catastrophe. No doubt the world would have known other struggles, but nothing allows us to conclude that those struggles would have produced the hellish machinery of Hitlerism and Stalinism. On the contrary every indication points to the conclusion that a victorious German revolution at the close of the First World War would have been infinitely fertile for the social progress of humanity as a whole. Such speculations on the hypothetical variants of history are legitimate and even necessary if we wish to understand the past and orient ourselves in the present. To negate the value of such speculation is to claim that history is nothing but a chain of fatalistic, mechanical occurrences and not the unfolding of human life in the flow of time.

In fighting for revolution, the German Spartacists, the Russian Bolsheviks, and all their worldwide comrades were struggling to prevent the global cataclysm that we have just lived through. They understood what was approaching. They were moved by a great will to liberation. Anyone who ever rubbed shoulders with them will never forget it. Few men in history have ever been so devoted to the cause of men as a whole. It is fashionable now to impute to the revolutionaries of 1917–27 a desire for hegemony and world conquest, but it is not difficult to see what kind of bitterness and interests are at the root of such attempts to denature historical truth.

At the time, however, the errors of Bolshevism were obvious. Europe was unstable, and socialist revolution seemed theoretically possible and perhaps rationally necessary; in fact it was not. The overwhelming majority of the working classes in the West refused to support the struggle; they believed instead in the return of the social progress of the period before the war. They managed to recapture enough of a feeling of well-being to be afraid of the risks involved. They allowed themselves to be fed with illusions. Led by moderate and mediocre leaders, the German social-democrats feared the costs of a revolution, which could easily have been brought about in November of 1918. Instead they chose to follow the democratic paths of the Weimar Republic. When we reproach Bolshevism for having brought about a revolution by violence and the dictatorship of the proletariat, it would only be fair to consider also the historical alternative—the path of reformist, moderate socialism in Germany, which in attempting to exhaust the possibilities of bourgeois democracy led directly to the victory of Hitlerism.

The Bolsheviks were mistaken about the political understanding and the energy of the working classes in the West, principally in Germany. This error, which was brought about by their militant idealism, engendered the most serious possible consequences. They lost contact with the working classes in the West. The Communist

International became a creature of the Soviet party-state. Finally the fallacious doctrine of "socialism in one country" was born out of the deception. In time the idiotic and sometimes villainous tactics of the Stalinized International were to facilitate the triumph of nazism in Germany.

*VI.*

A first accounting of the Russian Revolution must be made at about 1927. Ten years have passed. The dictatorship of the proletariat has since 1920–21 (the dates are approximate and arguable) become the dictatorship of the Communist Party, itself under the dictatorship of the "Bolshevik old-guard." Speaking generally this "old-guard" constitutes a rather remarkable elite: intelligent, altruistic, active and opinionated. The results it achieves are formidable. Abroad the USSR is recognized, respected, and often admired. Domestically, economic reconstruction has been accomplished upon the ruins of years of war, through nothing but available resources and the energies of the masses. A new system of collectivized production has been substituted for the old capitalist one and is functioning reasonably well. The Russian working classes have proved their ability to win the struggle, to organize, and to produce. New beliefs and a new feeling of the dignity of the worker have settled in. The instinct toward private property, which bourgeois philosophers consider innate in men, is on its way to a natural extinction. Agriculture has been reconstituted on a level that equals and is beginning to surpass that of 1913. The salaries of workers, in real terms, are significantly higher than those of 1913. A new literature full of life and vitality has appeared. The balance of the proletarian revolution is clearly positive.

But now it is no longer a question of "reconstruction", but of construction—of progress and new development in industry (autos, aviation, chemistry, aluminum, etc.); it is now essential to remedy the imbalance between a revitalized agricultural sector and a relatively weak industrial sector. The USSR is isolated and under threat. It is important to see to its defense. The Marxists have no illusions about the Briand-Kellog pact which "outlaws" war. The regime is at a crossing of the ways. The party is torn by struggles for power, and over the program to be instituted by that power; struggles which pit the "old-Bolsheviks" against each other. The most lucid of the inheritors of the "heroic times" are grouped around Trotsky. They are capable of tactical errors, of insufficiently worked-out theories, of hesitations—still their courage and merit are unquestionable. They comprehend the necessity for industrialization and planification, as well as the need to fight the forces of reaction and, above all, of bureaucratization. They see a clear need for militant internationalism and the democratization of the regime—beginning with the party itself. They are to be beaten by the hierarchy of secretaries, in a kind of interlocking directorate with the commissars of the GPU under the guidance of the General-Secretary, the so-recently obscure Georgian, Stalin.

Thousands of founders of the USSR, in an example of devotion to the socialist ideal, pass from power into prison or deportation. The things they are accused of are contradictory and irrelevant. The essential, overwhelming fact is that in 1927–28, by means of a "coup de force" within the Party, the revolutionary Party-State becomes a bureaucratic police state, a state that is reactionary in every important way with respect to the ideals of the revolution. Ideological changes speed up brutally. A marxism of dead slogans born in offices takes the place of a critical marxism of thinking men. The cult of the Leader begins. "Socialism in one country" becomes the password of newcomers who intend by it no more than the protection of their new privileges. What opponents of the regime see with a kind of anguished myopia is the profile of a new, emerging state, a totalitarian regime. The majority of the old-Bolsheviks opponents of the Trotskyist Opposition—Bukharin, Rykov, Tomski and Riutin—are horrified at the sight and pass over to the resistance. Too late.

The struggle of the revolutionary generation against totalitarianism lasts ten years, from 1927 to 1937. The confused and sometimes disconcerting path taken by this struggle should not hide from us its real importance. Its leading figures confronted, fought, reconciled, even betrayed each other; they got lost on the path, humiliated themselves before the tyranny, tried to outwit the thugs, wore themselves out, revolted desperately. The totalitarian regime used them one against the other, all the more efficiently since it had a hold on their souls. Patriotism toward the party and the revolution, cemented by devotion for the sacrifices, the dedication, the actual results, the prodigious vision of a grand future, the sense of common peril—all this obliterated any sense of reality in even the clearest minds. Despite this, the fact is that the resistance of the revolutionary generation, headed by the old socialist Bolsheviks, was so tenacious that in 1936–38 (the period of the Moscow trials) it was necessary for the entire generation to be eliminated, in order that the new regime could consolidate itself. This was the bloodiest takeover in history. Bolsheviks perished by the tens of thousands, civil-war veterans by the hundreds of thousands, and Soviet citizens who were tainted by the condemned ideals by the millions. A few dozen companions of Lenin and Trotsky found themselves capable of dishonoring themselves by a supreme act of devotion to the party before being shot. Thousands more were shot in basements. The largest concentration camps in history were set up to oversee the physical elimination of the vast masses of condemned.

Thus the bloody rupture was complete between Bolshevism, a kind of ardently Russian and creative form of socialism, and Stalinism, equally Russian, which is to say conditioned by all the totalitarian past and present of Russia. In order that this latter term take on its precise meaning, let us define it: Totalitarianism, in the form taken in the USSR, the Third Reich, and, much less completely in fascist Italy and elsewhere, is characterized by the despotic exploitation of labor, collectivization of production, monopoly of power by the police (more exactly, by terrorists) and the bureaucracy, corruption of free thought, mythification of the leader/symbol. Any regime of this type will tend naturally to expansion through force, which is to say, wars of conquest. This is because such regimes are incompatible with the existence of different—and, above all, more humane—neighbors because they inevitably suffer from their own psychoses and paranoias, and because they survive upon the permanent repression of explosive internal forces.

An American author, James Burnham, has taken it upon himself to uphold the idea that Stalin is the true heir of Lenin. Pushed to such a level of hyperbole, paradox tends to acquire a stimulating attraction to lazy and ignorant minds. Of course it goes without saying that a parricide remains the biologic continuation of his father. On the other hand, it is equally obvious that a movement is not continued by massacring it nor is an ideology continued by denying its premises. Neither is a worker's revolution continued through the blackest exploitation of workers, or the work of Trotsky through ordering his assassination and grinding his books back down to pulp. Either that or the words continuation, rupture, negation, denial, and destruction lose all intelligible meaning—which may in fact prove convenient to certain brilliantly obscurantist intellectuals. I would not think of including James Burnham in this category. The paradox that he has developed—no doubt out of love for the controversial and nonconformist theory—is as false as it is dangerous. In a thousand dead formulations, it can be found in the press and in books in this time of preparation for the Third World War. The reactionaries have a clear interest in confusing Stalinist totalitarianism—exterminator of the Bolsheviks—with Bolshevism itself and thus eventually with socialism, Marxism, and even liberalism.

The personal case of Stalin—ex-Bolshevik himself, just as Mussolini was one of the ex-old socialists of *Avanti!*—is entirely secondary from the sociological point of view. Who would contest the view that the authoritarianism, intolerance, and certain errors of Bolshevism furnished a fertile breeding ground for Stalinist totalitarianism? A society, just like an organism, always contains within it the germs of death. In addition, however, it requires favorable historical circumstances to ensure their germination. Neither the intolerance, nor the authoritarianism of the Bolsheviks (and most of their adversaries) can cast into doubt their socialist mentality and the accomplishments of the first ten years. Such real accomplishments, in fact, that, in looking at them, two American thinkers studying the cyclical development of organisms and societies pointed out that, "in 1917–18, Russia entered an era of expansion and growth, so that today it stands as the youngest of the great nations of the globe" (Edward R. Dewey and Edwin F. Dakin, *Cycles* [New York, 1947]). We would like to know to what degree the Stalinist totalitarianism weakened the new vitality of Russia. In this connection, David J. Dallin gives us an indication. During the First World War, Russian loss of lives equalled 30 percent that of the Allies; in the Second World War, the Russians are estimated to have lost 12 to 16 million dead,[1] or 80 percent of the allied nations. On the battlefields, the Red armies lost about four times as many dead as the invader.)

At the outbreak of the Russian Revolution, the actual organized membership available to all the revolutionary parties was less than one percent of the population of the Empire as a whole. Of this one percent, the Bolsheviks constituted only a fraction. This infinitesimal agent of fermentation served its purpose and was exhausted. The revolution of October-November 1917 was guided by a party of young men. The oldest among them, Lenin, was 47 years old; Trotsky was 38, Bukharin, 29, Kamenev and Zinoviev both 34. Ten to twenty years later, the resistance to totalitarianism was carried out by an aging generation. And this generation did not succumb only under the weight of a young police–bureaucracy determinedly hooked on the privileges of power, but also because of the passivity of masses exhausted to the point of breakdown; undernourished, paralyzed by the terrorist regime, and drunk on propaganda. In addition it found itself without the slightest support on the outside. While it was resisting inside the USSR, the rise of worldwide forces of reaction continued almost uninterruptedly. The great democracies accommodated or encouraged Hitler and Mussolini. The life force of the Popular Fronts, that rear-guard struggle of the Western working classes, was broken in Spain by a coalition of Nazism, fascism, and Franco at the very moment when Stalin's thugs were moving to liquidate Bolshevism in Russia.

*VII.*

What, after its ten exultant first years and the ten black years following, is left to defend in the Russian revolution? An immensely important historical experience, the proudest memories, examples beyond value—these would already be a lot. But the doctrine and tactics of Bolshevism require a critical analysis. There have been so many changes in this chaotic world that not a single marxist—or socialist, for that matter—concept could be applied today without being undated first. I don't think that in a system of production where the laboratory is taking precedence over the workshop, the hegemony of the proletariat can assert itself, unless in moral and political ways that in fact imply a renunciation of hegemony. I do not think the "dictatorship of the proletariat" will reappear and be viable in the struggles of the future. No doubt there will be revolutionary dictatorships of one kind or another in the future; I am convinced that the role of the worker's movements in these cases will be to guarantee the democratic character of these regimes—not just for the sake of the proletariat alone but for the sake of all workers and even nations. In this sense proletarian revolution is no longer to be our aim; the revolution that we are waiting to serve can only be socialist—in the humanist sense of the word—or, more precisely, *socializing*, through democratic, libertarian means. Beyond the borders of Russia, the Bolshevik idea of the party has failed completelz. The variety of interests and psychological backgrounds has made impossible the grouping of such a homogeneous cohort of militants all dedicated to the ideals so nobly praised by the poor Bukharin. Centralization, discipline, and guided ideology should inspire in us a healthy suspicion, no matter how badly we need an organizational framework.

And what is left to the Russian people in all this to support? By an overwhelming irony of history they are now the people who have nothing to lose but their chains! I hope that someone will soon translate into French the objective and uncompromising work by David J. Dallin and Boris I Nikolaevski on *Forced Labor in the Soviet Union*. It tells us that in 1928, during the Soviet Thermidor, the GPU concentration camps held no more than about thirty thousand inmates. Today, though, it is impossible to estimate the number of the millions of slaves in Stalin's camps. The most modest estimates put the number at 10 or 12 million, that is, according to these authors, at least 16 percent of the adult male population (and a considerably lower percentage of women). Recently in *Masses* I underlined the decisive importance of these figures. Taking 15 percent as the proportion of the population having the privilege of enjoying the equivalent of a modest European standard of living (the figure is probably overly optimistic at this moment, and in any case would have to be halved to obtain the percentage of workers in that category), I wrote: "Thus, 7 percent privileged workers, 15 percent pariahs,

78 percent exploited and living in misery and poverty." What can one say about such a social system? Is it defensible?

Beyond the borders of Russia, the influence of this "concentration-camp universe" was to block the development of socialism and social reorganization in Europe. Thus the tragedy is no longer Russian alone, it is universal in proportion. The logical conclusion of this process seems to be the Third World War. Still we mustn't resign ourselves to catastrophic outcomes, as long as other possibilities are in sight. The aggressiveness of the Stalinist regime in foreign affairs is conditioned by the gravity of its internal situation. The latent disposition of the Russian and non-Russian masses to revolt against this regime was proved by their defeatism at the beginning of the invasion, and the way in which they greeted the invaders as liberators. It is also proved by the "troubles" that followed upon the victory, and by the movements of the Vlasov army, which were far more complex then generally known, as it battled first for the Nazis, then against them. It is proved by the two to three hundred thousand Russian refugees in Germany, and by the filling up of the concentration camps. It is my belief that totalitarian regimes constitute colossal factories of revolt. And this one all the more because of its revolutionary tradition.

Documentation on the morale of the Russian masses is increasing every day. Under the iron grip of the regime, there is still a profound vitality, as anyone knows who knows Russia. Nine tenths of the men who are working, building, inventing, administering could, if their chains were broken, become from one month to the next active citizens in a workers democracy. Will they be able to break their chains in time for a socialist Russia to head off the war?

The degree to which the Stalinist regime has managed to inculcate in its oppressed masses a horror and disgust for socialism is incalculable. Powerful forces of reaction are to be expected in Russia, and even more among the non-Russian peoples—above all among the Central Asian Muslims, who for many years have been permeated with pan-Islamic aspirations. Nevertheless I believe—on the basis of many observations carried out in the USSR during even the cruelest years of oppression—that the great majority clearly understand the imposture of official socialism. Because no return to the old regime—or even to large-scale capitalism—is possible because of the high degree of development attained by state-controlled production in Russia (at a time when throughout Europe nationalization and planification are on the rise), a true Russian democracy could only bring health and efficiency in reorganizing socialized production in the interest of the producers. The technical imperatives of production would combine with the desire for social justice and a newfound freedom to once again place the economy at the service of the community. Because this realistic and deeply felt hope remains to us, all is not lost.

VICTOR SERGE
Mexico,
July-August 1947

*Translated by Michel Bolsey*

# Note

1. The number of Soviet losses in World War II is now admitted to be 26 million. This figure was revised upward from 20 million by Soviet researchers during the period of *glasnost*, when the Stalin era came under intense scrutiny. (Ed.)

# Index